Texts in Philosophy
Volume 23

The Normative Structure of Responsibility
Law, Language, Ethics

Volume 14
Corroborations and Criticisms. Forays with the Philosophy of Karl Popper
Ivor Grattan-Guinness

Volume 15
Knowledge, Value, Evolution.
Tomáš Hříbek and Juraj Hvorecký, eds.

Volume 16
Hao Wang. Logician and Philosopher
Charles Parsons and Montgomery Link, eds.

Volume 17
Mimesis: Metaphysics, Cognition, Pragmatics
Gregory Currie, Petr Koťátko, Martin Pokorný

Volume 18
Contemporary Problems of Epistemology in the Light of Phenomenology. Temporal Consciousness and the Limits of Formal Theories
Stathis Livadas

Volume 19
History and Philosophy of Physics in South Cone
Roberto A. Martins, Guillermo Boido, and Víctor Rodríguez, eds.

Volume 20
History and Philosophy of Life Sciences in South Cone
Pablo Lorenzano, Lilian Al-Chueyr Pereira Martins, and Anna Carolina K. P. Regner, eds.

Volume 21
The Road Not Taken. On Husserl's Philosophy of Logic and Mathematics
Claire Ortiz Hill and Jairo José da Silva

Volume 22
The Good, the Right & the Fair – an introduction to ethics
Mickey Gjerris, Morten Ebbe Juul Nielsen, and Peter Sandøe

Volume 23
The Normative Structure of Responsibility. Law, Language, Ethics
Federico Faroldi

Texts in Philosophy Series Editors
Vincent F. Hendriks
John Symons
Dov Gabbay

vincent@hum.ku.dk
jsymons@utep.edu
dov.gabbay@kcl.ac.uk

The Normative Structure of Responsibility
Law, Language, Ethics

Federico L. G. Faroldi

© Individual authors and College Publications 2014.
All rights reserved.

ISBN 978-1-84890-141-4

College Publications
Scientific Director: Dov Gabbay
Managing Director: Jane Spurr

http://www.collegepublications.co.uk

Original cover design by Laraine Welch

Printed by Lightning Source, Milton Keynes, UK

All rights reserved. No part of this publication may be reproduced, stored in a retrieval system or transmitted in any form, or by any means, electronic, mechanical, photocopying, recording or otherwise without prior permission, in writing, from the publisher.

Niektóre pytania rodzą się dopiero po odpowiedziach.
Some questions come to being only after their answers.

Stanisław Jerzy Lec, *Myśli nieuczesane wszystkie,* p. 471.

ACKNOWLEDGEMENTS

Chapter 1 benefitted greatly from constant discussion and interaction with Paolo Di Lucia, and received very useful comments by Stefano Colloca. An earlier version was discussed at the St. Alberto di Butrio international philosophical seminars.

Chapter 3 received some useful criticisms and comments in several parts of the world. I thank Ken Levy for thought-provoking remarks and suggestions on an earlier draft of this chapter, Tim Scanlon and Serena Olsaretti for some hints, Elvio Baccarini, Helen Beebee, Simon Blackburn, Gianfranco Pellegrino, Stefano Predelli, and audiences in Padua, London, Pavia and Alghero for all their comments.

Chapter 4 benefitted from some conversations with Micheal M. S. Moore in Firenze and Sergio Seminara in Pavia. A modified part of this chapter appears as Faroldi, 2014b and benefitted from comments by an anonymous reviewer.

The ideas developed in Chapter 5 were initially discussed with linguist Φιλιώ Χασιώτη and received some fuel from discussions with Peter Simons. Two earlier drafts were scrutinized at the St. Alberto di Butrio international philosophical seminars — whose participants I warmly thank for their patience and critiques. A modified part of this chapter appears as Faroldi, 2014a and benefitted from comments by two anonymous DEON2014 reviewers.

The bibliography wouldn't have been possible in its current form without the immense resources of Trinity College Library, Dublin. The EU Erasmus Program, the University of Pavia/Trinity College fellowship, and Almo Collegio Borromeo also supported this work.

Many thanks go also to Giampaolo M. Azzoni, Luca Fonnesu, Matthias Maring, Kevin Morris, Katarzyna Nowicka, Rafał Urbaniak, Peter Vranas, Wojciech Żełaniec.

Mattia Bazzoni and Guglielmo Feis were instrumental for this work, and with Giulia Fanti, Dario Mazzola, Enrico Grosso, Andrea M. Marcelli and Emil Mazzoleni made my life in and out Borromeo worth remembering.

Sergio Filippo Magni was involved in this project from the beginning, commented sharply on many drafts and encouraged me when hope seemed lost.

I cannot thank enough Amedeo Giovanni Conte. My intellectual debt goes well beyond his teachings, the countless hours we spent together discussing and the example he set before me with his life. His influence is apparent throughout the book.

My mum Emanuela, my dad Stefano and Sara were immensely supporting during this endeavor.

All *responsibilities* remain mine — whatever responsibility turns out to be.

SUMMARY

0 INTRODUCTION   1

I The Concepts of Responsibility   9

1 RESPONSIBILITY: CONCEPTS, CONCEPTIONS, CONDITIONS   11

II The Rules of Responsibility: Law and Ethics   37

2 RESPONSIBILITY AND MENS REA   39

3 RESPONSIBILITY AND NEUROSCIENCE   71

4 RESPONSIBILITY AND CAUSATION   101

III The Language of Responsibility: Semantics and Pragmatics   137

5 ASCRIPTION OF RESPONSIBILITY   139

6 THE NORMATIVITY OF CONTEXT   185

Appendices   189

A ANSELM'S "DEBĒRE"   191

B RUDZIŃSKI'S "Z LOGIKI NORM": A FRAGMENT   193

C SORAINEN'S "DER MODUS UND DIE LOGIK": A FRAGMENT   195

D SZTYKGOLD'S "NEGACJA NORMY"   197

BIBLIOGRAPHY   203

INDEX OF SUBJECTS   245

INDEX OF NAMES   249

CONTENTS

0 INTRODUCTION 1

I The Concepts of Responsibility 9

1 RESPONSIBILITY: CONCEPTS, CONCEPTIONS, CONDITIONS 11
   1.0 Introduction: Concepts, Conceptions, Conditions 13
   1.1 Responsibility CONCEPTS: Four Dichotomies 15
      1.1.1 I: Praxical *vs.* Non-Praxical Responsibility 16
      1.1.2 II: Nomophoric *vs.* Non-Nomophoric Responsibility 17
      1.1.3 III: Regulative-Rule-Related *vs.* Constitutive-Rule-Related Responsibility 17
      1.1.4 IV: Role-Related *vs.* Role-Unrelated Responsibility 18
      1.1.5 List of Responsibility Concepts 19
   1.2 Normative Responsibility CONDITIONS 19
      1.2.1 *Eidologic* Conditions of Responsibility 20
      1.2.2 *Eidonomic* Conditions of Responsibility 21
   1.3 CONCEPTIONS *vs.* JUSTIFICATIONS of Responsibility 23
      1.3.1 Conceptions of Responsibility 23
      1.3.2 Justifications of Responsibility 26
      1.3.3 Relationships among Concepts, Conceptions and Justifications: Dimensions of Responsibility 28
   1.4 Two Senses of 'Normativity': Nomophoric *vs.* Axiological 29
      1.4.1 Nomophoric Normativity 30
      1.4.2 Axiological Normativity 30

1.4.3 Nomophoric *vs.* Axiological Responsibility   30

II The Rules of Responsibility: Law and Ethics   37

2 RESPONSIBILITY AND MENS REA   39
- 2.0 Introduction: How Criminal Systems Work   41
- 2.1 Lady Wootton's Strict Liability System   42
    - 2.1.1 Retribution *vs.* Prevention   43
    - 2.1.2 Criminal Liability = Strict Liability   44
    - 2.1.3 Mental Abnormality and the Elimination of Responsibility   47
    - 2.1.4 Side Remarks: Taxonomies, Determinism, Semantics   48
    - 2.1.5 Lady Wootton's Proposal: recap   50
- 2.2 Hart's Reply   50
    - 2.2.1 Hart's Moderate Proposal   50
    - 2.2.2 Hart's Threefold Critique to Lady Wootton   51
    - 2.2.3 Hart's Two Critiques to Strict Liability   54
- 2.3 A. Ross's Reply   56
    - 2.3.1 Ross's Conception of Responsibility   57
    - 2.3.2 Ross' Fourfold Critique to Lady Wootton   61
    - 2.3.3 J. Glover's Double Critique   63
- 2.4 Five Criticisms from a Contemporary Perspective   65
    - 2.4.1 Assessing Lady Wootton's Proposal   65
    - 2.4.2 Ascription of Responsibility Seems Normative   69

3 RESPONSIBILITY AND NEUROSCIENCE   71
- 3.1 Introduction   73
- 3.2 Criminal Liability Without Responsibility?   75
    - 3.2.1 Criminal Liability Has No Necessary Connection with *Moral* Responsibility   77
    - 3.2.2 Capacity Responsibility and Neuroscience   80
- 3.3 Law without Capacity Responsibility   85
    - 3.3.1 Law, Games, Conventions   86

3.3.2 Strict Liability-Responsibility   91
3.4 Punishment & Consequences   97
  3.4.1 Some Consequences   97
  3.4.2 Conclusion   99

4 RESPONSIBILITY AND CAUSATION   101
  4.0 Introduction   103
  4.1 FIRST Argument: Queer Responsibilities   106
    4.1.1 Strict Liability *vs.* Collective Responsibility   107
    4.1.2 The Various Cases of Collective Responsibility   108
    4.1.3 Accomplice & Corporate Responsibility   109
    4.1.4 Qualified Responsibilities   110
  4.2 SECOND Argument: Responsibility and Causation   111
    4.2.1 A Bird's Eye View   112
    4.2.2 Causation as Normative   129

III The Language of Responsibility: Semantics and Pragmatics   137

5 ASCRIPTION OF RESPONSIBILITY   139
  5.1 Two Paradigms: Ascription *vs.* Description, Ascription *vs.* Prescription   143
    5.1.1 First Paradigm: Ascription *vs.* Description in Hart   144
    5.1.2 Second Paradigm: Ascription *vs.* Prescription in Kelsen   146
    5.1.3 Ascription, Responsibility, Imputation   149
    5.1.4 Ascription and Thetic Acts   150
  5.2 Phenomenology of Responsibility Judgments   152
    5.2.1 Attribution of Responsibility (Accusation)   153
    5.2.2 Denial of Responsibility (Excuses, Absolutions)   156
    5.2.3 Ascription *vs.* Description of Responsibility   159
    5.2.4 FIRST Argument: Axiological Evaluation   163

                5.2.5   SECOND Argument: Normative Relationships   163
                5.2.6   THIRD Argument: Discretionality   163
        5.3   FOURTH Argument: Denial of Responsibility   164
                5.3.1   Negation, Negations   167
                5.3.2   Normative Negation   173
                5.3.3   Denial of Responsibility, Formalized   176
        5.4   The Relevance of Context: Pragmatics and Normativity   183

6   THE NORMATIVITY OF CONTEXT   185

Appendices 189

A   ANSELM'S "DEBĒRE"   191

B   RUDZIŃSKI'S "Z LOGIKI NORM": A FRAGMENT   193

C   SORAINEN'S "DER MODUS UND DIE LOGIK": A FRAGMENT   195

D   SZTYKGOLD'S "NEGACJA NORMY"   197

BIBLIOGRAPHY   203

INDEX OF SUBJECTS   245

INDEX OF NAMES   249

LIST OF FIGURES

Figure 0.1   Aitionyms/1   7
Figure 0.2   Aitionyms/2   8
Figure 1.1   Dimensions of Responsibility   35
Figure 1.2   Four Dichotomies of Responsibility   36

0 | INTRODUCTION

OVERVIEW

In this work I defend *two* main theses, relevant both for ethics and for legal philosophy: that responsibility is fundamentally normative and that responsibility should be normative.

Part I ('The Concepts of Responsibility') aims at:

(i) *first*, clarifying what kinds of entity 'responsibility'[1] refers to, and, using a structured taxonomy, distinguishing *concepts*, *conceptions*, *conditions* and *justifications* of responsibility;

(ii) *second*, clarifying what 'normative' in the phrase 'normative responsibility' means.

In the remainder of this work, I shall put forward four arguments to back up my thesis.

In Part II, I shall put forward three *negative* arguments. In particular:

In Chapter 2 (*Responsibility and Mens Rea*), I consider the claim that since responsibility should have a descriptive content, it cannot be based on *mens rea* (on mental elements) because *mens rea* is not objectively or scientifically ascertainable.

In Chapter 3 (*Responsibility and Neuroscience*), I then consider the claim that cognitive sciences (ie. neuroscience) would

---

[1] A convention on the use of quotation marks: quotation marks are simple (' ') only for terms used *in suppositione materiali*; quotation marks are double (" ") for all other uses: scare quotes, irony, etc. Here is an example: 'When talking about "use", use 'use'.'

be able to objectively measure mental states, thus giving a plausible descriptive foundation to responsibility. I refute this claim both for theoretical and practical reasons. I propose, instead, to endorse a normative notion of responsibility.

In Chapter 4 (*Responsibility and Causation*), I consider (and refute) an even more extreme argument: that responsibility attribution should be completely descriptive because it is based on (one of its conditions:) causality. The evaluative component would then (almost) disappear.

In Part III (*The Language of Responsibility*), I shall put forward a fourth and *positive* argument: using a pragmatic analysis of *negation* (of normative statements), I shall consider negations of responsibility and shall show the normative nature of responsibility judgments.[2]

In the Appendices, I make available part of four works (especially important for my last chapter and for philosophical deontics) hard to find or not yet translated into English.

RESPONSIBILITY: THE NAME, THE THING

Names of Responsibility

At the end of this Introduction (Figures 0.1 and 0.2), I shall provide the reader with a list of some xenonyms, of some counterparts, of 'responsibility' in 50 natural languages, most of which are Indo-European.

In most Indo-European languages, the words for "responsibility" are connected to the words for "answer". I shall present five examples and then try to give an etymological sketch, to show

---

[2] This is by no means the standard theory. When judgments of responsibility are kept separate from responsibility or concepts of responsibility, they are usually considered *non*-normative; for example, judgments of responsibility are considered *explanatory* by Björnsson and Persson, 2012, forthcoming.

that while the connection with 'answer' may seem immediate, the matter is more complicated.

The word for "responsibility" is connected to the word for "answer" in at least *five* different groups of Indo-European languages. *First*, it is obviously connected to answer in *Romance languages*. *Second*, it is connected to answer in most *Germanic* languages. *Third*, it is connected to answer in most *Slavic* languages. Polish *'odpowiedzialność'* ["responsibility"] is obviously connected to *'odpowiadać'* ["to answer"]. *Fourth*, it is connected to answer in some *Goidelic* languages. Irish Gaelic *'freagracht'* ["responsibility"] is connected to 'a fhreagairt' ["to answer"]. *Fifth*, the word for responsibility is connected to the word for answer in some *Baltic* languages, such as Lithuanian. Lithuanian 'atsakomýbė' ["responsibility"] is connected to 'atsakýti' ["to answer"].

But things are more complicated than that. Hart (Hart, 2008, Postscript) points out the connection between 'responsibility' and Latin *'respondēre'*, not in the sense of answering questions, but in the sense of responding to accusations. Latin 're-spondēre' is obviously a compound made by *'re'* and *'spondeō'*. *'Spondeō'* has been sharply investigated by Benveniste, 1969.

'Spondeō' has, in fact, the primary meaning of "to pledge, promise, make a contract";[3] briefly: engaging oneself in an obligation (like a promise), and likely responding for that.

Germanic languages — at least according to Benveniste, 1969 — show a parallelism with Romance languages and Latin: *'Verantwortung'*, *'ansvar'*, *'answerability'* all come originally from a verb akin to Gothic *'swaran'* (cf. German *'schwören'*, English 'to swear') with the sense of "swear", "undertake an oath", but whence we got Icelandic *'svara'* "to answer", Old High German *'and-swara'* "to re-spond", akin to the meaning of Latin *'respondēre'*.[4]

While doing philosophy from etymology can be risky or useless, I think that both Latin (and mediately Romance languages)

---

3 Cf. Vaan, 2008, p. 582 and for the related Greek 'σπένδω' *'spéndō'* "to offer a libation, pour" cf. Beekes, 2009.
4 For this line of reasoning, cf. Benveniste, 1969, pp. 165, 209–221.

and Germanic languages suggest that responsibility's (linguistic) ancestor is connected to a normative entity, be it an obligation, a promise or an oath.

In the rest of this work, I shall try to show that there is more to be added to this (partial) *philological* evidence. I shall try to show that there are *philosophical* reasons to think that responsibility is primarily a normative notion.

Aitiologics

For the study of responsibility, I would propose the term 'Aitiologics' ['Aitiologique', 'Aitiologica', 'Aitiologik', 'Ajtiologyka' vel 'Aitiologyka'].

But why use 'aitia', if 'aitia' means "cause", such as in 'etiology'? Even intuitively, "cause" and "responsibility" are not the same.

'Αἰτία' 'Aitía', in Ancient Greek meant both "guilt" (one could try to say, employing contemporary categories: "responsibility") and "cause".[5]

So, why use 'aitiologics' to designate the study of responsibility? For *three* main reasons.

First, the primary meaning of 'αἰτία' 'aitía' is something akin to modern "guilt".[6]

Second, the primary use of 'αἰτία' 'aitía' was in social, legal and medical contexts, in order to mean "guilt".

Third, the conceptualization of "causality", from blame or guilt, developed in medical thinking. It is from medicine that 'αἰτία'

---

5 Cf. for instance Beekes, 2009, ad vocem.
6 The word 'αἰτία' 'aitía', from a reconstructed '*αἶτος' 'aîtos' "share" (cf. Beekes, 2009, p. 45), was already used in Homeric texts (cf. for instance Iliad, XIX, 86) but it is does not seem likely that the concept expressed is comparable to the modern "guilt", because of the notorious lack of subjectivity in archaic Greek thought. On this last aspect, see at least Adkins, 1960; Gernet, 1917, Snell, 1946, Vernant, 1971; Vidal-Naquet and Vernant, 1972, Saïd, 1978 and Vegetti, 2007b, 2010.

'aitía' in the sense of "cause" (the idea of causality) passed on to natural thinking (for instance in physics).[7]

LINGUISTIC/SEMANTIC REMARKS

My work has been carried out mostly in an English-speaking setting and with primary sources mainly in English or concerned with an English-based legal system and categories. Nonetheless, the author's personal background is from continental law — a domain with different categories and a different semantics. This cross-contamination seems a useful experiment, because it forces me to look anew and from different perspectives at both the "lived" and the "learnt", in a process of mutual enlightenment.

It may therefore be useful to give a sort of linguistic and semantic map for the reader from another legal system, with the usual caveat that all translations are imperfect and approximative: not all xenonyms are also synonyms.

The non-bijectivity of these terms is splendidly shown by the very eponym of my work: 'responsibility'. In Romance languages, the xenonyms for 'responsibility' cover not only what in English is called 'responsibility' but also what is called, respectively: 'answerability', 'accountability' and, most importantly I think, *'liability'* (German: *'Verantwortung'*, Swedish, Danish and Norwegian: *'ansvar'*; Dutch: *'verantwoordelijkheid'*, *'aansprakelijk'*, *'toerekeningsvatbaar'*).[8]

METHODOLOGICAL REMARKS

Now, *four* methodological remarks.

---

7 These theses are backed up, in various forms, by Snell, 1946, Vernant, 1971; Vidal-Naquet and Vernant, 1972, Saïd, 1978, Irwin, 1980, 2007–11, Frede, 1980, 1987, B. A. O. Williams, 1993, Vegetti, 2007a,b, 2010 and Mondolfo, 2012.

8 For an early analysis of these words in Dutch from a legal semiotic perspective, see de Haan, 1912, 1916, 1919. I owe Paolo Di Lucia this clue.

First, the word 'responsibility' is usually qualified: moral responsibility, legal responsibility, criminal responsibility. Furthermore, responsibility is kept separate — if not distinct — from liability. When the word 'responsibility' is not qualified, I usually refer to the general phenomenon.

Second, 'responsibility' is an umbrella term in the sense that it covers both blame and praise. Usually praise is ignored to focus only on blame. I shall follow this general use somewhat, but the scope of the following considerations should hopefully also be symmetrically applicable to praise.

Third, I am aware of at least two latent issues: the relationship between moral and legal responsibility, and, more generally, between law and morals. For both, personal and external constraints suggest that I do not engage directly with these points.

Fourth, I shall try to investigate responsibility and not one of its (possible) conditions: freedom of the will. For this reason I shall not be concerned directly with the debate on freedom and (moral) responsibility.

This dissertation hopes to be philosophical, if not in nature, at least in its intention. Occasional examples or doctrines taken from the law are considered mainly from a philosophical perspective and for their philosophical import.

As always (at least in analytic philosophy), the arguments I offer in the following pages are in no way definitive proof of anything.

I shall try to highlight those issues arising from various philosophical (and non-philosophical) theories I think problematic. I shall picture a detailed theory to account for these issues and my aim is to offer an alternative possible solution. I then try to address obvious and not so obvious objections and counter-arguments and argue why this particular approach might be the best explanation.

My proximate aim then will be to show that the position defended here has at least some pros (or less cons) than its main rivals.

Language	Aitionym(s)	Transliteration	Notes
Afrikaans	verantwoordelikheid		
Albanian	përgjegjësi		
Arabic	مسؤولية		
Basque	erantzukizun		
Belarusian	адказнасць	adkaznasć	
Bulgarian	отговорност	otgovornost	
Catalan	responsabilitat		
Chinese	责任	zérèn	
Croatian	odgovornost		
Czech	odpovědnost		
Danish	ansvar, ansvarlighed		
Dutch	verantwoordelijkheid aansprakelijk, toerekeningsvatbaar		
English	responsibility, accountability, answerability, liability		
Estonian	vastutus		
Finnish	vastuu		
French	responsabilité		
Galician	responsabilidade		
German	Verantwortung, Verantwortlichkeit		
Greek (modern)	ευθύνη		
Hebrew	אחריות		
Hindi	जिम्मेदारी	Jim'mēdārī	
Hungarian	felelősség		
Icelandic	ábyrgð		
Irish	freagracht		

Figure 0.1: Aitionyms/1

Language	Aitionym(s)	Transliteration	Notes
Italian	responsabilità		
Japanese	責任	sekinin	
Korean	책임	chaeg-im	
Latvian	atbildība		
Lithuanian	atsakomýbė		
Macedonian	одговорност		
Maltese	responsabbiltà		
Norwegian	ansvar		
Occitan	respondoiretat		
Persian	مسؤولیت		
Polish	odpowiedzialność		
Portuguese	responsabilidade		
Romanian	responsabilitate		
Russian	ответственность	otvetstvennost'	
Sardinian	responsabbilidàde		
Serbian	одговорност	odgovornost	
Slovak	zodpovednosť		
Slovenian	odgovornost		
Spanish	responsabilidad		
Swedish	ansvar		
Turkish	sorumluluk		
Ukrainian	відповідальність	vidpovidal'nist'	
Urdu	ذمہ داری		
Welsh	cyfrifoldeb		
Yiddish	אַכרײַעס	'akryya's	

Figure 0.2: Aitionyms/2

Part I

The Concepts of Responsibility

1 RESPONSIBILITY: CONCEPTS, CONCEPTIONS, CONDITIONS

Distingue frequenter.

1.0 Introduction: Concept, Conceptions, Conditions

1.1 Responsibility CONCEPTS: Four Dichotomies

    1.1.1 I: Praxical *vs.* Non-Praxical Responsibility

    1.1.2 II: Nomophoric *vs.* Non-Nomophoric Responsibility

    1.1.3 III: Regulative-Rule-Related *vs.* Constitutive-Rule-Related Responsibility

    1.1.4 IV: Role-Related *vs.* Role-Unrelated Responsibility

    1.1.5 List of Responsibility Concepts

1.2 Normative Responsibility CONDITIONS

    1.2.1 *Eidologic* Conditions of Responsibility

    1.2.2 *Eidonomic* Conditions of Responsibility

1.3 CONCEPTIONS *vs.* JUSTIFICATIONS of Responsibility

    1.3.1 Conceptions of Responsibility

    1.3.2 Justifications of Responsibility

    1.3.3 Relationships among Concepts, Conceptions and Justifications: Dimensions of Responsibility

1.4 Two Senses of 'Normativity': Nomophoric *vs.* Axiological

    1.4.1 Nomophoric Normativity

    1.4.2 Axiological Normativity

    1.4.3 Nomophoric *vs.* Axiological Responsibility

1.0 INTRODUCTION: CONCEPTS, CONCEPTIONS, CONDITIONS

> *We are up against one of the great sources of philosophical bewilderment: we try to find a substance for a substantive. A substantive makes us look for a thing that corresponds to it.*
> Wittgenstein, 1958

'What is responsibility?' is a misleading question. It is misleading because it has *two* false presuppositions.[1]

First, it concedes that *there is* at least such a thing as responsibility.[2]

Second, it assumes that there is at most *one* thing such as responsibility.[3]

Undeniably there are several phenomena referred to, collectively or separately, as responsibility. I shall start from the phenomena to try and clarify not what the word 'responsibility' means, but what the constellation of concepts umbrella-termed 'responsibilities' consists of.

The thesis of this work is that responsibility is normative. Now, in this equation there are (at least) two unknowns: responsibility and normativity. One of the aims of this work is to shed light on the concept of responsibility through a close study of its relationships with normativity.

In this chapter I therefore shall conceptually explore both *responsibility* and *normativity*, whereas in the rest of this book I

---

[1] In this work 'presupposition' is used technically with reference to the theory of presuppositions (for an introduction see Beaver and Geurts, 2011, for other works on the topic see for instance Atlas, 1977; Balasubramanian, 1984; Carston, 1998; Karttunen, 1976, 1977; Kripke, 2009; Peters, 1979). For the non-technical usage, I shall adopt such words as 'supposition', 'assumption' and so on.

[2] That there is *no* such thing as responsibility has been maintained at least by G. Strawson, 1994, 2009 and Waller, 2011.

[3] That there is more than one such thing as responsibility has been argued at least by Di Lucia, 2013b; Hart, 2008; Heller, 1988; Ross, 1975; Vincent, Van De Poel, and Van Den Hoven, 2011.

shall investigate their mutual relationship from different perspectives.

This chapter is organized in *two* parts.

In the *first* part (Sections 1.1, 1.2 and 1.3), I shall investigate *responsibility*. In particular I shall show that responsibility is not a unitary entity.

Firstly, in Section 1.1, I show that the concepts of responsibility are at least four-fold. *Secondly*, in Section 1.2, I try to separate the investigation on responsibility from the enquiry on its *conditions* (such as free will). *Thirdly*, in Section 1.3, I put forward some reasons to keep separate the concepts of responsibility ("what is responsibility?") from the *justification* of the social practices of holding responsible ("why responsibility?") and from general *conceptions* of responsibility ("how should responsibility be?").

Concepts [*concetto, concept, concepto, Begriff* and *Konzept, pojęcie, ponjatie*], however, differ from *conceptions* [*concezione, conception, concepción, Auffassung, koncepcja* and *ujęcie, koncepcija*].

I shall focus on the various *concepts* of responsibility in Section 1.1.

I shall focus on the various *conditions* of responsibility in Section 1.2.

I shall focus on the various *conceptions* of responsibility in Section 1.3.

In the *second* part (Section 1.4), I shall investigate *normativity*. 'Normativity' and 'normative' have several different senses.[4]

In particular, I shall contrast two senses of 'normativity': normativity explicitly related to rules (*nomophoric* normativity) with normativity conceived as an evaluation (*axiological* normativity).

Arguably, the *two* most pregnant for this kind of inquiry are thus the following.

---

4 An investigation of normativity is beyond the scope of the present work. I shall, however, attempt an heuristic dichotomy in Section 1.4. To get a glimpse of the broadness of this subject, see: http://philpapers.org/browse/normativity.

First, 'normative' is something somewhat[5] related to norms.[6] I shall suggest for this concept the term 'nomophoric' (or 'nomological') [*'nomoforico'*, *'nomophorique'*, *'nomophorisch'*, *'nomoforyczny'*].

Second, 'normative' as something *prima facie* opposed to the 'descriptive', 'non-normative' and thus involving an evaluation.[7] I shall suggest for this concept the term 'axiological' (or 'axiotic') [*'axiologico'* or *'assiologico'*, *'axiologique'*, *'axiologisch'*, *'aksiologiczny'*].[8]

1.1 RESPONSIBILITY CONCEPTS: FOUR DICHOTOMIES

I shall not investigate what responsibility is, its essence or nature (*das Wesen der Verantwortung*), but — for starters — I shall consider what kinds of entities it can be predicated of. I shall try to show that among these different concepts of responsibility there are *Familienähnlichkeiten* [*Family Resemblances*] — common traits hard to identify analytically.

If we see responsibility as a *trivalent*[9] concept (subject *a* is responsible for thing *x* to person(s) *b*), then in this section I shall limit my enquiry mostly to the "things" one may be responsible for.[10]

---

5 I shall explore in particular two types of relationship to norms: responsibility-related norms, and norm-related responsibility. Vide *infra*, Section 1.4.3.1.
6 For the polysemy of the term 'norm', see Conte, 2007b.
7 For a similar suggestion, see Finlay, 2010.
8 The disciplines studying the nomological and the axiotic are, respectively, *nomologics* (for which vide Conte, 2013b) and *axiotics* (in a related, although different, sense, vide Conte, 2008.)
9 I refer here to the concept of *valency* in linguistics, proposed by Tesnière in Tesnière, 1959. In recent literature, this thesis is echoed by Duff, especially in Duff, 2008, 2009.
10 But note that Lenk and Maring, 1993 deals with responsibility as a *hexa*valent concept. In particular, the authors maintain that the concept of responsibility [*Verantwortung*] has the following six *valencies*:
"*jemand*: Verantwortungssubjekt, -träger (Personen, Korporationen) ist;

I shall propose these dichotomies not because I have seen them, but in order to see (*ut videam*) — to better see the phenomena I shall investigate in the remainder of this work.

1.1.1 I: Praxical *vs.* Non-Praxical Responsibility

Praxical responsibility is responsibility for (human) actions, deeds. The etymology of 'praxis' is straightforward: the verb 'πράσσω' ('πράσσειν'), meaning "(I) do", especially contrasted to 'ποιέω', "(I) make".[11]

Non-praxical responsibility is responsibility not exclusively for human actions, but for intentions, thoughts or more generally, outcomes. Example of non-praxical responsibility are *causal* responsibility (for instance as described by Hart, 2008, Postscript) and *virtue-responsibility*, that is, responsibility for one's character (for instance as described by Vincent, in Vincent, Van De Poel, and Van Den Hoven, 2011) or *blameworthiness* (for instance as proposed by P. A. Graham, forthcoming). Other examples include responsibility for believing (Hieronymi, 2008) and beliefs (sometimes referred to as *doxastic* responsibility) or dreams (Mullane, 1965) and for mere intentions (Jackson, 1975).[12]

---

für: etwas (Handlungen, Handlungsfolgen, Zustände, Aufgaben usw.);
gegenüber: einem Adressaten;
vor: einer (Sanktions-, Urteils-) Instanz;
in bezug auf: ein (präskriptives, normatives) Kriterium;
im Rahmen eines: Verantwortungs-, Handlungsbereiches verantwortlich (p. 229)."

11 The distinction between a manipulative/creative aspect and a mere bringing about of something apparent in Ancient Greek is echoed, I suppose, in a similar distinction at least in modern English and German: πράσσειν prássein : to do/tun = ποιεῖν poieîn : to make/machen. For philosophical remarks on these verbs, see Conte, 2001b. For the semantics of the verbs of doing and making in Indo-European languages, see Yoshioka, 1908. Varro, in *De lingua latina*, notes that besides 'agere' and 'facere' there is a third word in Latin for 'officia': 'gerere'. On this point, see also Di Lucia, 2013b.

12 To expand fully on this point I'd need a developed philosophy action I do not have.

1.1.2 II: Nomophoric vs. Non-Nomophoric Responsibility

Nomophoric responsibility (or rule-related responsibility) is responsibility arising because of a rule (or a set of rules). I shall focus on nomophoric responsibility *infra* in Section 1.4.3.1.

Non-nomophoric responsibility is responsibility but not because of moral or legal rules, implicitly or explicitly stated.

As an example of praxical, non-nomophoric responsibility, I propose to consider *moral* responsibility (broadly understood), as investigated for instance by Strawson.[13] The attribution of responsibility depends on (moral) reactive attitudes and it is not reducible to a system of (moral) rules.

1.1.3 III: Regulative-Rule-Related vs. Constitutive-Rule-Related Responsibility

Regulative-rule-related responsibility is responsibility for the violation of a regulative rule. An example of regulative-rule-related responsibility is responsibility arising because of the violation of a rule prohibiting murder.

Constitutive-rule-related responsibility is responsibility arising because of some interaction with a constitutive rule. An example of constitutive-rule-related responsibility is responsibility arising because of the violation of anakastic rules on canonic marriage.

Regulative rules "regulate antecedently existing forms of behavior", whereas constitutive rules "create or define new forms of behavior [...] The activity of playing chess is constituted by action in accordance with these rules. Chess has no existence apart from these rules".[14] All constitutive rules are conditions

---

13 Cf. especially P. F. Strawson, 1968 (2008).
14 Searle, 1964, p.55. The distinction between constitutive and regulative rules comes from Rawls, 1955, but has had various sources in the history of thought. Many ideas on constitutive and regulative rules are indebted to Amedeo Giovanni Conte. See for instance Conte, 1995c, 2007c.

of their content: conditions of conceivability and conditions of the possibility of their content.[15].

Those rules ruling on responsibility must be distinguished from responsibility arising because of a "violation" of a rule. Of these rules, those I call (eidologic) conditions of responsibility shall be discussed in Section 1.2.

1.1.4 IV: Role-Related vs. Role-Unrelated Responsibility

Role-related responsibility is responsibility arising because of the presence of rules codifying a *type* of conduct, a role.

Examples of type-responsibility include all *role*-responsibilities, such as the responsibility of bearing the role of a ship captain, a firefighter, a GP.

Role-unrelated responsibility is — instead — responsibility arising because of the presence of norms "ruling" on the validity of a single act, but non-relatedly to roles.

Think of a catholic priest. The *role*-responsibilities (the *type*-responsibility) of a catholic priest include, among others, celebrating baptisms, masses and marriages according to the Church's law. In this respect, this is comparable to the duties of a ship captain.

Now, say our catholic priest marries two people. Let's say that the Bishop forbids wedding ceremonies in a given period, but our priest goes ahead and marries our two friends. The priest can be punished because he disobeyed that (regulative) rule. One of the necessary conditions for the validity of that marriage according to canon law (let's imagine) is the fact that these two people can't be close relatives. The priest knows, but he goes ahead and celebrates the wedding, which turns out to be

---

15 Constitutive rules can be further divided in deontic and adeontic constitutive rules. An example of the former is: 'The Bishop ought to move any number of squares diagonally, provided it does not leap over other pieces'. An example of the latter is: 'Stolicą Rzeczypospolitej Polskiej jest Warszawa' [Warsaw is the capital city of Poland]' (art.29 of the Polish Constitution) cf. Passerini Glazel, 2007. Apart from Conte's works, see also Carcaterra, 1974, Searle, 1964, Azzoni, 1988 and Roversi, 2006, 2012

invalid. He hasn't broken any regulative rules, but it seems he is still responsible for having celebrated an invalid marriage — he is *token*-responsible, responsible for that specific invalid act.

Can he be punished? And if so, according to which rules?

Examples of type-responsibility include the responsibility of doing invalid acts (marrying people against *impedimenta dirimentia* according to 1917 Canon Law, signing a sentence if one is not the judge), acts that do not carry with them common sanctions if invalidly done (marrying people against *impedimenta impedientia* is forbidden and carries sanctions with it).[16]

I shall focus on these two kinds of responsibility (type- *vs.* token-responsibility) *infra* in Section 1.4.3.1.

1.1.5 List of Responsibility Concepts

Here, I summarize the four dichotomies I have introduced. Their interplay may be seen in Figure 1.2.

1. Praxical responsibility *vs.* non-praxical responsibility;

2. Nomophoric responsibility *vs.* non-nomophoric responsibility;

3. Regulative-rule-related responsibility *vs.* Constitutive-rule-related responsibility;

4. Role-related responsibility *vs.* role-unrelated responsibility

1.2 NORMATIVE RESPONSIBILITY CONDITIONS

From concepts of responsibility must be distinguished the *conditions* [condizione, condition, condición, Bedingung, warunek, sostojanie] of (a concept of) responsibility.

---

16 The situation with catholic marriage according to 1917 Canon Law is studied with reference to constitutive and anankastic rules by Azzoni, 1988.

Conditions can pertain necessarily to a concept of responsibility, or can pertain non-necessarily to that concept but, for instance, be dependent on rules or laws.

Accordingly, I distinguish *two* kinds of conditions of responsibility:

- (i) *eidologic* conditions (necessary conditions for that concept), in Section 1.2.1;

- (ii) *eidonomic* conditions (conditions posited by rules or laws), in Section 1.2.2.

Of course, conditions may be different for different concepts of responsibility (for instance, those I highlighted in the last section). I shall rhapsodically enumerate some of these for illustrative reasons.

1.2.1 *Eidologic* Conditions of Responsibility

Eidologic conditions of responsibility are necessary conditions for that concept. For the concept of moral responsibility, for instance, several necessary conditions have been required:

- (i) *freedom*: especially in modern contexts as the possibility to do otherwise;

- (ii) *voluntariness*: for instance by *Ethica Nicomachea*, Book III;[17]

---

17 This is disputed. The first thematization of the debate on responsibility (better: blameworthiness) is considered *Ethica Nicomachea*, Book III. There, Aristotle begins an analysis of the conditions of responsibility. Blame and praise, he argues, apply to voluntary actions. But — with a strategy followed as recently as those by Hart, 1948 and Austin, 1956 — he does not define voluntary except in reference to the involuntary, that is, what is done under duress or by ignorance.
Both duress and ignorance are topics still debated nowadays in moral philosophy and criminal law, as it is clear from discussion in other parts of my work.
While the discussion on *duress* seems fit to stand for modern excuses, it is especially the discussion on *ignorance* which seems to capture all those ele-

- (iii) *identity of a person over time*: for instance by Ingarden, 1970, 1987.

It is important to notice that necessary conditions of a concept *must* be kept separate from that concept. The investigation of *freedom*, for instance, is not automatically an investigation of *responsibility*, closely connected as the two may be. This observation will become particularly significant when I consider scientific investigations in Chapter 3.

1.2.2 *Eidonomic* Conditions of Responsibility

Eidologic conditions of responsibility are conditions posited by a rule or a group of rules.

While in Section 1.4.3.1 I refer to *nomophoric* responsibility, that is, responsibility related to rules, I am considering here the opposite relation, namely, rules related to responsibility.

An example of *nomophoric* responsibility is the responsibility arising from the violation of a rule prohibiting murder.

An example of a rule on responsibility is Art. 27.1 of the Italian Constitution: "La responsabilità penale è personale".

These rules related to responsibility I call eidonomic conditions of responsibility.

Those norms ruling directly on responsibility in a given system differ, then, from responsibility arising for the violation (in some sense) of generic rules, being its conditions.

But since there are different *kinds* of rules (for instance regulative and constitutive rules), there are *different kinds* of rules conditioning responsibility.

---

ments captured by the expression 'mens rea' or combined in 'colpa' and 'dolo', namely intention, knowledge, recklessness and negligence.

Now, *two* problems with Aristotle's approach: *first*, a metaphilosophical problem. It is not at all clear whether his approach is descriptive or prescriptive, whether he merely reports what is the case (blamable actions are those voluntary) or what must be the case (blamable actions must be those voluntary). *Second*, it is not clear at all whether what is blamable are voluntary or deliberately chosen actions. In the first case (blamable are voluntary actions) praise and blame should be attributed also to animals and small children — which seems neither the case nor acceptable.

I shall distinguish between *regulative* rules, eidetic-constitutive and anankastic-constitutive rules conditioning responsibility, with the warning that these are only some possible rules. A full analysis has not yet been completed.

1.2.2.1 (Responsibility-Related) Regulative Rules

I define regulative-rule-related responsibility (in short, regulative responsibility, RR) as responsibility for actions, behaviors or state-of-affairs prescribed by regulative rules.

Here are two possible examples: (i) "Ogni reato, che abbia cagionato un danno patrimoniale o non patrimoniale obbliga al risarcimento il colpevole e le persone che, a norma delle leggi civili, debbono rispondere per il fatto di lui (Art. 185, It. Penal Code)."

(ii) "Qualunque fatto doloso o colposo, che cagiona ad altri un danno ingiusto, obbliga colui che ha commesso il fatto a risarcire il danno (art. 2043, It. Civil Code)."

1.2.2.2 Responsibility-Related Constitutive Rules

I define constitutive-rule-related responsibility as responsibility related to constitutive rules.

RESPONSIBILITY-RELATED EIDETIC-CONSTITUTIVE RULES I define re-sponsibility-related eidetic-constitutive-rules as responsibility constituted by *eidetic-constitutive* rules, rules that define the *concept* of responsibility, rules that are *necessary conditions* of (that concept of) responsibility.

Here is an example, taken from the Italian Constitution, Art. 27.1: "La responsabilità penale è personale".[18]

If eidetic-constitutive rules change, the concept of responsibility itself changes accordingly. Take the example above. If the article were to change, then we would get another concept of "responsabilità penale", quite different from the original one.

---

18 Here I am not interested in the meaning of this article, but in the fact that it is a condition of criminal responsibility in Italian law.

(RESPONSIBILITY-RELATED) ANANKASTIC-CONSTITUTIVE RULES

I define responsibility-related anankastic-constitutive-rules as responsibility constituted by *anankastic-constitutive* rules, rules that *posit* a necessary *condition* to responsibility.

Here is an example, taken from the Italian penal code, Article 97: "Non è imputabile chi, nel momento in cui ha commesso il fatto, non aveva compiuto i quattordici anni."

If an anankastic-consitutive rule changes, the concept of responsibility does not change: what changes are the conditions of applicability of that concept. In our example, if the minimum age for imputability were 13 or 15 there would be no change in the concept itself, but only in its condition(s) of application.

As a matter of fact, of course, since its (necessary) conditions change, also the resulting *synolon* changes as well — but not conceptually.

1.3 CONCEPTIONS *VS.* JUSTIFICATIONS OF RESPONSIBILITY

I distinguish *conceptions* of responsibility from *justifications* of responsibility.

While conceptions try to answer the question: 'how should responsibility be?', *justifications* presuppose a given conception of responsibility, and answer the question: 'why is one held responsible?'

Justifications thus presuppose a given conception, but cannot be reduced to it, nor be deduced from it.

1.3.1 Conceptions of Responsibility

I distinguish *two* main conceptions of responsibility: one *descriptive*, one *normative*.[19]

---

19 Two caveats: *first*, there are different ways of conceptualizing these positions. Vargas, 2013, p. 137, for instance, describes (i) a *characterological* account of responsibility "if the action in some way expresses a deep fact about the

1.3.1.1 *Descriptive Responsibility*

> (*DR*) A's being responsible for x depends on facts[20] prior to/independent from our assessment or evaluation.

Descriptive responsibility can be declined in *two* sub-positions: (i) the metaphysical realist; (ii) the eliminativist.

THE REALIST POSITION   The metaphysical realist holds that (DR) responsibility depends on natural facts independent from us, *and* that those facts exist.[21]

The "Ledger View"   A particular stream of thinkers representing this position is that called the "ledger view", usually identified with Feinberg, 1970,[22] Glover, 1970 and Zimmerman, 1988.

To give a gist of the theory, I shall sketch here the position of Feinberg in *a part* of Feinberg, 1970. This position does not exhaust Feinberg's theory of responsibility.

As opposed to *legal* responsibility, moral responsibility should be:[23]

- independent from practical considerations (for instance the specific aim of punishment one has);[24]

---

agent (Vargas, 2013, p. 137)" (for instance Hume, 1902, 2011, Watson); (ii) a *reason-responsiveness* one ("a particular power to respond to the world (Vargas, 2013, p. 137)"); and (iii) an *attributionist* one (for instance: Scanlon, 1998 and Angela Smith).
Second, parsimony leads me to identify only these two neat ones: a *descriptive* conception; and a *normative* conception.

20 These facts need not be natural, of course.
21 This of course does not imply that the attribution of responsibility isn't itself an evaluation.
22 I should warn the reader that Feinberg explored this conception of responsibility and in the end found it untenable for several reasons, one of which was the existence of moral luck.
23 Please note that Feinberg does not *describe* moral responsibility (he's not saying that responsibility is so-and-so); he is telling the reader how moral responsibility *should* be. There are evaluative considerations involved here.
24 Cf. Feinberg, 1970, pp. 52-3.

- absolute: independent from social policy (ie the aim of punishment);[25]

- luck-independent.[26]

Responsibility judgments are (or should be) — according to Feinberg — *descriptive*, that is, consisting in merely looking up a given individual's moral *ledger* and "seeing" whether his responsibility is written there.[27]

The "ledger view", however, is more complex. All these factual elements we have seen constitute what is called by Feinberg "*imputability*". But imputability is only a part of the problem of responsibility.

In fact, imputability is distinguished from *liability*, which is responsibility in its fuller sense: while imputability is an objective judgment such as "He is *blamable*", liability is a judgment — expressed or not — as "He is *to blame*". Liability is more akin to an evaluation and is bound to social interactions and social policy, so to speak, but refers to a series of *factual* conditions (those qualifying for imputability).[28]

To sum up, this interpretation of the "ledger view" may be considered descriptive not because responsibility is not evaluative, but because evaluating responsibility requires a necessary reference to *factual* elements that are objective.[29]

THE ELIMINATIVIST POSITION   The metaphysical realist holds that (DR) responsibility depends on natural facts independent from us, *and* that those facts do *not* exist.

For the eliminativist responsibility could only be rooted out there in the physical world — but since there are no facts point-

---

25 Cf. Feinberg, 1970, pp. 31.
26 Cf. Feinberg, 1970, pp. 32.
27 For this interesting metaphor of the register — and the most appropriate verbs 'to impute' [*imputare*] and 'to ascribe' [*ad-scribere, zuschreiben*] — taken to be the conceptual ancêtre of responsibility (at least by Ricœur, 1994, but see Fonnesu, 2013) — see my note on *Zurechnung* in Chapter 5.
28 Feinberg contrasts imputability and liability explicitly in Feinberg, 1970, pp. 119–151.
29 I thank S. F. Magni for discussion on this point.

ing in that direction, then there is no such a thing as responsibility.

Examples would be G. Strawson, 1994, 2009 and Waller, 2011.

1.3.1.2 Normative Responsibility

> (NR) A is responsible for x iff it is appropriate to hold A responsible.

Normative Responsibility can be declined in at least *two* fashions: (i) an objectivist position; (ii) a conventionalist position.

THE OBJECTIVISTIC POSITION The objectivist holds that (NR) responsibility depends on some standard of appropriateness, *and* that this standard both exists, is unique, and can be known.

THE CONVENTIONALIST POSITION The conventionalist holds that (NR) responsibility depends on some standard of appropriateness, *and* that this standard is merely conventional, depending on the social community we are considering.

Among proponents of a normative concept of responsibility, there are at least Bayertz, 1995 and Lenk and Maring, 1993, Wallace, 1994 and McGrath, 2005; Thomson, 2003.

Ingarden, 1970 may be included here with some doubts.

1.3.2 Justifications of Responsibility

We have seen that conceptions of responsibility try to answer to questions such as "what is responsibility?", whereas *justifications* of responsibility are concerned with aim of responsibility, and try to answer to questions such as "why do we consider someone responsible?"[30]

Historically, at least *three* distinct justifications of responsibility have been emerging. In this section I aim to give a minimal account of them.

---

[30] I urge the reader not to mistake justifications of *responsibility* for justifications of *punishment*. Responsibility may be considered equal to punishment (as Mill, 1865 alleged) — but this need not necessarily be the case.

In Section 1.3.2.1, I shall sketch a retributionist justification of responsibility;

In Section 1.3.2.2, I shall present a predictive (consequentialist) justification of responsibility;[31]

There is also a more recent, subject-centered justification of responsibility, for instance the *agency cultivation model* — cf. Vargas, 2013, Ch. 6, that I cannot engage with here.

1.3.2.1   *Retributionist Responsibility*

A retributive justification of responsibility is (usually) concerned with *reward* (retribution): an individual must be held responsible because of what he has done, because of his guilt. Using a rather worn out motto of Seneca, one is held responsible *quia peccatum est*.

The prototype of this stance in modern philosophy is usually considered Immanuel Kant — cf. (Kant, 1797, Ch. 49)[32],[33]

---

[31] Note that a hard-line distinction between retributionist and consequentialist theories of responsibility is hard to come by. Contemporary writers seem to have taken a sort of *via media*. This middle way is exemplified — for justifications of punishment — by Hart, 2008, Postscript, §3.

[32] Judicial or juridical punishment (poena forensis) is to be distinguished from natural punishment (poena naturalis), in which crime as vice punishes itself, and does not as such come within the cognizance of the legislator. juridical punishment can never be administered merely as a means for promoting another good either with regard to the criminal himself or to civil society, but must in all cases be imposed only because the individual on whom it is inflicted has committed a crime. For one man ought never to be dealt with merely as a means subservient to the purpose of another, nor be mixed up with the subjects of real right. Against such treatment his inborn personality has a right to protect him, even although he may be condemned to lose his civil personality. He must first be found guilty and punishable, before there can be any thought of drawing from his punishment any benefit for himself or his fellow-citizens. But what is the mode and measure of punishment which public justice takes as its principle and standard? It is just the principle of equality, by which the pointer of the scale of justice is made to incline no more to the one side than the other. It may be rendered by saying that the undeserved evil which any one commits on another is to be regarded as perpetrated on himself (Kant, 1797, Chapter 49, translation by W. Hastie).

[33] Richterliche Strafe (*poena forensis*), die von der natürlichen (*poena naturalis*), dadurch das Laster sich selbst bestraft und auf welche der Gesetzgeber gar

1.3.2.2 *Consequentialist Responsibility*

A consequentialist or predictive justification of responsibility is (usually) concerned both with *prevention* and *correction*: an individual must be held responsible to avoid the repetition of what he has done and to better him and/or to benefit society in general.[34] Following Seneca, one is held responsible *ne peccetur*.

The prototypes of this stance in modern philosophy are usually considered Jeremy Bentham and John Stuart Mill — cf. Mill, 1865.

1.3.3 Relationships among Concepts, Conceptions and Justifications: Dimensions of Responsibility

I have distinguished *supra* among conceptions, concepts and justifications. In this subsection, I shall explore their mutual relationships by way of combinatorics and illustrate their interplay in a three-dimensional figure (1.1).

In particular, I shall limit my investigation to pairs of conceptions (normative and descriptive), pair of justifications (backward-looking and forward-looking) and pair of concepts (here moral and legal concepts of responsibility).

If we have three pairs of elements to combine, we shall obtain

---

nicht Rücksicht nimmt, verschieden, kann niemals bloß als Mittel ein anderes Gute zu befördern für den Verbrecher selbst, oder für die bürgerliche Gesellschaft, sondern muß jederzeit nur darum wider ihn verhängt werden, weil er verbrochen hat; denn der Mensch kann nie bloß als Mittel zu den Absichten eines Anderen gehandhabt und unter die Gegenstände des Sachenrechts gemengt werden, wowider ihn seine angeborne Persönlichkeit schützt, ob er gleich die bürgerliche einzubüßen gar wohl verurtheilt werden kann. [...] Welche Art aber und welcher Grad der Bestrafung ist es, welche die öffentliche Gerechtigkeit sich zum Princip und Richtmaße macht? Kein anderes, als das Princip der Gleichheit, (im Stande des Zünglein an der Wage der Gerechtigkeit) sich nicht mehr auf die eine, als auf die andere Seite hinzuneigen (Kant, 1797, §49).

34 As S. F. Magni suggests (private conversation and Magni, 2005, Ch. 4) a consequentialist justification of responsibility needs not be purely forward-looking: in fact, consequentialists are concerned mostly with one already did, and not only with future actions.

$2^3 = 8$ combinations

In particular,

1. Normative, backward-looking, moral responsibility;

2. Normative, forward-looking, moral responsibility;

3. Descriptive, backward-looking, moral responsibility;

4. Descriptive, forward-looking, moral responsibility;

5. Normative, backward-looking, legal responsibility;

6. Normative, forward-looking, legal responsibility;

7. Descriptive, backward-looking, legal responsibility;

8. Descriptive, forward-looking, legal responsibility;

These 8 combinations are illustrated in three dimensional graphic 1.1.

1.4 TWO SENSES OF 'NORMATIVITY': NOMOPHORIC *VS.* AXIOLOGICAL

'Normativity' and 'normative' have several different senses.[35]
Arguably, the *two* most pregnant for this kind of inquiry are *first*, the *nomophoric*; *second*, the axiological.

---

35 An investigation of normativity is beyond the scope of the present work, and the heuristic dichotomy I sketch here is by no means exhaustive. To get a glimpse of the broadness of this subject, see: http://philpapers.org/browse/normativity.

1.4.1 Nomophoric Normativity

First, 'normative' is something somewhat[36] related to norms.[37] I shall suggest for this concept the term 'nomophoric normativity' (or 'nomological normativity') [*normatività nomoforica, normativité nomophorique, nomophorische Normativität, nomoforyczna normatywność*].

1.4.2 Axiological Normativity

Second, 'normative' as something *prima facie* opposed to the 'descriptive', 'non-normative' and thus involving an evaluation.[38] I shall suggest for this concept the phrase 'axiological normativity' (or 'axiotic normativity') [*normatività axiologica* or *assiologica, normativité axiologique, axiologische Normativität, aksiologiczna normatywność*].[39]

1.4.3 Nomophoric *vs.* Axiological Responsibility

In which sense, then, can responsibility be normative, as in the phrase 'normative responsibility'?

Since I have distinguished *two* senses of 'normativity', I maintain that responsibility can be considered normative in *two* senses:

- (i) *nomophoric* responsibility, when it is related explicitly to norms;

- (ii) *axiological* responsibility, when it is considered in an evaluative dimension.[40]

---

36 I shall explore in particular two types of relationship to norms: responsibility-related norms, and norm-related responsibility. Vide *infra*, Section 1.4.3.1.
37 For the polysemy of the term 'norm', see Conte, 2007b.
38 For a similar suggestion, see Finlay, 2010.
39 The disciplines studying the nomological and the axiotic are, respectively, *nomologics* (for which vide Conte, 2013b) and *axiotics* (in a related, although different, sense, vide Conte, 2008).
40 There is further room for inquiry here. According to some reasons are fundamental in the normative domain, and thus responsibility can be considered normative in the further sense of being tied to reasons. Since it's not clear

1.4.3.1 *Nomophoric Responsibility*

The *first* sense of "normative responsibility", that is, *nomophoric responsibility* is rule-related responsibility.

In this subsection, I shall consider three kinds of rule-related responsibility:

- (i) regulative-rule-related responsibility (in Section 1.4.3.1);

- (ii) constitutive-rule-related responsibility. In particular,
    - (ii.i) *eidetic*-constitutive rule-related responsibility (in Section 1.4.3.1);
    - (ii.ii) *anankastic*-constitutive-rule-related responsibility (in Section 1.4.3.1)

REGULATIVE-RULE-RELATED RESPONSIBILITY   I define regulative-rule-related responsibility as responsibility for actions, behaviors or outcomes regulated by regulative rules.

Two examples: (classical) moral responsibility, Aquilian responsibility (liability to pay damages).

CONSTITUTIVE-RULE-RELATED RESPONSIBILITY   I define constitutive-rule-related responsibility as responsibility arising for some sort of interaction with constitutive rules.

Eidetic-Constitutive-rule-related Responsibility   I define eidetic-constitutive-rule-related responsibility as responsibility arising from interactions with eidetic-constitutive rules, rules that *are* condition(s) of (the concept of) something.

An example is the responsibility of a cheater: eidetic-constitutive rules of that game are necessary for him to cheat, but can exhaust his responsibility.

---

whether the nomophoric or the axiological route are more basic than the reason approach, I leave this path open for future research.

Anankastic-Constitutive-rule-related Responsibility I define anankastic-constitutive-rule-related responsibility as responsibility arising from a "violation" of anankastic-constitutive rules, rules that *posit* condition(s) of (the validity of) something.

An example is the responsibility of doing an invalid exam, when this option is not already considered by regulative rules.

1.4.3.2 *Axiological Responsibility*

The *second* sense of "normative responsibility", that is, *axiological responsibility* is responsibility considered in its evaluative dimension, with reference to values.[41]

This is the most difficult to characterize, because any qualification cannot be neutral and has to build on a meta-normative theory. In some respects (that is, according to some — but not all — metanormative theories) it can be characterized as opposed to what is descriptive.

It is in this sense that I primarily refer in the rest of this work. By the end of my investigation, I hope that a clearer sense of normative responsibility will emerge.

Further Problems Now, it seems that these *two* senses of normativity (and of responsibility) can be distinguished at least heuristically.

But are they irreducible to one another?

As far as I know, several attempts have been made to explore the relationships between what I call the nomophoric and what I call the axiological.

I only sketch here the possible stances on the relationships between the axiological and the nomophoric. I suppose they can be distinguished — at least *prima facie*.

First, deontic panagathism: normativity coincides with the axiological, and therefore the nomophoric is reduced to the axiological. An example of deontic panagathism is Judith Jarvis Thom-

---

[41] Of course the reference to "values" does not clarify the matter. In fact, what kinds of values? Are epistemic values akin to moral values? I leave this problem open here.

son's stance: *duties* and *oughts*, for instance, can be reduced to *goodness*.⁴² "Teleological" theories usually also hold that deontic concepts are to be explained with reference to values (for one G. E. Moore, 1922, p. 25; for a direct argument against this thesis, besides supererogation, see Sesonske, 1964, pp. 70, 75; cf. Schroeder, 2012 and van Fraassen, 1973).

Second, pandeonticism: normativity coincides with the nomophoric, and therefore the axiological is reduced to the nomophoric. An example of pandeonticism is Uberto Scarpelli's work (Scarpelli, 1981); another example is the family of theory called "fitting attitudes account", including Scanlon's famous buck-passing account of value, according to which (roughly) value can be explained with other reasons-providing properties (cf. Scanlon, 1998).

It seems to me that this is a fundamental problem I can only touch on here, hoping for more research to come. For instance, I haven't touched on the relationship between reasons and normativity. Reasons are taken to be fundamental (in the normative domain) by more than one prominent theorists such as Scanlon, 1998, 2014 and Skorupski, 2010.

CONNECTION WITH THE REMAINING PARTS OF THIS WORK   In this chapter, I have engaged in *two* different conceptual investigations:

- in the *first* part, I have considered the nature of responsibility, distinguishing among concepts, conceptions, justifications and conditions of responsibility;

- in the *second* part, I have considered the nature of normativity.

The rest of this work deals with the mutual interactions of responsibility and normativity.

In Part II, I shall consider and try to refute three *negative* arguments, against the thesis that responsibility is normative. In particular:

---

42 For Thomson's stance, see Thomson, 2007, 2008, 2010.

in Chapter 2 (*Responsibility and Mens Rea*), I consider the claim that since responsibility should have a descriptive content, it cannot be based on *mens rea* (on mental elements) because *mens rea* is not objectively or scientifically ascertainable.

In Chapter 3 (*Responsibility and Neuroscience*), I then consider the claim that cognitive sciences (ie. neuroscience) would be able to objectively measure mental states, thus giving a plausible descriptive foundation to responsibility. I refute this claim both for theoretical and practical reasons. I propose, instead, to endorse a normative notion of responsibility.

In Chapter 4 (*Responsibility and Causation*), I consider (and refute) an even more extreme argument: that responsibility attribution should be completely descriptive because it is based on (one of its conditions:) causality. The evaluative component would then (almost) disappear.

In Part III, I consider directly what I call the *pragmatics* of responsibility. I try to put forward an argument for the thesis that responsibility is normative, based on an analysis of responsibility judgments and *norm negation* (negation of normative statements).

1.4 TWO SENSES OF 'NORMATIVITY': NOMOPHORIC VS. AXIOLOGICAL

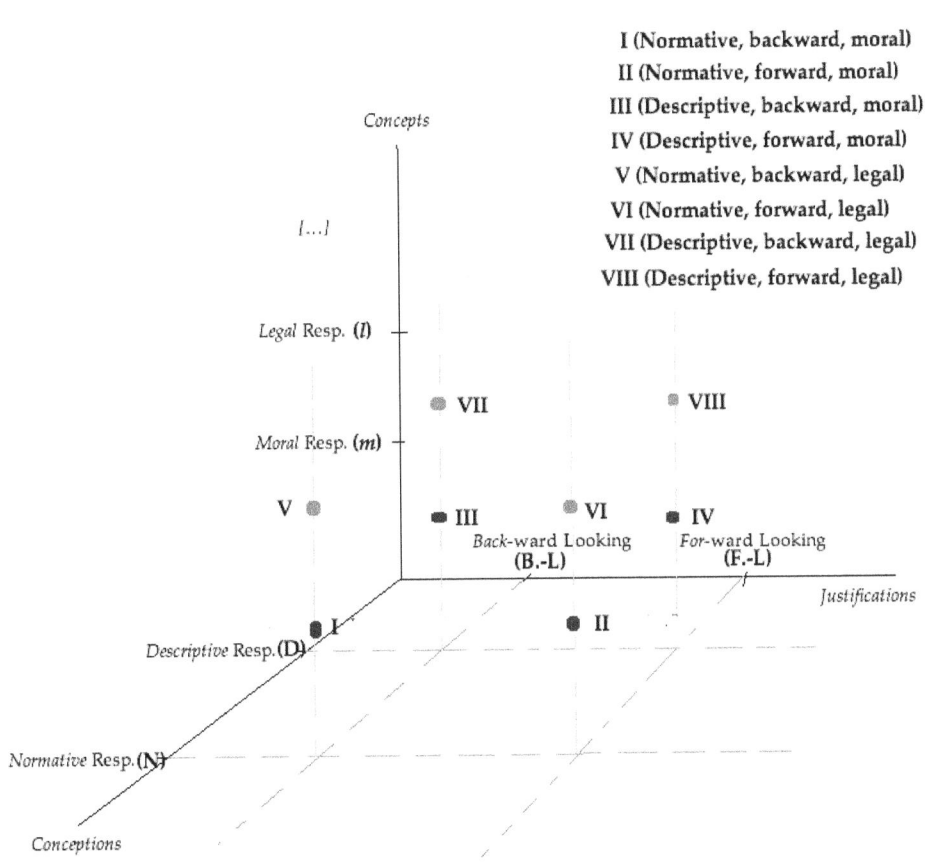

Figure 1.1: Dimensions of Responsibility

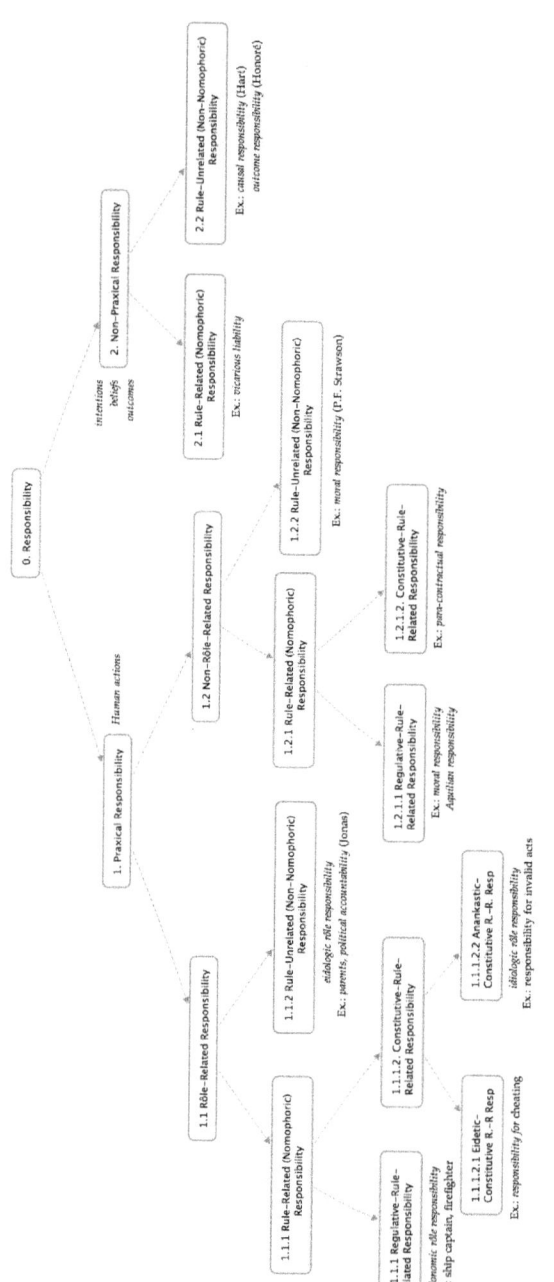

Figure 1.2: Four Dichotomies of Responsibility

Part II

The Rules of Responsibility: Law and Ethics

2 | RESPONSIBILITY AND MENS REA

2.0 Introduction: How Criminal Systems Work

2.1 Lady Wootton's Strict Liability System

    2.1.1 Retribution *vs.* Prevention

    2.1.2 Criminal Liability = Strict Liability

    2.1.3 Mental Abnormality and the Elimination of Responsibility

    2.1.4 Side Remarks: Taxonomies, Determinism, Semantics

    2.1.5 Lady Wootton's Proposal: Recap

2.2 Hart's Reply

    2.2.1 Hart's Moderate Proposal

    2.2.2 Hart's Threefold Critique to Lady Wootton;

    2.2.3 Hart's Two Critiques to Strict Liability

2.3 A. Ross's Reply

    2.3.1 Ross's Conception of Responsibility

    2.3.2 Ross's Fourfold Critique to Lady Wootton

    2.3.3 J. Glover's Double Critique

2.4 Five Criticisms from a Contemporary Perspective

    2.4.1 Assessing Lady Wootton's Proposal

    2.4.2 Ascription of Responsibility Seems Normative

"Otro demérito de los falsos problemas es el de promover soluciones que son falsas también."
Jorge Luis Borges

In this chapter, I consider (and, eventually, try to refute) the claim that the *attribution* of responsibility — if done without reference to *mental* elements — is a *value-free*, *non*-normative task.

Attributing responsibility without considering mental elements has been suggested, for instance, by Lady Wootton. Wootton proposed to abolish the *mens rea* requirement for criminal responsibility and to attribute liability only for the outward conduct, with reference to the behaviorism dominating in her age. Since establishing *mens rea* has traditionally been an (the?) evaluative task *par excellence*, Wootton's proposal — if enacted — would then understand the ascription of responsibility as a purely behavioral-based (almost mechanical) process.

I critically assess the Hart–Wootton debate on whether criminal trials should be based on strict liability, waiving the *mens rea* requirement. In Section 1, I present Lady Wootton's stance: she argued for getting rid of *mens rea* to define criminal offences. In Sections 2 and 3, I consider Hart's and Ross' criticisms: neither agreed with Lady Wootton's proposal but for different reasons. In Section 4, I try to assess Lady Wootton's arguments and I note that even a mental-free liability attribution would still be normative, because it is based on many kinds of evaluations.

2.0 INTRODUCTION: HOW CRIMINAL SYSTEMS WORK

This is how a criminal legal system works, in the words of one of the most prominent legal philosophers of last century, Herbert Lionel Adolphus Hart [Harrogate, 1907 — Oxford, 1992]:

> [i]n all advanced legal systems liability to conviction for serious crimes is made dependent, not only on the offender having done those outward acts which

the law forbids, but on his having done them in a certain frame of mind or with a certain will. These are the mental conditions or 'mental elements' in criminal responsibility and [...] they are broadly similar in most legal systems. Even if you kill a man, this is not punishable as murder in most civilized jurisdictions if you do it unintentionally, accidentally or by mistake, or while suffering from certain forms of mental abnormality.[1] Lawyers [...] use [...] *mens rea* as a comprehensive name for these necessary mental elements; and according to conventional ideas *mens rea* is a necessary element in liability to be established *before* a verdict (Hart, 2008, p.187).

2.1 LADY WOOTTON'S STRICT LIABILITY SYSTEM

This section explores Lady Wootton's [Barbara Adam, later Baroness Wootton of Abinger, Cambridge, 1897 – Surrey, 1988] contribution to the debate on responsibility and criminal liability. This debate is very often overlooked by both scientific and philosophical literature. This is unfortunate. In fact, Lady Wootton's stance (which dates back to 1963) is mirrored — sometimes with pretence of novelty — by very fortunate writers and papers more than forty years later, such as Greene and Cohen, 2004, Sapolsky, 2004, Dawkins (passim), Cashmore, 2010 (see the introduction of Vincent, 2013 and Chapter 3 for a general survey).

In particular, Lady Wootton's main thesis is that responsibility (defined as reference to *mens rea*, i. e. mental elements) should be eliminated from criminal law as we are heading towards a

---

[1] Please note Hart's begging of the question. It is clear that if *murder* (murder and not: killing) is defined as killing with mens rea (i. e. intentionally, knowingly and so on), a killing without those requirements cannot be consistently punished as murder. It is *not* a murder. In other words, mental elements are part of the wrong and partly characterize it. I shall touch on the question in full with constitutive rules below.

preventive system. Her strategy is threefold: (i) she shows that the aim of a modern criminal system must be fundamentally preventive (Section 2.1.1), and (ii) since the current system of responsibility and punishment attached to mental elements is tied up with a fundamentally retributive system (Section 2.1.2), then (iii) responsibility *via mens rea* should be eliminated from the criminal system, as the cases of negligence and mental abnormality already show (Section 2.1.3).

2.1.1 Retribution *vs.* Prevention

The starting point of the relevant portion of the 1963 Hamlyn Lectures[2] I am interested in is the sharp contrast Lady Wootton sees between modern "forensic science in the detection of a crime" and the "prescientific character of the criminal process itself", together with the "extreme conservatism of the legal profession". Testimony for instance, still widely used, has been shown by psychology to be unreliable.

The ultimate contrast, however, is about the *aim* of punishment. The "traditional", historical idea for Lady Wootton is that of retribution, of justly punishing the guilty *qua* guilty: everyone would get what he deserves. The modern idea she favors is that of reform or prevention of further harm for the offender and for society.

The implications of the traditional view are necessarily linked to an objective moral content: "the wickedness which renders a criminal liable to punishment must be inherent either in the actions which he has committed or in the state of mind in which he has committed them (p. 38)." Lady Wootton moreover quotes Lord Devlin[3] as a supporter of this view and his distinction between criminal (roughly: morally wrong, *mala in se*) and quasi-criminal (roughly: conventional, *mala prohibita*) acts as untenable. Since for Wootton this distinction is the byproduct of a traditional view, what is morally wrong (and therefore fully criminal) is what has been always considered as such (*mala antiqua*);

---

2 Given in 1963 and reprinted definitely in Wootton, 1963, whence I shall quote.
3 Devlin, 1965. Devlin was a famous opponent of Hart's views

whereas what is only conventionally wrong (and therefore quasi-criminal) is what is (technologically) new. But what is *considered* to be morally wrong or not is subject to change — even with the help (or under the push) of technology.[4]

More interestingly, Lady Wootton points out that there is nothing inherent in the physical actions alone that makes them "wrong" or at least criminally punishable. The action of firing a gun or of driving are in themselves perfectly legal; furthermore, one could have had the *intention* to perform exactly those actions that lead to criminal consequences, without intending those consequences.

This is even more apparent in stealing: as a physical sequence of actions, stealing consists merely in the translation of an x from region of space s_1 at time t_1 of the same x to region of space s_2 at time t_2. But it is only the circumstances (plus the mental elements, presumably) that make this physical translation a "real" theft.

The very same talk about "punishment" — even by people otherwise non-retributivist such as Hart in (Hart, 1962) — presupposes a punitive view of the courts functioning. But all these concerns must be discarded, because they are all attached to a backward looking function of courts, whereas the sole justifiable aim of the criminal system is to prevent harm and to reform criminals.

2.1.2 Criminal Liability = Strict Liability

Even the fear or repulsion for a possible spread of strict liability crimes, i. e. crimes without reference to mental elements (*mens*

---

[4] Let me note here in passing two things: first, the greatly different (metaethical) premises of Devlin and Wootton — which leads to a *de facto* impossibility to discuss — Devlin in fact would probably reply that moral principles used to tell what is wrong and what is right do not change at all; whereas Wootton's criteria for what is wrong and what is right probably depend on what people in general deem wrong or right; second, the splendid *straw man* of Wootton's discussion: she quickly and imperfectly summarizes Lord Devlin's arguments in a fashion such that she can accuse him of the faults of another theory.

rea), is maybe meaningful, Wootton goes on, only in a retributive framework. In fact,

> [i]f, however, the primary function of the courts is conceived as the prevention of forbidden acts, there is little cause to be disturbed by the multiplication of offenses of strict liability. If the law says that certain things are not to be done, it is illogical to confine this prohibition to occasions on which they are done from malice aforethought; for at least the material consequences of an action, and the reasons for prohibiting it, are the same whether it is the result of sinister malicious plotting, of negligence or of sheer accident (p. 46).

Here you can read an act-consequentialist. In a more refined way, Hart would have specified that the *voluntariness* of an action adds more to its effects than the mere consequences. Voluntariness is therefore an important element of moral and social life — even if it turns out to be illusory.[5]

Is Lady Wootton ignoring this remark? Not really. As a matter of fact, she does not argue for a total elimination of the *mens rea* requirement. *Mens rea* should not be taken into consideration for the definition of a crime, because if we aim for prevention, every harm — voluntary or not — is to be taken care of:

> If the object of the criminal law is to prevent the occurrence of socially damaging actions, it would be absurd to turn a blind eye to those which were due to carelessness, negligence or even accident (p. 47).

Mens rea, however, makes a comeback later, after the conviction stage. The presence or absence of a guilty mind is relevant for the *sentence*, that is, not to give criminal liability, but to decide *what kind* of liability, for instance imprisonment *vs.* medical treatment. In her words,

---

5 This seems echoed in P. F. Strawson, 1968 (2008) and cf. Nichols and Knobe, 2007 on intuitions about moral responsibility.

> [where] this argument leads is, I think, not that the presence or absence of the guilty mind is unimportant, but that *mens rea* has [...] *got into the wrong place*. [...] The question of motivation is in the first instance irrelevant. But only in the first instance. At a later stage, that is to say, after what is now known as a conviction, the presence or absence of guilty intention is all-important for its effect on the appropriate measures to be taken to prevent a recurrence of the forbidden act (pp. 47-8).

Offenses of strict liability do not lead directly to punishment, but only to a sort of liability to further consequences that "must be taken to prevent the occurrence of such actions (p. 49)" The gravity of (strict liability) offenses is estimated more by their consequences than by the offender's state of mind. A fit example is (very characteristically for Lady Wootton) a driving offense: careless driving is criminally relevant only if it had some (serious) consequences; otherwise is in fact seldom prosecuted.

Since (i) the general aim of the criminal system is that of prevention and minimization of social harm, it does not really matter, *prima facie*, if this harm was voluntary (i.e guilty, with *mens rea*) or not. And since (ii) in technologically advanced societies "much and more damage is done by negligence, or by indifference to the welfare or safety of others, as by deliberate wickedness (p. 50)",[6] then (iii) if those offenses are to be judged by criminal courts, than most of them should be offenses of strict liability. But apparently mental elements are a problem only at the beginning, because it is on them that the choice of treatment is made.

---

6 And again, "an increase in strict liability offenses would be merely the latest adaptation of the long evolution of our legal system to the changing conditions of human life and to the growth of human understanding. That system is already outdated in a world in which negligence, careless- ness and indifference cause more injury and damage than the total that is attributable to deliberate intent (p. 63)."

To sum up, according to Wootton, "the concept of guilty mind has become both irrelevant and obstructive" (p.51), especially in the cases of negligence and even more of mental abnormality.

2.1.3 Mental Abnormality and the Elimination of Responsibility

Mental abnormality is the epitome of Wootton's theory.[7]

The very neat distinction between punishment as retribution and treatment as prevention (and the absolute absence of any *via media*, in Wootton's view) becomes apparent in the case of mentally abnormal offenders.

The traditional retributive system is linked to guilt and culpability: the more mentally ill an offender, the less culpable he is, the less he deserves punishment.

The proposed preventive system is linked to future risk and treatability: the degree and severity of mental illness entails medical or other kinds of treatment.

But the traditional is the wrong approach and the concept of responsibility should be eliminated from criminal law: in fact,

> any attempt to distinguish between wickedness and mental abnormality was doomed to failure; and that the only solution for the future was to allow the concept of responsibility to "wither away" and to concentrate instead on the problem of the choice of treatment, without attempting to assess the effect of mental peculiarities or degrees of culpability (p. 71).

And a key reason for this is Lady Wootton's idea that it is scientifically impossible "to get inside another man's skin":

> neither medical nor any other science can ever hope to prove whether a man who does not resist his impulses does not do so because he cannot or because he will not. The propositions of science are by definition subject to empirical validation; but since it is not

---

[7] For a thorough analysis of mental illness and law, see Morse, 1977.

> possible to get inside another man's skin, no objective criterion which can distinguish between "he did not" and "he could not" is conceivable (p. 78).

This (nowadays) radical position of Lady Wootton should be understood in reference to *behaviorism*.[8] If we consider that behaviorism was dominant in philosophy and social sciences at the time Lady Wootton was writing,[9] then it is easier to see why she was trying to avoid all potentially dangerous references to the inner sphere, and in particular to intentions and volitions to impartially attribute responsibility.

Responsibility was to be based on external observable behavior.

2.1.4 Side Remarks: Taxonomies, Determinism, Semantics

Taxonomical approaches such as the later Hart's postscript (Hart, 2008), Fisher's physiognomy (Fischer and Tognazzini, 2011) or Vincent's structured taxonomy (Vincent, Van De Poel, and Van Den Hoven, 2011) are *de facto* irrelevant for criminal courts:

> I cannot think that anyone can listen to, or read, the sophisticated subtleties in which legal disputations about degrees of responsibility persistently flounder and founder, without reaching the paradoxical conclusion that the harder we try to recognize the complexity of reality, the greater the unreality of the whole discussion. Indeed it is hardly surprising that in practice most of these subtleties probably pass over the heads of juries, whose conclusions appear to be reached on simpler grounds (p. 76).

---

8 Behaviorism is the theory that human and animal behavior can be explained in terms of conditioning, without appeal to thoughts or feelings, and that psychological disorders are best treated by altering behavior patterns, cf. *New Oxford American Dictionary*, ad vocem.

9 Think of Ryle's *The Concept of Mind*. I thank S. F. Magni for discussion on this point.

But there is a difference, or distinction, Lady Wootton deems fit to preserve: that between *causal responsibility* (concerning authorship of an act: perfectly fine in criminal law) and *capacity responsibility* (concerning the mental state in which the act was committed: to be eliminated).[10]

It is the latter, capacity responsibility, that raises all the concerns we have explored in this section. The capacity responsibility requirement is to be eliminated in all cases (and not only when mental abnormalities are detected) but *not* because of a metaphysical impossibility, such as a possible incompatibility with determinism *via* absence of free will. Lady Wootton is in fact clear in denying her acceptance of determinism.

Lady Wootton, consequently, wishes for a progressively blurred distinction between prison and hospital and that

> eventually obliterated altogether. Both will be simply "places of safety" in which offenders receive the treatment which experience suggests is most likely to evoke the desired response (p. 82).[11]

A very natural question follows, given (a) Wootton's refusal of determinism and (b) her wished "medical treatment for all": how would you know that your treatment was going to be effective, if there were no minimal causal or deterministic connection? This should not be a problem: it is one thing to deny that there is freedom of the will (that the will is deterministically caused), another to deny that determinism is true *tout court*. More problems with Lady Wootton's approach will be dealt with in the comment section, *infra* in Section 2.4.1.

---

10 These terms are not used in the original Hamlyn lectures and have been popularized by Hart, 2008.
11 Then of course you will loose the social, expressive, function of punishment, as highlighted by Feinberg, 1970, 1990.

2.1.5 Lady Wootton's Proposal: recap

In Wootton, 1963, pp. 47–52 Lady Wootton maintained that the *mens rea*[12] requirement was to be ignored in convicting criminal offenders. The crime was to be defined only as the outward conduct, without any reference to the mental state at the time of the offense. All offenses then were strict liability offenses.

Lady Wootton's thesis came from a very neat premise: the sole aim of criminal law is "the prevention of socially damaging actions". Punishment is justified inasmuch as it causes the best consequences for society and for the offenders.

The offender's state of mind at the time of the offense (i.e. his *mens rea*) is therefore irrelevant to determine now his liability to be punished. His state of mind would be relevant if the aim of criminal law were retribution for past wrongs.

In Lady Wootton's approach, the offender's *mens rea* is used only *after* conviction, in order to establish penal punishment, medical treatment or nothing altogether.

2.2 HART'S REPLY

2.2.1 Hart's Moderate Proposal

H. L. A. Hart addresses his first Jerusalem 1964 lecture[13] to reply to Lady Wootton's proposal.

He makes clear that there are *two* of Lady Wootton's assumptions he does not share:

First, she thinks that the doctrine of *mens rea* is tenable only if accompanied by a retributive theory of punishment. Since she refutes this and endorses a consequentialist understanding of punishment, then she can discard the *mens rea* requirement on

---

12 *Mens rea* stands for purpose, knowledge, recklessness and negligence, at least in the Model Penal Code, §2.02 (1985). Other formulations apply, depending on jurisdiction.
13 In Hart, 1964, pp. 5–29, reprinted in Hart, 2008, §8.

that basis. Hart believes this is a philosophical confusion, as he argues in Hart, 1962.

Second, Lady Wootton holds that the question of what was the offender's state of mind is "in principle unaswearble (Hart, 1964, p.22)" because "it is not possible to get inside another man's skin (Wootton, 1963, p.74)".

Hart calls Lady Wootton's tenets the "extreme form" (p.14) of this new theory (because it would do away with the entire *mens rea* requirement) and moves on to consider only a "moderate" form concerning "the legal responsibility of the mentally abnormal".

Hart, then, is not interested in a new system of attributing liability for criminal punishment, but more modestly in a reform of the existing system with respect to mental illness, the Achilles' heel often used to force current jurisprudence. In fact, since most critics of responsibility have been concerned with mentally abnormal offenders, Hart proposes to keep the *mens rea* requirement as a condition to liability, in order to show that one need not to throw the baby out with the bath water and discard the whole theory of responsibility because of some problems with one of its parts.

Hart's moderate reform is thus conceived. He keeps separated conviction and sentencing: mental illness would be irrelevant at conviction (an "accused person would no longer be able to adduce any form of mental abnormality as a bar to conviction (p.25)") but investigated at the sentencing stage in order to decide the most efficacious punishment (or treatment), and thus the defendant's abnormal state of mind is only relevant at the time of the trial, and irrelevant at the time of the offense. I shall not discuss Hart's proposal — with the very obvious problems it raises — here, but will focus on his critiques to Wootton.

2.2.2 Hart's Threefold Critique to Lady Wootton

I shall now present Hart's objections to the abandoning *mens rea* as a necessary condition for criminal liability and offer some thoughts on them.

In particular, Hart puts forward three objections to Lady Wootton's model: (i) a threat to individual freedom; (ii) moral and sociological objections to Lady Wootton's identification of punishment and medical treatment; (iii) a practical consequence of Lady Wootton's model for criminal law.

(I) HART'S FIRST CRITICISM: INDIVIDUAL SOCIAL FREEDOM In a system like Lady Wootton's "every blow, even if [...] purely accidental or merely careless [...] would be a matter for investigation (p.26)" with the associate effect of greater discretionary power of the authority and great possibility of intervention in everyday life that constrains individual freedom.

> If the doctrine of *mens rea* were swept away, [...] very considerable discretionary powers would have to be entrusted to them [the police] [...]. No one could view this kind of expansion of police powers with equanimity, for with it will come great uncertainty for the individual: official interferences with his life will become more frequent but he will be less able to predict their incidence if any accidental or careless blow may be an occasion for them (Hart, 2008, p. 206).

(II) HART'S SECOND CRITICISM: IDENTIFICATION OF PUNISHMENT AND TREATMENT Wootton thinks that both penal punishment and medical treatment are equal forms of social hygiene, enforced to obtain the best consequences for society and the offender. Hart raises two objections: penal punishment and medical treatment cannot be considered alike. Morally speaking, Hart believes that we need a moral justification (or "licence", p.27) to use a man for the benefit of society (i.e. with deterrence or example by imprisoning him when he has broken the law). These moral grounds are for Hart to be sought in the "demonstration that the person so treated could have helped doing what he did (p.27)" — a proof we cannot obtain from the mentally abnormal.[14]

---

14 This seems a reference to what Hart calls capacity-responsibility and indeed, to some notion of freedom of the will.

Sociologically speaking, Hart notes, "a sentence of imprisonment" — unlike a medical treatment — "is a public act expressing the odium [...] of society for those who break the law (p.28)".[15] With the identification of the two, the law would lose a powerful instrument of deterrence, both for society and the offender.

(III) HART'S THIRD CRITICISM: PRACTICAL CONSEQUENCES   Hart notes that there are some crimes identified only by reference to mental elements, such as attempted crimes. In Lady Wootton's model these are likely to disappear.

> Consider the idea of an attempt to commit a crime. It is obviously desirable that persons who attempt to kill or injure or steal, even if they fail, should be brought before courts for punishment or treatment; yet what distinguishes an attempt which fails from an innocent activity is just the fact that it is a step taken with the intention of bringing about some harmful consequences (Hart, 2008, p. 209).

It seems to me that none of Hart's objections are decisive, since they rest either on further implicit (moral) premises to be proved or on required psychological and sociological empirical research. Hart himself admits this (Hart, 2008, p. 209) and calls only for an answer to his objections, without claiming that they defeat Lady Wootton's proposal. In fact, it has to be said that the first two objections are peculiar to Lady Wootton's model, and do not apply to a strict liability system more utilitarian-free than Wootton's. But Hart crafted several other arguments against strict liability tout court, without any (specific or direct) reference to the "extreme" model we have so far taken into account. The next subsection is devoted to analyzing and evaluating them.

---

15 For similar remarks, see Feinberg, 1970.

2.2.3 Hart's Two Critiques to Strict Liability

In this subsection, I summarize two Hart's arguments against strict liability and offer a critical evaluation of them. Strict liability, I recall, is defined as criminal liability without *mens rea* required for the offense to take place — where the actual "components" of *mens rea* vary according to jurisdiction.

(A) MENS REA AND THE RULE OF LAW   The Rule of Law as a general ideal and aim for the law to pursue had always been dear to Hart in his writings. But it is his Hart, 2008, Chapter 2 that the Rule of Law is explicitly linked to the *mens rea* requirement.

The Rule of Law[16] is concerned with protections against the possible absolute power of the State *via* "unjust" means such as vague, secret and retroactive laws, in particular *via* the legal maxim: *actus non facit reum nisi mens sit rea*.

Hart therefore thought that the *mens rea* requirement was another assimilable warrant of the Rule of Law, a requirement that excludes the punishment of an "innocent", that is when there are no "subjective elements" (p.152) and relevant "mental conditions" (p.35). Why is it so? Because the law — according to Hart — ought to give its subjects a fair warning to let them organize and live their lives, clearly in order to be law in the name of the rule of law.

(B) MENS REA, THE RULE OF LAW AND FREEDOM   Furthermore, not punishing the innocent (he who lacks *mens rea*) "maximizes individual freedom within the coercive framework of law" (p.23).[17]

These critiques, as far as I can understand them, are two sides of the same coin: Hart's liberal concern that citizens can live as free from the coercive power of the state as much as they can.

---

16 Rule of Law is a formula peculiar to common law countries. To my understanding, it is comparable to Fr. *état de droit*, Ger. *Rechtsstaat*, It. *stato di diritto*, Pol. *praworządność*, Russ. *pravavoe gosudarstvo*.

17 For an interesting discussion on this point over the contemporary political framework, see Gardner's introduction to Hart, 2008, pp. xxxvii–xliv.

The law should also serve as an instrument to organize one's life — a tool giving certainty and security.

In this respect, strict liability crimes (crimes without *mens rea* required) seriously endanger one's plan, because one is never sure that a punishment could not follow for an action he did not intend or want and this, in turn, may jeopardize one's life plan.

Hart's concerns are reasonable, but there are at least *two* different issues here.

First, the fact that *mens rea* has not to be proven to hold someone liable for an offense is not the same as punishing an innocent. The equivalence between *mens rea* and guilt[18] is not self-evident and must be proved.

Hart seems unable to see the conceptual difference between absence of *mens rea* (volition, intention, etc.) and absence of *guilt* (i.e. a criminal offense — with the required *mens rea* — but an excused one: duress, provocation, etc.). A *mens rea* element (eg intention to kill) is an element *of the* wrong; an *excuse* is instead a *defense* for the wrong already committed (eg duress when killing). But in no way can legal excuses guide our lives as a priori principles — they serve only a posteriori. Hart's failure to distinguish the two made him implausibly stretch the rule of law to also include excuses — excuses are not exceptions, and were someone to adapt his behavior to "benefit from excuses that he believes the law will grant him, the law is likely to react by denying him the excuse" (p.xlvii).

Second, as long as people consider themselves rational and in self-control, the law can still be their ally in planning their life as they want, even if there are strict liability crimes. People would be able to think that as long as they act rightly criminal law won't touch them. *Mens rea* elements are not required for the offense to take place, but an offense (even if only material, or "external") still needs to happen. Even if the law ignores

---

18 I take as a working definition that innocent is one who is not guilty. I am not able to provide the reader with reliable synonyms in other languages, due to differences in legal systems. In fact, the obvious xenonyms are not synonyms. Sp. *culpa*, Fr. *faute*, It. *colpa* are a part of what would be called *mens rea*, along with Sp., Port. and It. *dolo* at least according to a plausible interpretation of Art. 42, Italian Penal Code.

mental elements, people might still feel that mental elements are there and can be controlled, and that mental elements in the end determine external acts. So if they control their mind, they roughly control their actions, even if the law is ultimately concerned only with their material, external actions, and not with those mental elements that brought them about. Moreover, it has been argued[19] that strict liability crimes may even increase law's deterrence.

Interestingly and at a more general level, Hart shifts the argument from within (formal) philosophy of law towards more substantive moral claims. In a way, it seems that from the mere *form* of punishment one ends up with the general justifying principle of the whole social activity of punishment. In other words, it seems (I won't argue for it here) that Hart is loosing sight of his own positivism to root the practice of *legal* (*rectius*: criminal) punishment in the *moral* practice of blaming, as if he were to "institutionalize certain moral practices", as Gardner subtly notes (p.xlix).[20]

To sum up, Hart's two main critiques to strict liability crimes (they are against the rule of law, they are against freedom) have not proven definitive. I pointed out that one is misleading because of Hart's failure to discriminate between *mens rea* and guilt; the other — apart for being confused and ill-directed — is (surprisingly perhaps for a legal positivist like Hart) founded on a defeasible moral claim.

2.3 A. ROSS'S REPLY

Alf Ross [1899 – 1979], one of the leading legal philosophers of the 20th century, linked his critique to Lady Wootton's proposal to the wider and richer picture of his understanding of moral and legal responsibility.

---

19 Cf. Simester, 2005.
20 For some interesting remarks on positivism and the separation of law and morals, see Gardner, 2012, §2 and L. Green, 2008.

This section is organized in two parts. In Section 2.3.1, I present Ross's conception of moral and legal responsibility; in Section 2.3.2, I present and assess Ross's critique to Lady Wootton.

2.3.1 Ross's Conception of Responsibility

Ross, 1975 is very careful in keeping separate guilt, responsibility and punishment. Guilt [*skyld*][21] (pp. 1–12) is when one can be blamed according to the normative system in question. Guilt is different from *feelings* of guilt, which can be sometimes lacking (in psychopaths, for instance); it does not refer to a tangible, or measurable, state-of-affairs: it is a *tû-tû* concept, i.e. an empty concept, without natural reference, that nonetheless is still meaningful in a given linguistic community.[22]

2.3.1.1 The Conditions of Responsibility

The conditions of responsibility are profoundly different from its concept or its meaning: analyzing the former does not exhaust analysis of the latter. Some conditions of responsibility are, for instance, free will and alternative possibilities. These are just part of the problem: they in fact may be one of the "*criteria* [...] for the presence of responsibility (p.16)" but not the *meaning* of responsibility itself.

Moreover, the conditions of responsibility are *normative* rather than descriptive. Among other reasons, this is apparent because different sets of morality are at stake. Choosing one out of them (even before conditions for responsibility apply) is an evaluative, rather than descriptive, task.

That "moral responsibility is excluded when the conditions for it are not fulfilled" is not a *descriptive* account, but "is itself

---

21 For an analysis of guilt and culpability in speech acts, see *infra* at §5. For a philosophical analysis of the names of guilt, see Conte, 2001a.
22 For *tû-tû* concepts, see Ross, 1957; for a critical reconstruction, see Roversi, 2012.

a moral statement which says that under these conditions it is unjustified (*immoral*) to invoke responsibility [...] (p.113)."

But what about determinism then? I shall not tackle the issue here, but it is not a great problem for Ross, who doubts both that determinism is true and that, were it true, in a relevant formulation it would be compatible with the conditions required for responsibility.

2.3.1.2 The Concept of Responsibility

Responsibility is a trivalent[23] concept:[24] it is always someone who is responsible *for* something *to* someone else. $R(a, X, b)$ hereby means that " person *a* is responsible for X to person(s) *b*".[25]

Ross distinguishes between two senses of responsibility:

- Responsibility$_1$ = accountability [*tilregnelighed*] = be rightfully accused;

- Responsibility$_2$ = liability [*ansvarlighed*] = be rightfully sentenced.[26]

Accountable or responsible$_1$, then, is the person who can *rightfully* be brought to account for some *state-of-affairs*.

Liable or responsibile$_2$ is the person who can *rightfully* be sentenced for some *state-of-affairs*, i.e. one that "fulfil[l]s all the conditions, subjective and objective, which are jointly necessary and sufficient for his being convicted and sentenced (p.20)."

'Rightfully' and some 'state-of-affairs' are necessary requirements both for accountability and liability. In other words, there cannot be any kind of responsibility but in (i) a certain presupposed normative system (either legal or moral) and (ii) for a certain, definite act or action someone committed or omitted.

---

23 I refer here to the concept of *valency* in linguistics, proposed by Tesnière in Tesnière, 1959.
24 In recent literature, this is echoed by Duff, especially in Duff, 2008, 2009.
25 But cf. Ladd, 1992; Lenk and Maring, 1993, 2011 for *hexavalent* responsibility.
26 I owe the Danish terms to the kindness of professor Alastar Hanney, who worked with Ross to Ross's English translation. I have not been able to find the original Danish book.

Ross focuses on liability [*ansvarlighed*]: liability is the connection between "conditioning facts" (i. e. guilt) and "conditioned legal consequences" (i. e. punishment) (p.21). But this

> "connection is not a 'natural' (causal or logical) one, but exists only by virtue of the legal rule [...].
> Responsibility[2] is an expression of a legal judgment, and the latter consists of a directive (normative) demand that occurs as the conclusion of an inference: since such and such facts obtain (in short, A's guilt), and since the law is such and such, it follows that A is punishable (p.21)."

Responsibility is therefore a *tû-tû* concept: not an objective state-of-affairs but rather a "legal connection between facts and consequence (p.23)." Responsibility "lacks semantic reference" but it is still a meaningful concept, because it lets us "express the connection between facts and consequence (p.23)."[27]

2.3.1.3 The Concept of Moral Responsibility (and the Aim of Punishment)

Even if primarily legal, Ross's analysis of responsibility can be extended to the moral domain with some adjustments. Moral responsibility presupposes the existence of moral norms, their violation, accusations, trials and judgments — even if in a non-institutionalized manner. In *morality*, however, judgment and sanction coincide in censure (i. e. disapproval), while in *law* conviction and sentence occur at different stages.

Interestingly, censure (or disapproval) as punishment retrospectively enlightens the very aim of punishment itself. Censure is justified both because it is "a form of retribution (an emotive, hostile reaction) for guilt" and because it has a "guiding, preventive effect upon actions (p.28)." Punishment is a mixture of retribution and prevention: the traditional opposition between these

---

27 On this point, see how Kelsen, 1943 characterizes in an analogous fashion (that is, as purely normative) the "primitive" notion of imputability [*Zurechnung, Zurechenbarkeit*] and the "modern" notion of causation [*Kausalität*].

two aims is therefore "meaningless". This thesis is fundamental for Ross's subsequent criticism of Lady Wootton's assumption of an exclusively preventive aim for punishment (see *infra*, Section 2.3.2).

Ross, then (cf. Ch. 5, Chapters 2 and 3) argues that even the conditions that would exclude the possibility of deeming someone morally or legally responsible are in fact normative, i.e. pertaining to a moral or legal system. This requirement (say, a particular kind of mental incapacity) merely affirms that would be immoral (illegal) to blame (punish) someone subject to those conditions (say, who is mentally ill). But in themselves, they are not any more than an empty container with a normative shell.

2.3.1.4 Ross' Two Problems: a Relational Critique

I see *at least two* relevant issues in Ross's account of moral and legal responsibility. *One* is — so to speak — horizontal: (a) the relationship (and connection, if any) between moral and legal responsibility. *The other* is rather vertical: (b) what is (if any) the connection between responsibility$_{[1]}$ and responsibility$_{[2]}$, i. e. between accountability and liability?

As for (a), Ross's moral responsibility mirrors legal responsibility. The former differs only at the sanctioning stage: censure for moral responsibility *vs.* sentence and conviction for legal responsibility. Is this a *legalistic* bias? Moral and legal responsibility seem different concepts. Even if they are formally or genetically (so to speak) related, it is still to be argued which is modeled on which.

A natural law theorist (such as John Finnis, for one) may well think that legal (criminal) responsibility comes after *moral* responsibility, because of the very fact that law is part of morality.[28]

As for (b), Ross does not explain if *liability* presupposes *accountability* and if *accountability* entails *liability*.

---

[28] See for instance Finnis, 1991: "[...] the moral theory which the criminal law as we know it more or less steadily embodies and enforces (p.38)."

The distinction Gardner, 2008 drawn between a basic and a consequential responsibility seems to parallel Ross's accountability *vs.* liability — even though it is different in many relevant senses.

2.3.2 Ross' Fourfold Critique to Lady Wootton

Ross harshly criticizes Lady Wootton's arguments, finding them implausible and ill-founded (1975, pp.72–100). His strategy is twofold: he lays bare Wootton's assumptions and subsequently tackles them.

The *four* assumptions Ross points out are (iv) the misunderstanding of retribution — "if retribution for guilt is not the purpose of punishment, then retribution and guilt have no place at all in the philosophy of punishment (p.83)"; (v) the unnecessary connection between guilt and metaphysical freedom: "if guilt (imputation and imputability) is to be accorded any relevance in penal law, [...] man's will [must be] free in the metaphysical sense (p.83)"; (vi) the impossibility of knowing the offender's state of mind — his "mental responsibility" and (vii) the impossibility of making sense of actions without reference to mental elements.

(IV) ROSS'S FIRST CRITICISM: MISUNDERSTANDING OF RETRIBUTION According to Ross, "it is altogether unreasonable to suppose that retribution should be an aim, that is to say an intended and deliberately pursued effect of criminal legislation (p.88)" and that Wootton simply assumes, without explanation, that the purpose of criminal law should be preventive. From this assumption, she jumps to the conclusion that responsibility should be dropped because it can be only retributive. Ross instead argues that the current system based on guilt and responsibility is already (at least partially) preventive and this would work as a counterexample to Wootton's assumption.

(V) ROSS'S SECOND CRITICISM: DETERMINISM AND FREE WILL
On this unjustified assumption, men can be guilty (and respon-

sible) only if they could have acted freely. Responsibility is directly linked with free will: if the latter is not real, then the former is ill-founded. In general, Ross believes that "metaphysical problems have no significance for practical criminology (p.84)". Moreover he argues that determinism is scientifically unproven (p.85) and anyhow he adopts a compatibilist stance.

(VI) ROSS'S THIRD CRITICISM: IMPOSSIBILITY OF A SCIENTIFICALLY RESPONSIBILITY ASCRIPTION   Wootton thinks that (ir-)responsibility cannot be established with scientific objectivity, and therefore it is too high a cost to carry on punishing people without any certainty. Ross reckons that the criterion of responsibility ascription is not as scientifically objective as diagnosing cancer.

But this is the "normal condition" pertaining to many human practices. The "normal condition" of moral and juridical judgment (including but not limited to responsibility) is blurry and imprecise. As far I can see, it may be said that Ross holds responsibility is partially a normative concept that in the end depends on estimates and judgments more than on accurate description of states-of-affairs.[29]

(VII) ROSS'S FOURTH CRITICISM: ACTS AND ACTIONS   A very powerful, but underestimated, remark of Ross' must be taken into account. Ross, *contra* Wootton, who pushed to deem relevant for criminal conviction only outward conduct, replied that an act cannot be "described objectively as a purely physical sequence of events, without introducing into its description a reference to mental components (p. 80)."

Throwing a stone to someone is manifestly different, Ross tells the reader, if this same act is done in a game between two friends, or when the stone is targeted at a police officer during a revolt. Intention is what differs (and matters) here: "[t]he distinction

---

29 But this is not necessarily the case — there are no conceptual reasons to infer this from Ross' premises. In fact, there may be *opaque facts*, that is, facts than don't let you see only one evaluation. I thank S. F. Magni for discussion on this point.

between the act itself and its attendant mental circumstances is an artificial and impossible abstraction. The act is grasped immediately as having a definite "sense" and only in this way becomes an act of a definite kind (p. 80)."

Ross's argument goes further and objects to Lady Wootton that outward conduct is not at all objective, and it is also hardly understandable if considered alone, without reference to mental elements.

Three objections: *First*, a hard physicalist may well think that those "mental elements" (intention, will, etc.) are all well reducible to physical (i. e. cerebral) elements (if, of course, he admits their existence). This would make them as objective and describable (with the right techniques) as outward conduct is, thus cutting Ross's objection of any relevance. Clearly, this is subject to accepting the bold assumptions of a hard physicalist.

Second, it sounds funny to me that Ross, who advocates for a pan-normative understanding of responsibility (guilt, imputability, imputation and so on), is concerned with an "objective description" of outward conduct — that seems like a daunting task.

Third, it may be replied to Ross that an activity, or an action, can be judged fairly well by looking at (and assessing) circumstances: a stone-throwing game and a stoning occur in very different — and fairly objectively recognizable — circumstances, even if there is a part of stipulativeness involved. I reckon that there might be cases where the difference is tiny or non-existent: but that is a risk in every human enterprise, probably.

2.3.3 J. Glover's Double Critique

In his *Responsibility*, Jonathan Glover moves a twofold critique to Lady Wootton's system, in his broader discussion of the issue of mental illness and the foundations of punishment.[30]

In particular, he focuses on the distinction between penal punishment and medical treatment. As I explained above, Lady

---

30 Thanks to M. Bazzoni for bringing this passage to my attention.

Wootton thinks this distinction should gradually blur to become non-existent in the near future. Glover, instead, thinks this distinction fundamental for society and is reluctant to accept it as a doable way to go, mainly for two reasons: (ix) punishment for a helpless act is unjust and (x) the fact that medical treatment and penal punishment have different aims.

(IX) LIABILITY FOR HELPLESS ACTIONS   In his own words, "[u]nder a system where someone who could not help his act is not convicted, he is spared this stigma (Glover, 1970, p. 170-4)" that typically characterizes conviction. In Wootton's system, Glover adds, even he who could not have avoided what he did would be convicted (because of the elimination of responsibility and mental elements, capacities etc.) and therefore stigmatized. And among other considerations, it might well be the case that this stigma has a *preventive* dimension (and thus it could be acceptable to Wootton) inasmuch as it contributes to deterring people from breaking the law.

(X) TREATMENT AND PUNISHMENT HAVE DIFFERENT AIMS   Treatment and punishment have different aims: medical treatment is to directly benefit the treated, whereas penal punishment — according to one's point of view and to one's country laws — is either retribution, benefit to society at large and re-education for the convicted or a mixture of the two.

Glover thinks it is important medical treatment and punishment be kept separate because of the different principles they can be justified with. Penal punishment can be justified with retribution, benefit to society at large and re-education for the convicted or a mixture of the two, whereas *compulsory* medical treatment can be justified much more convincingly on paternalist grounds, than on the grounds of a general benefit to society. One may prefer to act on paternalist grounds, the other on the grounds of benefit to society, and therefore argue for or against compulsory medical treatment.

But this kind of discussion would be swept away in a system such as Lady Wootton's.

2.4 FIVE CRITICISMS FROM A CONTEMPORARY PERSPECTIVE

This section is roughly split in two. In Section 2.4.1, I put forward *five* criticisms against Lady Wootton's arguments. I shall not be concerned with her *formal* arguments, but rather with the philosophical import of her discussion. Section 2.4.2, along with the next chapter, is devoted to expanding Lady Wootton's model and to seeing the extent to which these criticisms apply to a possible modern strict liability-based criminal system.

2.4.1 Assessing Lady Wootton's Proposal

In this subsection, I assess Wootton's proposal from a philosophical, rather than legal or practical, perspective. I am not concerned with her actual formal arguments. I see three major flaws in Wootton's argumentation: (i) one in the system's premise, (ii) one in the system's very machinery, and (iii) one in the wished consequences.

2.4.1.1 *(i) Prevention vs. retribution: a blurred distinction*

As Hart and Ross also noticed, all Lady Wootton's hatred against the traditional criminal system is founded on the premise of it being completely retributive. But since responsibility based on mens rea is necessarily tied to a retributive system, and since retribution is not a fair aim for criminal law, then with the aim of the system we must change also its functioning, with the elimination of traditional responsibility.

The thesis that punishment cannot be retributive is held for instance by Moritz Schlick, because "[...] the opinion that with more sorrow, past sorrow can be made again good is completely barbarous (Schlick, 1930, Ch.7. trans. mine)." Of course Schlick thought the aim of punishment to be totally preventive — but this did not lead him to discard responsibility; quite on the contrary, he tried to provide a compatibility account between (preventive) responsibility and determinism.

Unfortunately for Lady Wootton, and as several commentators pointed out, her very first presupposition is manifestly wrong. The criminal system she takes into account (and by extension all western modern legal systems at least) are neither factually nor theoretically exclusively retributive.

In fact, there is always a mixture of retribution *and* prevention in criminal systems: at times, the aim of prevention is even stated formally as a constitutional provision, maybe as a reform provision for the offender[31] — even when the punishment seems *de facto* only retributive, it might be argued that this prevents the offender from committing further crimes and serves as an example to society as a whole.

Since the major premise of Wootton's argument is patently wrong, her subsequent theses are shaky. But there are reasons independent of (i) to doubt her argument.

2.4.1.2 *(ii) Mens rea: culpability* vs. *imputability*

Let us put aside (i) and focus on the second premise: problems with *mens rea*. *Mens rea* is scientifically non-provable. This has nasty consequences for the legal system and in the end for society: criminal law remains antiquate, criminal liabilities are discretionary and there is a risk of punishing the mentally ill with the sane, because the difference between: "he had not resisted his impulse" and "he could not have resisted his impulse" is practically unascertainable.

For those reasons, Lady Wootton proposes all crimes be crimes of strict liability, that is, without *mens rea*, without reference to mental elements.

Mens rea, however, makes a spectacular comeback not for conviction, but for sentence, in order to choose among different kinds of treatment, i. e. penal or medical.

Now, if assessing *mens rea* is scientifically undoable, it is always undoable: it cannot be the case that one is not able to establish *mens rea* for conviction, but one can for sentence.

---

31 For instance Art. 27 of the Italian Constitution: "La responsabilità penale è personale. [...] Le pene [...] devono tendere alla rieducazione del condannato."

Therefore it is clear that we are considering two distinct things: *culpability* and *imputability*. Both have to do with the mind, but while *culpability* is concerned with the actual state of mind at the time of the offense (say: intention, knowledge and so on), *imputability* is concerned with those requirements the law deems sufficient to stand trial. Of course imputability and culpability are related — in several ways. It is plausible, for instance, that absence of imputability may entail no (legal) culpability. But these connections are to be proven.

Failure to take into account the distinction between culpability and imputability leads Lady Wootton to have the very same problems about the provability of *mens rea* for conviction with the provability of *mens rea* for sentence.

It is true, however, that hypotheses on *mens rea*, although untenable from a scientific perspective, may be used as clues to advise on the severity of sentences.

2.4.1.3 *(iii) Past crimes and forward-looking punishment*

Now I consider (iii), namely, issues on the last part of the system. For argument's sake, let us admit that our criminal law is completely preventive. I shall not enter a thorough discussion on punishment and its justifiability, but merely touch upon flaws I see in Wootton's book concerning this topic.

PAST CRIMES   *Prima facie*, it seems counterintuitive to punish, or to treat, criminal offenders for past crimes on the basis of pure prevention, because one would need *positive* evidence of a correlation of no *mens rea* crimes with future criminal behaviors. Of course this practice might be justified if to this "liability" is attached a strong communicative message to the rest of society, warning them about possible consequences of criminal acts.

However, this does not seem the case, given that Lady Wootton *passim* wishes for the removal of any blame attached to criminal liabilities. Ideally, criminal liabilities should not serve as examples for the rest of society anymore.

But then, in order to punish, or treat, past offenders, one needs to have very strong evidence that these past offenders are extremely likely to commit future offenses. If so, then Lady Wootton's strategy might be assimilable to preventive custody and be plausible — or at least justifiable given certain premises.

If my line of reasoning is correct, then there is no need to punish (in whatever form) any *mens rea* offenses (such as accidental, casual and so on) for the benefit or society: since they are accidental or casual, there cannot be any convincing evidence that the perpetrators are likely to "commit" them again in the future, and there is no point in punishing or treating them. Otherwise, in order to prevent future harm for society, one would need to punish everyone in advance, because everyone can commit harms (or, in a strict liability framework, criminal wrongs) accidentally or casually.

The only reply Lady Wootton can have is this: past crimes are sufficient evidence to compel us to cure or treat offenders for their own good. To this is addressed the following paragraph.

COMPULSORY MEDICAL TREATMENT   Medical treatment is what Lady Wootton wishes for, for "normal" and abnormal offenders alike. She insists this is not a form of penal punishment. So what would happen if those offenders refused medical treatment? Can you impose it, in the same way you impose a penal sentence? If you can, is this not viewed as a punishment, both by the offender and by society: as a limitation of freedom instead of as a treatment or a cure?

ABNORMALITY   A final remark may be a problem for Lady Wootton's approach: on one hand, she is a strong advocate of a "modernization" towards scientific methods to be used in criminal courts to ascertain abnormality; on the other, she forgot to notice that what an illness is, science cannot tell. Especially in the case of a mental illness, values and preferences other than those found "in the physical world" are necessary.

One may statistically deviate from the mean. But by how much? For instance it is conceivable that in a hundred years, people whose IQ is less than 100 (which is now the average) will be treated like mentally ill people because, due to possible betterment of life conditions, the average IQ would steadily rise as it did in the past century (cf. Lynn and Vanhanen, 2002). Moreover, were one to know the exact frequency of a given x in the general population, one might come to consider it more normal than abnormal (take myopia, for instance).

One significant difficulty here is that Wootton has not defined *mental abnormality*, and in particular the very same word 'abnormality'. Abnormality — as Morse, 1977 reminds us — may refer to statistical abnormality, dysfunctional, psychological, or irrational (delusional) abnormality.

And again, defining abnormality is a *normative* evaluation.

2.4.2 Ascription of Responsibility Seems Normative

In this chapter, I have considered a possible way of ascribing responsibility based on observable facts, namely Lady Wootton's proposal. I assessed Hart's and Ross's replies and objections and eventually I directly engaged and evaluated Wootton's arguments.

I tried to show, both with Hart's and Ross's arguments and with mine, that even if the attribution of responsibility were based only on observable facts, considering it non-normative and *value-free*[32] is a self-defeating claim.

In sum, I see two main overarching reasons to refute that claim:

(i) first, the very choice of one system of responsibility ascription over another (say strict liability over *mens rea*, not to mention prevention over retribution or a mix of the two) is itself evaluative (at least);

(ii) second, even ignoring (i), if the ascription of responsibility were based on a somehow factual system, one would still need (substantial) norms (moral or legal) to categorize what to consider punishable.

---

32 The adjective 'value-free' is a calque of Max Weber's *'wertfrei'*, It. 'avalutativo'.

In this chapter, I hinted that attribution of responsibility may be normative. The next chapter will be devoted to defending Lady Wootton's intuitions from contemporary criticisms (based on current scientific techniques such as neurosciences) and to expanding her view into a coherent normative proposal.

3 | RESPONSIBILITY AND NEUROSCIENCE

3.1 Introduction

3.2 Criminal Liability Without Responsibility?

    3.2.1 Criminal Liability Has No Necessary Connection with Moral Responsibility

    3.2.2 Capacity Responsibility and Neuroscience

3.3 Law without Capacity Responsibility

    3.3.1 Law, Games, Conventions

    3.3.2 Strict Liability-Responsibility

3.4 Punishment & Consequences

    3.4.1 Some Consequences

    3.4.2 Conclusion

This chapter can be read both independently from and as an expansion on the last chapter about responsibility attribution.

In the *first* part, I assess and try to refute the claim that contemporary sciences (ie cognitive sciences, neuroscience) can ascertain those mental elements required for a crime (*mens rea*) objectively, both for factual and theoretical reasons.

In the *second* part, I put forward a theory of responsibility attribution based on strict-liability responsibility, both expanding on Lady Wootton's proposal and defending it from some possible objections.

3.1   INTRODUCTION

The last chapter was devoted to analyzing Lady Wootton's claim that (legal) responsibility should be based on *strict liability* (ie external, behavioral elements), without attention to mental elements (*mens rea*). This should be the case — among other reasons — because *mens rea* is impossible to prove (for instance) scientifically.

This view of responsibility as based on internal (mental) elements may presuppose a descriptive conception: were these mental elements objectively ascertainable, then responsibility would collapse on one of its condition (*mens rea*).

And cognitive sciences (ie neuroscientific techniques) may be thought to do just this: measuring those mental elements Lady Wootton believed impossible to ascertain, thus giving a plausible basis to responsibility as involving descriptive internal contents.

The purpose of this chapter is to weigh up these claims.

First, I shall clarify the terms of the question, distinguishing between *mens rea*, capacity responsibility and moral or legal responsibility.

Second, I show that there is a categorial mistake: *mens rea* and capacity responsibility are (possible) *conditions* of responsibility, whereas moral or legal responsibility are *concepts* of responsibility.

Third, I shall consider the use of neuroscientific techniques, showing that they have little or no import to the philosophical question of responsibility.

Fourth, I shall put forward (and defend) a normative notion of responsibility in line with Lady Wootton's: strict liability responsibility.

THE TERMS OF THE QUESTION   *Mens rea* (standing for purpose, knowledge, recklessness and negligence, depending on the particular jurisdiction), is one of the *conditions* of responsibility in common law countries.[1]

Capacity responsibility is the stable possession of all those abilities or powers required to be a "responsible" agent. In continental systems it may be referred to, for instance, as 'imputability' (ie Italian: 'imputabilità').

Both *mens rea* and *capacity* responsibility are *conditions* of responsibility.

Moral and legal responsibility are instead *concepts* of responsibility.[2]

Unfortunately — and wrongly, as I hope to make apparent in the rest of this chapter — there are *two* underlying ideas in the analytical debate on criminal responsibility:

(i) that moral responsibility is necessary for criminal responsibility; and

(ii) that it is the very presence of mental elements, if (morally) wrong (or morally good), that makes up moral responsibility.

Given those assumptions, it is easy to reduce criminal responsibility to mental elements (*mens rea*). And if mental elements

---

1 This particular formulation is drawn from the Model Penal Code Section 2.02 (1985). *Mens rea* refers to Anglo-American systems. In continental legal systems one finds a (or more) mental requirement(s) akin to 'guilt' (Fr: *faute*; Sp. and Pt: *dolo*; It: *dolo* and *colpa*; Ger: *Fahrlässigkeit* and *Vorsatz* (or *Absicht*). In extra-legal language: *Schuld*). See for instance Arts. 42-3 of the Italian Penal Code.

2 For the distinction between concepts and conditions of responsibility, see my taxonomy *supra* at Chapter 1.

were objectively ascertainable, then (criminal) responsibility would also be objective.

The fundamental categorial mistake here is to identify capacity responsibility — one of the *conditions* of responsibility and *possibly* ascertainable objectively by neuroscience — with moral (or criminal) responsibility. Moral and criminal responsibility aren't conditions of responsibility, but *concepts* of responsibility.

3.2 CRIMINAL LIABILITY WITHOUT RESPONSIBILITY?

The aim of this section is to argue that basing legal liability on moral responsibility (if conceived as I explained above) (Section 3.2.1) and that the very notion of (capacity) responsibility (Section 3.2.2) are utterly questionable and problematic to justify descriptively in the law. In Section 3.3, I shall positively argue for a criminal law system based on a normative notion such as strict liability-responsibility.

Current legal systems, especially those parts dealing with criminal misdeeds, are very much alike. In most jurisdictions, criminal punishment normally requires moral responsibility, either directly or indirectly.[3] Directly if criminal liability depends on

---

[3] See for instance Hart, 2008, pp. 35-6 reporting on the state of the criminal system: "[...] for criminal responsibility there must be 'moral culpability' [...] the maxim *actus non est reus nisi mens sit rea* refers to a morally evil mind." G. Dworkin (Dworkin, 2011, p.7) for instance writes "[...] conduct that has to be forbidden must be wrong, immoral, a violation of rights, or something along these lines." Ferzan, 2008; Fischette, 2004; Lippke, 2008 all point in this direction, as K. Levy, 2011, p.1304-5n notes. Again: "legal liability (in torts and criminal law) falls only on those who are morally responsible (M. S. Moore, 2009, p. vii)." For similar remarks, cf. M. S. Moore, 1997. Alexander, Ferzan, and Morse, 2009 in building a system of criminal law founded on desert, briefly discuss the issue of moral responsibility. Though the authors cannot agree on the status of moral responsibility in regard to determinists' and incompatibilists' objections, it seems fair to infer that moral responsibility is the lying principle which sustains their whole architecture. Feinberg, 1990, p. 151: "A system of criminal law, whether or not it is assigned a moral

moral responsibility without intermediaries; indirectly if criminal liability requires criminal responsibility which in turn is based on moral responsibility.

It could be interesting to draw examples of moral responsibility, moral liability, legal responsibility and legal liability in an intuitive way, without providing definitions or discussion — for the time being. While in everyday situations they often overlap, sometimes we can appreciate cases when they are unrelated to one another.

When one promises her friend he will read and revise her paper, he has a duty to do it, unless other relevant conditions apply. It seems one has a prima facie *moral responsibility* when one contracts a promise. Unless otherwise stated, this example does not imply legal issues, so it is a case of moral responsibility without corresponding legal responsibility. Blaming, censure or other types of sanction, both social and internal (such as remorse), constitute what is often termed *moral liability*.

When my mother took my grandfather to the hospital she was in a hurry and there were no parking spots, she left her car under a "no parking" sign and she got a fine. She did not have any moral fault, but she had nonetheless to bear legal consequences — she was in fact legally responsible without being morally responsible.[4]

Current legal systems, both in civil and common law, have periods of prescription or statutes of limitations. If one has been judged responsible for a crime, say bribery, but is convicted when the terms have expired, one is in fact legally responsible without being liable for the crime, that is to say, without being given sanctions.

Punishment without legal responsibility is loosely termed strict liability-responsibility and it is usually given for particularly

---

justifying aim, employs an inherently moral (judgmental) constitutive process, and that process, in conjunction with the formal principle of fairness, is what underlies the concern with blameworthiness in sentencing."

[4] Even Hart, 2008, p. 215-6 corrected his earlier thought that one sense of responsibility is identical with liability; Raz, 2011, p.256 writes "that responsibility should not be identified with liability. Rather liability is — sometimes — a consequence of responsibility."

harmful or dangerous conducts, regardless of *mens rea*, such as statutory rape.

This section is divided into two parts. In the first one, I shall show the problems of founding criminal liability on moral responsibility. In the second part, I shall consequently argue that the very idea of capacity responsibility is questionable in criminal law for three sorts of reasons: (i) semantic, (ii) conceptual and (iii) factual.

3.2.1 Criminal Liability Has No Necessary Connection with *Moral* Responsibility

Legal liability[5] is usually rooted in moral responsibility[6] in two respects: as regards deciding when to give the liability and as regards the degree of liability imposed. In both respects, criminal liability could depend either directly or indirectly (*via* criminal responsibility) on moral responsibility.

I maintain that none of these should be the case, if we wish to keep our states as liberal and pluralist as we aim. *Two* caveats: *first*, I shall focus only on some structural/formal elements of ethics (i.e. beyond its possible contents) out of many possibilities; *second*, I shall not enter the contemporary debate on moral responsibility *stricto sensu*, on which the literature is immense.[7]

---

5 I am not maintaining here that morality and law must be kept separated *tout court*. As Hart, 2012, p. 185 notes, "[t]here are many different types of relation between law and morals": I shall try to narrow my claim only to one of these relations. See L. Green, 2008; Hart, 1957 and Gardner, 2003, 2009 for more detailed discussions.
6 Unless otherwise specified, with "moral considerations" I am referring to considerations regarding moral responsibility rather than general considerations of justice, fairness and so on that could inform legal systems. Every claim about "ethics" or "morality" should primarily be understood in the narrower sense.
7 For a general survey and some new proposals, see Björnsson and Persson, 2012; Denaro, 2012; Levy and McKenna, 2009, Fischer and Ravizza, 1993, Levy and McKenna, 2009 and Eshleman, 2009. Responsibility and moral responsibility are often dealt with in contemporary debates even without reference to the free will problem. See for instance Bok, 1998, 2002; Braham and van Hees, 2012; Brown, 2006; Bruckner, 2007; Burrington, 1999; Byrd, 2007, 2010;

3.2.1.1 Ethics as a Non-formalized System

It is reasonable to require that laws be as clear and explicit as possible, in order to have them enforced rigorously and consistently.

If criminal liabilities are to be based ultimately (or informally) on moral responsibility, and moral responsibility depends on moral theories that are usually hard to formalize and codify,[8] then there would be problems in drawing legal provisions — however indirectly — from moral theories, given their fluid and shapeless formulation.

I believe sound examples are provided by religious-inspired ethics. When these were dominant in a given culture or society and consequently enforced by civil authorities, parts of them were first enclosed and codified in legal codes.

3.2.1.2 Disagreement

Even if it could be demonstrated that there is only one objective and just theory of what moral responsibility is and when it should be ascribed, this does not seem the case. Moreover, there would be serious concerns in imposing this moral belief to all citizens, since what seems to be clear in pluralistic states is that

---

Campbell, 2008; Caruso, forthcoming; Chan, 2000; Ciurria, 2012; Clarke, 1997; Coates and Swenson, forthcoming; Cobb, 1959; Copp, 1997; Das, 2002; De Brigard, Mandelbaum, and Ripley, 2009; Denaro, 2012; Dodig-Crnkovic and Persson, 2008; Downie, 1964; Fischer, 1986, 1999a,b, 2006; Fischer and Ravizza, 1993, 1998a,b; FitzPatrick, 2008; Fletcher, 1967; Kershnar, 2004; King, 2012, 2013; King and Carruthers, 2012; Klampfer, 2004; Knobe and Doris, 2010; Lang, 1985; Macnamara, 2011; Mason, 2005; Moya, 2005, 2007; Parent, 1975; Paul, Miller, and Paul, 1999; Pink, 2009; Risser, 1996; Roskies and Nichols, 2008; Rosse, 1973; P. Russell, 2002; Sankowski, 1990; Sheehy, 2006; M. Smiley, 1992; Sommers, 2009; Swinburne, 1989; van den Beld, 2000; van Inwagen, 1997; G. Williams, 2003, 2004, 2008; Young, 1974; Zimmerman, 1988.

8 Because they are subject to inter-community negotiation, emotion-based judgments and other peculiar traits. There is also the problem of legal moralism, i.e. "the principle that it is always a good reason in support of criminalization that it prevents non-grievance evils or harmless immoralities (Feinberg, 1990, p.324)." See passim for discussion on how the state can distinguish illegal acts among immoral ones and immoral thoughts.

if the law is valid, one normally has to abide by it, even though he believes it is wrong or unjust. Instead, if one is unconvinced by a particular moral theory, he can freely choose whether to endorse it or not.

3.2.1.3 Partiality/Discretionality

If there was no agreed theory of moral responsibility, criminal legal systems could hardly be based upon a varying and inconsistent set of norms. The attribution of criminal liability would depend eventually on the moral system endorsed by the judge.[9] This seems against a principle of impartiality, because different judges endorsing different moral theories would *in principle* be allowed to take decisions upon them.[10] The criminal culpability cannot depend on the moral system adopted (if any) by the defendant or the claimant. Equally, we do not think that non-confessional states should officially endorse a certain moral system.

To reject the claim that criminal liability is to depend on *moral* responsibility seems fair for these reasons — namely difference of moral systems admitted in a non-confessional society, difficulty of enforcing a non-formalized system of norms, need of impartiality in judgment.

K. Levy, 2011 makes a compelling case regarding psychopaths. Psychopaths lack some of the conditions usually required to be held morally responsible (such as moral knowledge, empathy etc.).[11] On this basis, they are commonly thought not morally responsible and *therefore* often acquitted.[12] Both on consequen-

---

9 For similar but more detailed remarks, see Sinnott-Armstrong and Levy, 2011, p.303.
10 But see the interesting case of the Swiss Civil Code, where judges — in absence of rules or consuetudes — can assume the norm they will follow. See Di Lucia and Feis, 2013.
11 The weaknesses of this quite widespread view are quite obvious. I do not endorse it.
12 On responsibility, psychopathy and neuroscience, see for instance Adshead, 1996, 2003; Braude, 1996; Callender, 2010; Caruso, forthcoming; Ciocchetti, 2003a,b; De Brigard, Mandelbaum, and Ripley, 2009; Edwards, 2009; Elliott,

tialist and retributive grounds though — it is argued — they are to be held liable for criminal misdeeds, even if they cannot be morally responsible for them. Failure to acknowledge moral norms (on which the criminal system is built, it seems) does not prevent them from knowing what is forbidden by the law and what is not. Then they should be considered liable on the same grounds of "normal" people who endorse a different moral system (if any) and who know what is illegal but do not think what is forbidden is also morally wrong.

This example, however imperfectly, shows how it is unwise to build a legal system on moral provisions to attribute legal liability. In the case of psychopaths the lack of morality is somehow intrinsic. Normal people could endorse or engage in another set of moral norms, thus the lack of (relevant) morality is contextual and factual. The practical result is the same: for different reasons, both the psychopath and the weirdo do not abide by the common moral standard (and are allowed to do so in liberal and pluralistic states) but both must abide by the law.

In this section, I have highlighted several problematic issues for legal liability to be founded on moral responsibility. In the next section, I shall turn my attention to the very idea of responsibility in law.

3.2.2 Capacity Responsibility and Neuroscience

If the arguments developed in Section 3.2.1 are sound, then the moral-based responsibility system sketched above is seriously faulty. Nonetheless, let us put the moral part aside for a moment and consider criminal liability based on criminal responsibility.

1991, 1992; Faraci and Shoemaker, 2010; Fields, 1996; Fingarette, 1955; Frierson, 2008; Glannon, 2008; Greenspan, 1987, 2003; Grenander, 1982; Haji and Cuypers, 2004; Hindriks, 2011; Knobe and Doris, 2010; Maibom, 2008; Malatesti and McMillan, 2010; Martin, 2010; Mayerfeld, 1999; McMillan and Gillett, 2005; Meynen, 2010; Morse, 2008; Nadelhoffer, 2004; Nahmias et al., 2005; Pizarro, Uhlmann, and Bloom, 2003; Schauber, forthcoming; Schoeman, 1987; Shoemaker, 2009, 2011a,b; Sneddon, 2005; Sommers, 2012; Vargas, 2010a,b, forthcoming; Vincent, 2008; Wigley, 2007; G. Williams, 2003.

I shall tackle the issue of responsibility by itself, putting forward (i) semantic, (ii) conceptual and (iii) factual reasons to argue that the kind of responsibility required by the law is an unclear concept, theoretically defeasible and practically hard to ascertain, if it is identified with capacity responsibility from a purely *factual* perspective: capacity responsibility is at most one of the conditions of (legal) responsibility, and cannot exhaust it.

3.2.2.1   (i) Semantics

The word 'responsibility' is in itself well polysemic. One way to sum this up is the expression 'syndrome of concepts' coined by Vincent, 2009 to account for the several different meanings used in everyday life and language. Even in the legal discourse then, it is confusing if we refer to someone as 'responsible', meaning one or more of outcome-responsible, causal-responsible, role-responsible, capacity-responsible, to name but a few.[13]

The word 'responsibility' has not only different meanings, but arguably different and heterogeneous *referents* (cf. for instance Hart, 2008, Postscript).

Confusion in language leads to confusion in thought. Before ascribing responsibility, one should have in mind which responsibility he is ascribing, on which grounds and how he can do so. Certain scientific techniques, for instance, may let us measure or ascertain capacity-responsibility. From there, it is not great a leap to ascribing responsibility *tout court*, confusing a part for the whole. But that capacity-responsibility is by itself a sufficient condition for "full" responsibility is still to be proven.

This kind of semantic unclarity may well lead to conceptual and factual problems, as I argue in what follows.

3.2.2.2   (ii) Conceptual Issues

The very idea of responsibility seems theoretically questionable on deterministic grounds. Loosely, some think determinism would undermine alternative possibilities, i.e. the possibility to do otherwise, which is one of the condition usually required for

---
13 For other concepts of responsibility, see my taxonomy *supra* at Chapter 1.1.

freedom.[14] Without freedom one could not have done otherwise and therefore — the master argument goes — is blameless for an action he could have not chosen.[15]

Neuroscience would be able to prove (brain) determinism and this — as more and more judges seem to understand — would undermine (moral) responsibility and/or some sense of freedom. Levy 2011, for instance, argues that no one is ever responsible for anything and no one ever acts freely. Waller, 2011 argues for the total elimination of the idea of moral responsibility. If accepted, this line of argument would likely force our societies to reconsider not only our justifications of punishment, but the whole criminal system, since "current law envisions a criminal defendant as a free-willing, rational creature operating in a normal brain environment with the mental intent (either general or specific) to accomplish a crime (Gazzaniga, 2008)."

Increasingly, empirical scientists have started to investigate allegedly voluntary acts to see whether they are pre-determinated and hence not really "free". This, in turn, has been influencing the philosophical and legal sphere with respect to the ascription of responsibility. Results such as Libet's 2004 or Soon and colleagues' 2008 would pose a serious threat to the common understanding of voluntary acts and therefore to the possibility of ascribing any sort of responsibility.[16]

However, state-of-the-art science cannot provide us with conclusive or crucial reliable evidence for this complex matter on which current criminal law systems are heavily relying. It would be dishonest, then, to attribute serious liabilities based on a

---

14 For further discussion on the distinction between concepts of responsibility and conditions of responsibility, see *supra* at Chapter 1.2.
15 Of course the argument is much richer and many refined versions of determinism overcome this objection. For a recent account see Greene and Cohen, 2004. There are also philosophical theories arguing for compatibilism or semi-compatibilism between determinism and free will, and between determinism and responsibility. See for instance Fischer and Ravizza, 1998b; Kane, 2011. The discussion, however, exceeds the purpose of this work.
16 For a recent take on this issue, see Libet, Sinnott-Armstrong, and Nadel, 2011, in particular Alexander, 2011. But for an informative account of how neuroscience can be conciliated with traditional justifications of punishment, see Pardo and Patterson, 2013.

model we do not have deciding proofs thereof, conforming to it "as it were true". It would be fairer to recognize, at least, that the whole system is problematic and to try to rethink it on new conceptual bases.

3.2.2.3 (iii) Is-Ought Gap

While the ascription of responsibility is deemed normative,[17] it is increasingly done via scientific descriptive ways, especially with neuroscientific techniques. This factual gap is problematic and should not be underestimated.[18]

Were our social practices of holding responsible and of punishing not "mirroring nature" (according to our latest theories and practices), we should definitely reconsider them inasmuch as they are not rooted in a world empirically testable.[19] The general and common assumption here is that there is a natural (and therefore scientifically observable) or intuitively true basis on which we should ground our practices of ascribing responsibility.[20] If it is correct to say that ascription of responsibility is — at least partially — normativity-based, and if one follows the above line of reasoning, he is committing what has been known as "naturalistic fallacy" or in other terms, one is violating Hume's law, that is, deriving an "ought" from an "is". But how?

First — positively — neuroscience is thought useful for assessing whether an individual possesses the required set of men-

---

[17] Isolating a factual basis before and independently from the attribution of responsibility is problematic because it seems to require evaluative considerations. See for instance Ross, 1975, p.29 and Feinberg, 1970; Hart, 1948. For further discussion on this point, see *infra* in Chapter 5.

[18] The use and the admissibility of neuroscientific evidence in courtrooms has been discussed extensively. For instance Weisberg *et al.*, 2008 points out how neuroscientific evidence acquires an allure of truth — on this see also Aspinwall, Brown, and Tabery, 2012; Compton, 2010 discusses admissibility, current usage and risks. For other broadly skeptical takes, see Schleim, Spranger, and Walter, 2009; Schleim and Walter, 2007.

[19] Feinberg, 1970, pp.26-7 put it in this way: "Legal responsibility [...] cannot simply be "read off" the facts".

[20] As Gommer, 2010 very counterintuitively argues.

tal capacities to be held responsible for certain misdeeds. This builds on the unproven assumption that there is a minimum set of internal factors responsibility requires — cf. for instance Hart, 2008, p.218. Moreover, the issue of *naive physicalism*, according to which mental capacities would be directly and univocally reduced to neural states or correlates, is constantly underrated. This is far from obvious.[21]

Second (and negatively), some judiciary cases[22] employed neuroscientific evidence to assess whether an individual deviates from the standard of normality, thus having some excuse to be exempted from regular ascription of responsibility. This latter use is less theoretically demanding and builds on the assumption that everyone "normal" can be held responsible and thus responsibility (or in other terms liability or imputability) is the common standard condition (see famously Austin, 1956, 1966). Again it is a problem to define what is normal — which may not be so straightforward but might require an evaluation rather than a descriptive finding.

The use of (neuro)scientific techniques in ascertaining responsibility is increasing. I have underlined how this use presupposes problematic assumptions that are mostly unjustified. Arguably, in turn, those issues would factually undermine the whole practice.

In this section, I have highlighted that responsibility is more than one of its conditions (capacity responsibility) and therefore it cannot be scientifically ascertained in an objective manner. I have argued that its polysemy generates conceptual confusion, that it is questionable on grounds that are more and more endorsed by the scientific community and that its ascertainment through certain techniques can be both logically fallacious and factually doubtful.

---

[21] For instance Morse, 2011a,b define this approach as "fundamental psycholegal error". See in general Freeman, 2011. Others (among which there is Santoni de Sio, 2013) call this the "mereological fallacy".
[22] Notably the Albertani and Trieste cases in Italy.

The idea of capacity responsibility could be retained by criminal law at a high price: that of an uncertain, unclear, ill-founded belief, philosophically questionable, with little or no empirical evidence.

Lady Wootton's theses (influenced by behaviorism) on the scientific improvability of *mens rea* seem to hold even against current scientific techniques and, most importantly, they seem to hold not merely in a contingent way, but because of those conceptual reasons I underlined in this section.

3.3 LAW WITHOUT CAPACITY RESPONSIBILITY

The preceding skeptic critiques to responsibility are more than justified — but they presuppose a notion of responsibility that needs descriptive premises, and they work only against such a conception.

I am going to argue that our normative systems (and criminal legal systems, to begin with) can survive (and are probably better off) without this descriptive presupposition.

I'll show that a normative notion of responsibility can overcome the objections the skeptic may put forward (at least those that I summarized in the preceding section).

We have seen (in Section 3.2) that many problems with responsibility in (at least criminal) law are due to its mental "roots".

What if the skeptic is completely right, and then (capacity) responsibility is either non-existent or impossible to prove? What would happen if this kind of responsibility were not part of legal systems anymore?

In the rest of this chapter, I shall assume that skeptics are right and the concept of responsibility — at least as currently conceived in legal systems — is untenable.

I shall show that, instead, a normative conception (of responsibility) can do as well, without the downsides of non-normative conception of responsibility. In order not to confound the matter, I shall call this (mostly) normative notion 'liability-responsibility' — even if that phrase is already in use as a part for the general category of responsibility.

For the purpose of this chapter, I assume that the skeptic is right, and try to meet his challenges with a *twofold* strategy.

First, how to assign liabilities? This question goes deep into the structure of the criminal system and it is related to the justification of the criminal law as a whole. In what follows, I argue that criminal law is justifiable regardless of capacity responsibility, (a) by considering legal systems as groups coherent in themselves and not based on external factors (Sect. 3.3.1); and (b) by founding legal systems on strict liability-responsibility (Sect. 3.3.2).

Second, why assign liabilities? This one is the classic problem of justifying punishment. It will be dealt with briefly in Section 3.4 in regard to the arguments developed in this section.

3.3.1 Law, Games, Conventions

In this section, I try to put forward some analogies in order to show how a responsibility system may be justified without capacity responsibility.

Here, I shall hint at an analogy between legal systems and ludic systems. This analogy is neither new nor life-changing, but I contend that it is useful to our investigation with regard to the problems I discussed above.

3.3.1.1 *Chess as a paradigm*

Let's consider chess. Chess is a game where pieces, their moves and their actions are defined by a set of rules (some chess-rules are constitutive rules).[23] The king, whatever meaning it has out-

---

[23] What is defined is, of course, the type of action and the type of moving pieces are allowed to do, not the actual tokens of actions. I am referring here to what Ross, 1959, Ch.3 calls "primary rules", that is to say, rules governing the moves and the pieces and not to what is called "theory of the game", that

side the chess-world, is defined so-and-so *in* the game, according to its functional meaning.[24] It usually can only move one square in any direction, or — if under attack — it must move, if it can do so legally. In the chess-world it is not important that the King is king-shaped, but that it move and play as a King according to chess-rules.

However there are what we call, outside the chess-world, exceptions. The King, under particular circumstances, *can* move two squares (in castling). This is not an actual exception, but the fact that the King can move two squares is part of the definition of chess-King, i.e. what we mean by king in the context of the game of chess.

Moreover, were I — as a chess-player — to decide to move a Pawn backward, I would not be playing chess badly, but I would be playing another game.[25] Then, even if I am moving a piece called King, I do not have to consider what a real-life (outside the chess world) king is doing, in order to move my chess-King.

3.3.1.2 *Unfolding the analogy*

Now let's consider law. Law might be thought of as a game where agents, actions and sanctions are defined so-and-so by and in a set of rules.

- Those rules are the *necessary condition* of conceivability and existence of what they regulate: they are super-imposed on reality, but should not be logically dependent on and strictly adherent to it. On the contrary, regulative rules are a mere contingent conditioning of actions: they suggest a way to regulate a conduct already in existence. For instance, take enhancement of one's capacity. It can be defined, for legal purposes, as involving drugs (as opposed to private tutoring or particular alimentation). In sporting

---

is, strategies tied to the specific aim of winning the game. On chess, see also Schwyzer, 1969, 2012 and Roversi, 2006, 2012.

24 'Functional meaning' is a calque of '*funktionale Bedeutung*', Mally, 1971, Formalismus I, quoted in Conte, 1995c.

25 To play chess *badly*, one needs at least to play chess, i.e. following all the chess-rules. Cf. Wittgenstein, 1970, n.320, p.355

performance it is illegal and considered doping, while in academic or working settings it is not the case — until now. Therefore while in reality — descriptively — there is an enhancement of one's cognitive or physical capacities, in the first case it is cheating, in the second it is not. The rules of the game (opposed to other descriptive knowledge) create the nets of meaning we use to navigate our world for legal purposes.[26]

- Those rules may keep an *internal coherence*,[27] and need not to respond to external factors, exactly as a chess-king must move according to chess-rules, not according to what the King of X is doing right now. For instance, once a concept like responsibility has been established, scientific or philosophical objections should be ignored inasmuch as they are external to the system, i.e. based on determinism and incompatibilism grounds. This would prevent the law from continuous theoretical attacks and would move the debate to the process of crafting and agreeing laws (for which see 3.4).

This game-like architecture can answer to the issues raised against current legal systems in Section 2.1, namely formalism, disagreement and impartiality.

Games as Formalized Systems - Legal provisions should be stated as explicitly, consistently and rigorously as possible — just like game rules are — in order to avoid uncertainty and to keep the system less prone to in-group negotiation and the like.

Disagreement is not an issue in the game. Agents can ignore the (moral) value of regulative rules whose (theoretical) validity

---

26 On this point Czesław Znamierowski was probably the first to distinguish constructive norms [*normy konstrukcyjne*] from imperative norms [*normy imperatywne*], thetic acts [*akty tetyczne*] from psycho-physic actions — cf. Znamierowski, 1921, 1924.

27 On coherence and consistency, cf. Conte, 2007c, p.57-8. For instance, between two constitutive rules there cannot be antinomy. Consider (i) If the king is in check, castling is mandatory; (ii) if the king is in check, castling is forbidden. There is not any contradiction, because (i) and (ii) constitute two different games and different intensions of 'king' and 'castling': respectively king-(i) and castling-(i); king-(ii) and castling-(ii).

they recognize; this cannot evidently be the case with constitutive rules. The proper room for disagreement is when laws are crafted and agreed. Furthermore, disagreement can be also found in applying rules. This points us toward two aspects: a need for extreme clarity in setting the frame at the beginning and the room for discretionality of officials (or the game referees).

Impartiality Application of the rules is subject to interpretation and opens up the room for discretionality. Judges (or whoever has to decide) therefore have evaluative elbow room, which must be granted within the judiciary system and cannot be based on any (external) principles whatsoever.

Exceptions — what in the real world are seen as exceptions, excuses, justifications for K in the game become part of the definition of K. A King that cannot move two squares under the circumstances qualifying for castling, is *not* a chess-King, but something pertaining to another game, not to chess. In an analogous fashion, we must define L as so-and-so in the law game. What may be considered exceptions in the real (i.e. outside the game) world are part of the definition: L is not L in the game, unless considered so-and-so.

3.3.1.3 *Limits and Objections*

The example of chess is meant only to provide us with a clear instance of an organic group of rules: however enlightening, analogies are still imperfect. I am not claiming law should become chess-like; quite on the contrary, I am directing our attention to the logical structure of chess. One can raise several objections based on this analogy: the apparent uselessness of referees, the consciousness of playing a game *versus* being engaged in real life and the fact that chess is too perfect to serve as an analogon are just three possible instances.

Given the variety of laws even within the criminal domain, one could maintain that only some laws can be considered this way. What about power-conferring rules or rules describing the functioning of courts, for instance?[28] According to the thesis

---

28 Like those described by Hart, 2012, ch.3.

held here, those laws should be considered as adeontic constitutive rules, i.e. rules constituting states-of-affairs.

One could object that it is possible to keep a rule-based (chess-like, game-like) view of law *and* moral external grounds. There are *two* ways this might be done: *first*, by a strict legal moralism; *second*, by diminishing the autonomy and coherency of rules, having them referred or vaguely inspired to moral guiding principles judges can apply as and when. Both are prone to issues raised in Sect. 2.1, but the second is logically incompatible with such an architecture as put forward in this subsection, which needs to be closed and self-reliant.

But there is a *third*, middle way. While keeping the sharp distinction between moral principles and the group of legal rules in their application and enforcement, the moral dimension can intervene when legal rules are established or agreed. After that, the fact that some legal rules are morally shaded should be irrelevant.

The issue of our psychopath of Section 3.2.1 should therefore be solved: on the one hand, he should be able to follow game-rules free of (direct or indirect) moral references; on the other hand, the system can punish him for violations and crimes even if he cannot grasp the "wrongfulness" of his acts — which is not at stake in the proposed model.

Hart famously described an "internal" point of view (when people accept norms as regulating their behaviors, as reasons to do something) and an "external" point of view (when people refuse — or do not understand — norms, but take them as signs or clues of the fact that people will behave in a certain way or that certain sanctions will follow): those of psychopaths, who admittedly cannot understand norms as reasons for action, is an external point of view. A psychopath might think that a red light does not constitute a reason to stop, but it should be a clue that others will stop, and so should they. Inasmuch as they can do this reasoning, I think they can be subject to legal liability — even if they cannot be morally responsible.[29]

---

29 On the many problems of rule-following, see at least Kripke, 1982; Wittgenstein, 2009. On *nomotropic* behavior (that of a cheat, for instance) see the work

This subsection showed how the understanding of legal systems I proposed can help us in freeing the law of problematic considerations, in gaining in rigor, clarity and fairness. The next subsection is devoted to demonstrating how we can retain criminal liability regardless of a capacity-conceived responsibility.

3.3.2 Strict Liability-Responsibility

In this subsection, I offer a stipulative definition of strict liability-responsibility. Then I argue that legal strict liability-responsibility should substitute capacity responsibility in criminal law: criminal law should function regardless of a notion of responsibility that presupposes only descriptive elements.

The standard model reads that (some sort of) responsibility is necessary for legal liability.[30] If our society is to keep assigning sanctions and punishment, it first has to ascribe responsibility. But were it proven that — for any of above reasons — responsibility is seriously flawed, dubious or untenable, then should we stop assigning legal liabilities, because there must be no liability without prior responsibility? Or should we continue?

The problem needs careful evaluation. In what follows, I assume that the legal practices of punishing are to continue.[31] I hold that they are justifiable *regardless* of responsibility, that is (i) even if there is no moral (or legal) responsibility (as skeptics have it) or (ii) there are overwhelming difficulties in ascribing it. Criminal law systems are justifiable with the principle of strict liability-responsibility.[32]

---

on *nomotropism* of Conte (Conte, 2011) and others (Passerini Glazel in Colloca, 2013).

30 Except the limited number of strict liability-responsibility offenses already enforced.
31 I do not commit to any practical form or content of punishing — which I believe should be thoroughly re-thought anyway.
32 Even Hart, 2008, p. 226 notes that a legal system could require strict liability-responsibility for all crimes without ceasing to be a legal system — contrary to strict "moral" responsibility, there are no conceptual barriers. But for opposite claims, that is *for* some form of *strict* moral responsibility (better: liability) see Duff, 2008 and McKenna, 2012, pp. 187-95.

A variety of meanings have been attached to strict liability.[33] I will not enter the perilous meanders of various criminal systems described in works on strict liability, but I will content myself with a stipulative provisional definition of strict liability-responsibility.

Strict (criminal) liability-responsibility then is criminal liability *regardless* of *mens rea* for *any* material element of the offense. Regardless here means that (i) there are no mens rea elements required for the offense to take place; (ii) mental elements are irrelevant for the offense.[34]

We have seen in Section 3.2 that legal responsibility is deeply rooted in mental elements: some degree of *mens rea* is usually indispensable to attribute someone responsibility (and thus culpability) for criminal actions. If all crimes were redefined on a strict liability-responsibility basis, only material elements would play a role in criminal law, without references to mental elements. And without references to mental elements, all legitimate references to capacity-responsibility cease, taking with them all problems raised in Section 3.2.2. This proposal is comparable to Lady Wootton's.

Difference with Hart's Liability-Responsibilty

Hart, 2008, Postscript characterized legal liability-responsibility in a quite complex way. He made it more extended than legal responsibility. In fact (at least in my interpretation), legal responsibility requires three elements (mental elements — *de facto*, *capacity*-responsibility — a certain connection with the act and certain relationships between the agents), which are neither suf-

---

[33] See, for instance, Duff, 2009; S. Green, 2005; Honoré, 1999a; Husak, 1995; Perry, 2001; Simons, 1997. For a survey see Shen *et al.*, 2011, n.4, that presents an informative set of historical examples of strict liability-responsibility crimes, such as damages caused by one's property (including slaves) — an idea compared to today's products liability — and the old English and Norse *deodand*, according to which property that injured others was destroyed. For the origins of explicit strict liability crimes in common law jurisdictions, see Singer, 1988.

[34] Note that *mens rea* and fault are not the same thing. For instance cf. Gardner, 2005, p.69.

ficient nor necessary for legal liability. Legal liability can be assigned according to legal rules that may or may not require legal responsibility. Legal responsibility is, so to speak, reflecting people's intuitions, and keeps a descriptive or factual basis. Hart's model is subject to my earlier criticisms because of the factual component, and moreover it is not clear at all on the mutual relationship between liability and responsibility.

According to my definition then, mine and Hart's model are comparable insofar as his is deprived of the capacity-responsibility part — to leave room for normative elements (contingent as they may or may not be).

But why would we want to endorse such a counter-intuitive idea as strict liability-responsibility?

As a matter of fact, strict liability-responsibility is already *en force*, though in a limited number of cases: my proposal would be to generalize and extend what is already done in few circumstances to almost all criminal occurences.

I will now go through the issues I raised on responsibility in Section 3.2.2, namely (i) semantic, (ii) conceptual and (iii) factual problems, to show how this proposed shift in paradigm would account for them. Then I will consider a real life example and propose an analogy with fencing to explain my understanding of the issue.

3.3.2.1 (i) Semantics

Strict liability is hardly spoken of in everyday language: it is unlikely to cause confusion or obscurity. Moreover, strict liability-responsibility has to be founded on rules — rules that seem more conventional than their classic counterpart.

3.3.2.2 (ii) Conceptual Issues

While the idea of responsibility we considered before was said to be questionable on deterministic grounds, this is not the case for strict liability-responsibility. In fact, strict liability-responsibility is not based on a concept such as "freedom of the will" or "alternative possibilities" which can be put in question by certain empirical results (or by the idea of certain empirical results).

3.3.2.3   (iii) Is-Ought Gap

The strict liability-responsibility view does not commit to any descriptive notion, but it is purely a normative concept: it does not claim to be "out there" in the world, somewhat measurable. Clearly, it has a factual basis: the material elements of the action.

Neuroscientific techniques may still be used in criminal trials, but not with the purpose of telling something relevant for the ascription of responsibility, but only for the unfoldment of what took place.

PSYCHOPATHS   Let's consider the case "reported by Burns and Swerdlow, 2003 — namely, of a 40 year old school teacher who developed an obsession with child pornography due to a tumour that pressed on his orbitofrontal region, and who was unable to stop himself from acquiring such pornographic material (and doing various other things) despite knowing that what he was doing was wrong (Vincent, 2009)."

If "our brain makes us do it" (that is, there's no "I" different from my brain who is overall responsible for "my" actions), one might claim that it was the teacher's brain that "made him do it" no differently from how another person's brain (without the tumor) didn't.

While it's rather easy to see that this tumor caused the sufferer to deviate from the physiologically normal person, this is not always the case. Several neurological studies tell us there is no *normal* or *standard* brain. The expertise ordered in the Como case, to pick one, made a comparison between the defendant's brain and several other people's, drawn from girls about the same age, education and comparable backgrounds.

Were we to judge the school teacher for a criminal act (related to his pathology), we wouldn't hold him as liable as an individual without the brain tumor. But in our framework this is not the case *because* the teacher didn't possess the relevant mental capacities (i.e. self-control) to be held responsible, but *because* we originally stipulated in our law code certain requirements for liability, explicitly excluding cases like these.

It is more a matter of *imputability* rather than fault.

Neuroscientific (diagnostic) methods should be used not to establish whether he was responsible — an evaluative task — but to assess whether he was *liable* — i.e. that he fulfilled the factual requirements that constitute the offense.[35]

3.3.2.4 *An analogy with fencing*

Fencing seems like a good example. As a family of combat sports, it is a game. Nonetheless, there are different disciplines: foil, épée, sabre. Before entering the carefully ruled world of Olympic sports, sword combats have been used (and to an extent are being used) in wars and duels with different aims: to kill enemies, to re-establish one's honor etc. Roughly, in our analogy, real-life combats count as the moral system, while fencing games count as the legal system. In comparison to "real life" combats, these disciplines in fact are highly regulated and — so to speak — isolated. For instance the valid target, the allowed hits and even the scoring differ from weapon to weapon.

Compare each discipline to a legal system conceived — I suggest — as a game. Foil-system, for instance, has a so-called "right-of-way": when both opponents hit at the same time, the point is awarded to the one who started the offensive action. épée-system, instead, awards a "double-hit" (a point to each fencer) if both touch within 40ms. In most Romance languages, the "right-of-way" rule is termed with a word usually translated as "convention", or stipulation. What counts as point, as target or as allowed strategy is conventionally established by the rules of that specific discipline.

We could have a foil-like law-system that decides to recognize or to sanction only voluntary actions, or action consciously begun by the doer. On the contrary, we can allow for a épée-like law-system, that — regardless of how one hits — decides

---

[35] In other words, I maintained that a descriptive view of responsibility is untenable: this would mean using neuroscience to assess separately the state-of-affairs while leaving the evaluative dimension of ascribing responsibility.

to give credit for the simple touch, if it fulfills some requirements.[36] Loosely then, we may want to identify foil-systems as system sanctioning only voluntary or "meant" actions,[37] and épée-systems as attributing a sort of strict-liability, that is to say, sanctioning all hitting-actions regardless of other considerations, such as who started the attack.

This analogy shows two facets of my proposal: (i) legal systems as games bearing little reference to the outside moral universe can be seen in fencing as opposed to pre-Olympics, real-life combats (Sections 3.2.1 and 3.3.1); (ii) the principle of responsibility of current criminal systems opposed to the proposed principle of strict liability-responsibility can be seen in the opposition between foil and épée (Sections 3.2.2 and 3.3.2).

In this section, I have offered a stipulative definition of legal strict liability-responsibility and I have argued that criminal law systems might be based on strict liability-responsibility to overcome the problems of moral and legal responsibility underlined in Section 3.2.

The attribution of liability depends only on internal (to the law-game) conditions, and it is not subject (a) to the uncertainty and ambiguity of responsibility as a concept or ideal requirement; (b) to threats from empirical or theoretical extra-legal positions; (c) to different methods and criteria to ascertain responsibility as a state-of-affairs.

The next section replies to possible objections and discusses how this proposal would impact on the criminal system, were it to be adopted.

---

36 While in épée-fencing those could be something like the time span and the pressure of the hit, in law-systems other relevant characteristics (and exemptions) have to be agreed on.
37 Who voluntarily started an action may be inferred — exactly as in the criminal trial — by environmental clues, as it were.

3.4 PUNISHMENT & CONSEQUENCES

In this last section, I will summarize my argument and consider the problems my proposal leaves open and the objections aimed at (a) the idea of strict liability-responsibility; (b) the proposal in general.

I have argued that our criminal law systems are justifiable even if there is no objectively measurable capacity responsibility. In fact, I have suggested putting aside the concept of capacity responsibility (i.e. attention to mental elements): the guiding principle in assigning sanctions should be that of strict liability-responsibility (i.e. importance of material, external elements of the action, plus rules and evaluations). This strategy works *negatively* contra skeptics of moral and legal responsibility, undermining their argument against the criminal system; it works *positively* making our system more rigorous and harmonious with empirical findings, even in the worst-case scenario.

This shift of paradigm comes at a cost. *First*, along with responsibility, we probably have to put aside direct references to moral foundations of criminal punishment. This does not mean that morality has nothing to do with legal provisions, but its influence must be thought over. *Second*, we have to think of laws differently: they can no more regulate our conduct according to some other pre-existent (moral) principle, but should create what they prescribe.[38]

3.4.1 Some Consequences

Even if we take for granted the usefulness of my proposal, several issues remain to be addressed. In particular I try to isolate and answer objections directed to (a) strict liability-responsibility; (b) the system in general.

---

[38] In this sense I think that Hart's 2008, p.181 objection to strict liability-responsibility (namely, that it prevents us from planning the "future course of our lives") is ill-founded.

3.4.1.1 (a) Objections to Strict Liability-Responsibility

In a strict-liability framework, there would be no difference between crimes distinguished only by mental elements: the difference between voluntary (or first class) murder and manslaughter would formally vanish, roughly because in current jurisdictions the former requires intention to murder, while the latter is a result of some other activity not meant to murder. Clearly, then, the difference would not be one of kind, but of degree — at the sentencing stage by carefully accounting for the circumstances. This counter-objection should also serve to settle the question whether I need two senses of strict liability-responsibility, namely, to mirror the old distinction of responsibility without liability in case of periods of prescription or statute of limitations. My answer is on the negative side: one can be judged liable for an offense without being given a sentence for it — but the difference is simply one of degree.

If my model excludes mental elements for any material element of the offense, how do I account for "external" causal control of the agent, such as in cases of electrical stimulations, post-hypnosis, drugs raised by Scanlon, 1998, p. 277-8? It seems to me these cases do not significantly differ from the brain-tumor one I tackled *supra*.

Luck instead poses no particular objection to my model than to every other conception both of moral and legal responsibility.[39] In a way, the strict liability-responsibility model can be a *solution* to this problem, since it outsources — as it were — the basis of sanctioning from internal to external conditions: if one may say that an unlucky situation cannot bring blame on the poor fellow (since blame is based on will and will is independent from bad luck), unluckiness refers properly to external material elements, exactly those bringing strict liability-responsibility.

If strict liability-responsibility is not based on internal (i.e. mental) elements, such as alternative possibilities or freedom of

---

39 For the classical debate, see Nagel, 1979; B. A. O. Williams, 1981. Honoré 1999 discusses luck in responsibility for outcomes according to the principle of taking the rough with smooth: we cannot accept praise for lucky outcomes and repudiate blame or liability for unlucky ones.

the will, it must be based on external elements. Agreement on what to take in to account (i.e. causation?) may prove wearing and maybe worse than mental elements, which at least seem to have an intuitive basis.

Moreover, why not be hard materialists and think that "mental" elements are no more than material elements of the action, and therefore must be taken into account even under a strict liability-responsibility principle?

3.4.1.2 (b) Objections to the General Model

The analysis I conducted and the model I put forward are directly concerned with (criminal) law. Can my model be extended also to morality, as in fact Hart, 2008, Postscript did with his legal liability-responsibility to *moral* liability-responsibility? That I don't yet know.

Can this proposed system be discussed independently from a purely forward-looking notion of punishment as "social hygiene"?[40] Ultimately, it might be the case. But for the time being, I think it is more useful to assume the non-philosophical justification (and aim) of punishment embedded in western legal systems: a mixture of backward- and forward-looking (roughly, of retribution and prevention) conception of criminal sanctions.

I note here several issues I cannot answer. One may say that my model detaches law from its action-guiding and motivating dimension; that this model may bring about overcriminalisation; that without desert we lack a correlate to establish the length and severity of punishment; that we would need a never-ending list of regulations and exceptions, falling in a casuistic view of laws.

3.4.2 Conclusion

In this chapter, I have considered the *ascertainment* of responsibility, working on the proposal of Lady Wootton discussed in the preceding chapter. To start with, I put forward a distinction

---

40 Basically such as Lady Wootton, 1963 proposal. Cf. ch. 2.

between moral and legal responsibility, and moral and legal liability.

I then argued that several scientific and neuroscientific techniques can be (are) used to give a substantial contribution to the ascertainment of responsibility. Their use, however, already presupposes a *conception* of responsibility as made of elements *descriptively* ascertainable.

I tried to show this is not the case and that both the *concept* and this *conception* of responsibility should be normativity-based, thus seconding Lady Wootton's intuitions.

The next chapter is devoted to an analysis of the relationships between responsibility and causation, another element considered by some as a descriptive basis for responsibility.

4 | RESPONSIBILITY AND CAUSATION

4.0 Introduction

4.1 First Argument: Queer Responsibilities

    4.1.1 Strict Liability *vs.* Collective Responsibility

    4.1.2 The Various Cases of Collective Responsibility

    4.1.3 Accomplice & Corporate Responsibility

    4.1.4 Qualified Responsibilities

4.2 Second Argument: Responsibility and Causation

    4.2.1 A Bird's Eye View

        4.2.1.1 Kelsen: *Kausalität* und *Zurechnung*

        4.2.1.2 Hart's and Honore's *Causation in the Law*

        4.2.1.3 Moore: *Causation and Responsibility*

    4.2.2 Causation as Normative

> *Felix qui potuit rerum cognoscere causas.*
> Publius Vergilius Maro, *Georgicon* 2. 490

> *In jure non remota causa sed proxima spectatur.*
> Francis Bacon, *The Elements of the Common Law of England*, 1630

4.0 INTRODUCTION

This chapter deals with the relationships between causation, responsibility and normativity, both conceptually and in the works of Kelsen, Hart and Honoré, and M. S. Moore.

I consider the claim according to which responsibility is (i) ascribed on a causal basis, and (ii) therefore descriptive.

I offer two arguments to sustain my thesis: (i) there exist several *non*-causal forms of responsibility (and if they are actual forms of responsibility and *ab esse ad posse valet consequentia*...); (ii) causation is not completely descriptive, but subsumes an evaluative part, contrary to what many theorists and practitioners working in normative domains assume.

In this chapter causation will not be dealt with as an independent topic, ie causation tout court, but always in a certain normative system — excluding those within the domain of hard sciences. The non-descriptive aspects of causation are well-known in philosophy of science, starting clearly from Hume to Van Fraassen.[1]

'Cause' is a rich and polysemic term. Just using 'cause' or 'causation' does not explain anything — arguably, in fact, not only are there different concepts of causation, but also different *conceptions* of cause and causation, in different disciplines, used for different aims.[2]

Dealing with causation in the law is a complex task for two related terminological problems and not only for reasons intrinsic

---

[1] For a general introduction to the issue of causation in philosophy, see Beebee, Hitchcock, and Menzies, 2009.
[2] For evidence bearing on this point, see my discussion of 'αἰτία' — meaning both "guilt" and "cause" — *supra* in the Introduction (Chapter 0).

to the matter of causation. In law, there is no bijective relation between the words 'cause' and 'causation' and the things "cause" and "causation".[3] Every time the law speaks of 'cause' and 'causation', it does not necessarily refer to cause and causation (a well-known example is, in Italian civil law, the use of 'causa' to refer to the functions or reasons of contracts); [4]

Clearly, there is nothing special about the ambiguity of natural language employed in legal contexts, but we should be forewarned not to take this language at face value.

To discuss causation with a clearer focus below, I shall sketch here a brief taxonomy of causation in extra-scientific domain. We may be interested in causes with three different aims in mind. Those aims can significantly overlap sometimes, but what concerns us here is that they can be kept separate for philosophical inquiries.

Causation$_1$: forward-looking causation [*causalità prospettiva*]. This particular type is concerned with individuating possible future probable outcomes, given a certain state-of-affairs or a certain set of situations, ie "causes".

Causation$_2$: backward-looking causation [*causalità retrospettiva*]. This particular type is concerned with individuating those states-of-affairs or certain sets of situations whose prior existence necessarily(?) determined a given outcome. It has an *explanatory* aim.

Causation$_3$: causal responsibility [*responsabilità-causalità*].
This particular type is concerned with ascribing to an agent (not necessarily a living agent) a given outcome, "that his, her or its agency serves to explain and that can therefore plausibly be treated as part of the agency's impact on the world (Honoré, 2010)."[5]

---

3 S. F. Magni points out to me that this is the case also of the extra-legal word: it is the general problem of reference [*Bedeutung*]. This passing note was meant to show how *unreliable* it is to count too much on language — even legal language, by all means more formalized and accurate of everyday language, is potentially misleading.
4 Cf. Italian Civil Code, artt. 1325, 1343–45.
5 For similar remarks, see Hart, 2008 and Feinberg, 1965, 1970.

Clearly, causation is relevant in all three declensions, but while causation₁ is probably more considered in the legislative, law-making process, it is causation₂ and causation₃ that play the prime role in (criminal) courts. Causal responsibility especially concerns us here: it is arguably the most important of all three for criminal law (even though its importance it is not limited to law or morality, but extends to history for instance). As Honoré (Honoré, 2010) points out, it is not clear whether the concept of causation used in legal settings is different from other similar uses and requires a different understanding and explanation from causation₁&₂. Now, in order to better appreciate the subtle distinctions of philosophers and commentators, I ask the reader to keep in mind three different points, and to focus his attention on their mutual relationships:

(1) moral/legal responsibility;

(2) the relation between responsibility and causation;

(3) the notion of causation employed, varying among causation₁, causation₂ and causation₃.

To conclude the introduction, let's sketch a provisional map of the possible relationships between criminal liability and causation.⁶

CN: CAUSATION IS NECESSARY   On this view, causation is necessary for criminal liability, but *not* sufficient. It means that one can be punished *only* for those offenses one has caused, but not for *all* offenses one has caused. This seems to be Moore's view: he has to build up a complex theory of causation in order to be able to account for those threshold cases where apparently there are no traces of causation. Another vivid example of this view

---

6 The matter is complicated because we have three unknowns, so to speak: moral responsibility, criminal responsibility and causation. A general and convincing theory must of course fully take into account the relationships among all three unknowns. In Chapter 3.2.1, I defended the view that there is no necessary connection between moral responsibility and criminal liability. I will expand on this view with regard to causation *infra*.

is Antony Duff's jurisprudence, according to which causation is necessary (although not sufficient) for responsibility (cf. Duff, 2008, 2009). Example: justifications.

CS: CAUSATION IS SUFFICIENT On this rare view (possibly more common in tort law), one is liable for *all* offenses one has caused, but not only for them. The fact that someone has caused an offense leads directly to criminal liability, but this view does not exclude that there can be *other* foundations for criminal liability.

CNS: CAUSATION IS JOINTLY NECESSARY AND SUFFICIENT On this view, causation is jointly necessary and sufficient for criminal liability. It means that one is criminally liable for *all* and *only* those offenses he has caused.

NNNS: CAUSATION IS NEITHER NECESSARY NOR SUFFICIENT On this view, causation is neither necessary nor sufficient for criminal liability. The basis for liability may be causation, but it may not be. Example: vicarious responsibility.

4.1 FIRST ARGUMENT: QUEER RESPONSIBILITIES

Betrachte einmal die Vorgänge, die wir "Spiele" nennen. [...] Denn, wenn du sie anschaust, wirst du zwar nicht etwas sehen, was allen gemeinsam wäre, aber du wirst Ähnlichkeiten, Verwandtschaften, sehen, und zwar eine ganze Reihe. [...] Wir sehen ein kompliziertes Netz von Ähnlichkeiten, die einander übergreifen und kreuzen. Ähnlichkeiten im Großen und Kleinen.
Wittgenstein, 2009, §66.[7]

---

7 "Consider the activities we call "games". For it you look at them, you won't see something that is common to all, but similarities, affinities, and a whole series of them at that. We see a complicated network of similarities overlapping and crisscrossing. Similarities in the large and in the small (Wittgenstein, 2009, Ch.66)."

This section argues that responsibility is not only descriptive, for instance based on an alleged descriptive trait such as causation. In particular, I shall point out several kinds of non-causal responsibility. The phenomena — legal and moral — usually grouped under the umbrella term of 'responsibility' are so conceptually diverse that they cannot admit a common metaphysical basis.

4.1.1 Strict Liability vs. Collective Responsibility

I have investigated the phenomenon of strict liability *supra* in Chapters 3.3 and 3.3.2. It may be, however, of help to recall the definition I have provided *supra*. Strict (criminal) liability, then, is criminal liability *regardless* of *mens rea* for *any* material element of the offense. Regardless here means that (i) there are no mens rea elements required for the offense to take place; (ii) mental elements are irrelevant for the offense.[8]

In this subsection, I focus instead on other kinds of "queer" responsibility, namely those I group under the term 'collective responsibility'. While in *strict* liability the *actus reus* and the possible sanctions pertain to the very same individual, *collective responsibility* places the various elements (*actus reus*, *mens rea* and possible sanctions) across several individuals.[9]

---

[8] Of course *mens rea* and fault are not the same thing, as I already pointed out in Chapter 2.2.3.
[9] For a systematic analysis and classification of various forms of non-standard responsibility see Faroldi, 2013a.

4.1.2 The Various Cases of Collective Responsibility

In this section, I focus on collective responsibility.[10] I show that collective responsibility has at least three different "realizations": (i) group responsibility, (ii) shared responsibility, (iii) vicarious responsibility. I use this differentiation as a hint towards the idea that there cannot be a metaphysical property (or a state-of-affairs) common not only to various instantiations of collective responsibility, but to responsibility phenomena tout court.

> *DEFINITION*: Responsibility is collective when the *actus reus*, *mens rea* and possible liabilities are *not* pertaining to the very same individual.

4.1.2.1 Group Responsibility

Group responsibility is defined as when the responsibility for actions is imputed to members of that group *qua* group members, *regardless* of any *actus reus* or *mens rea* they could have or not have had, done or exercised.

A paradigmatic example is, I think, the responsibility for genocide imputed to Nazi party members following Nuremberg *regardless* of their intending or knowing the plan or putting it into practice.

4.1.2.2 Shared Responsibility

Shared responsibility is defined as when the responsibility for actions is equally imputed to members of a group *qua* members of that group, assuming that all of them need to do or intend to do the action in question; or in defect of this, everyone is held

---

10 For the concept (and consequences) of collective *moral* responsibility, see, for instance, Arendt, 1987; Feinberg, 1968; M. Smiley, 2011 and Benjamin, 1976, 1998; Bobzien, 2006; Braham and van Hees, 2012; Caruso, forthcoming; Corlett, 2001; Fischer, 2006, 2012; Gilbert, 2006; K. Graham, 2006; Isaacs, 2006, 2011; Mäkelä, 2007; Miller, 2001a,b, 2006; Miller and Mäkelä, 2005; Nahmias et al., 2005; Nelkin, 2007; Risser, 2009; Sheehy, 2006; Shoemaker, 2009; Silver, 2006; Soares, 2003; Tollefsen, 2003; Velasquez, 2003; G. Williams, 2006.

equally liable. Group responsibility differs from shared responsibility because the former requires a status (being member of a group) regardless of any action or intention, whereas the latter assumes actions and intentions as prior.

A paradigmatic example is, I think, the responsibility of cleaning a shared kitchen by members of an apartment block. All and single members need to clean the kitchen, but it might be the case that, for special arrangements, only a part of the group is entrusted with this task. Were the kitchen unclean, all members would be held equally liable, regardless of previous arrangements among the parties.

4.1.2.3 *Vicarious Responsibility*

Vicarious Responsibility is defined as when an individual is held responsible (and consequently presumably liable) for an *actus reus* someone else committed.

Vicarious Responsibility differs both from group responsibility and from shared responsibility because the individual held responsible or liable has — ex definition — no bearing on the act in question, either factually or mentally (no *actus reus* nor *mens rea*) — although he can (and often ought to) exercise control over those whom he is vicariously responsible for.

A paradigmatic example is, I think, the vicarious responsibility of an employer for his employees or that of a managing editor [Italian: *direttore responsabile*] for what has been published on the publication he edits.

4.1.3 Accomplice & Corporate Responsibility

Accomplice and corporate responsibility are examples of non personal responsibility.[11]

---

11 On the moral significance of corporate responsibility, see Dubbink and Smith, 2011; French, 1984; Garrett, 1989; González, 2002; K. Graham, 2001; G. Moore, 1999; Risser, 1985; Silver, 2006; Smith, forthcoming; Soares, 2003; Velasquez, 2003; Welch, 1992; Wilmot, 2001.

Corporate social responsibility seems to me a very complex and interesting form of responsibility (if it is a case of responsibility *stricto sensu*, of course), but I won't deal with it in this work.[12]

Accomplice responsibility will be dealt with in Section 4.2.1.3.

4.1.4 Qualified Responsibilities

The considerations in this subsection are merely of support to my general argument — I do not claim they are definitive.

Responsibility is often qualified through the use of adjectives, but in formal and informal contexts. Thus we have, in English law, the notion of "diminished" responsibility.

Over these past few days, we have heard — variously in the Italian press — acts qualified as "responsabilità *gravissima*", "assumerci *pesantissime* responsabilità".

Now, it is clear that ordinary speech is not the spring of good philosophy, but let's take these qualifications as a further sign of the fact that responsibility is not even *perceived* by ordinary men as purely objective.

All these forms of collective responsibility, however diverse, have enough traits in common to suggest they are not based on a traditional notion of causality (for instance, they are not based either on causation$_1$ or causation$_2$). This seems the case for two reasons: first, the source of responsibility is not individuated in agency, but rather in a given status of an individual or a group, a status more often than not resulting from normative relations; second, the contribution (or omission) of a particular individual cannot be singled out independently from the rules ascribing these people their responsibility.

In this section, I have shown that there are many substantially (and metaphysically) different phenomena grouped under the umbrella term of 'responsibility' — many of which are even non-causal. All these phenomena have nothing descriptive (factual) in common, and therefore (in these important cases) responsibil-

---

12 On corporate social responsibility, see for instance Azzoni, 2004, 2012.

ity cannot be explained away by pointing to a (common) metaphysical, descriptive trait of the world, such as causation (M. S. Moore), culpability, intention and so on.

The next section is devoted to exploring, and eventually refuting, the idea that the descriptive substratum of responsibility is causation.

4.2 SECOND ARGUMENT: RESPONSIBILITY AND CAUSATION

> *Wie ist denn der Begriff des Spiels abgeschlossen? Was ist noch ein Spiel und was ist keines mehr? Kannst du die Grenzen angeben? Nein. Du kannst welche ziehen: denn es sind noch keine gezogen.*
> Wittgenstein, 2009, §68[13].

This section deals with the relationship between legal responsibility and causation.[14] I argue that responsibility is *not* descriptive because the argument that it is rooted in causation fails.

The general claim I aim to disprove is that responsibility is objective or descriptive because it is fundamentally rooted in causality, and causality is metaphysically real and founded. My strategy is *twofold*.

First, I show that there are significant and independent non-causal forms of responsibility that cannot be reduced to causal responsibility; *second*, I show that the very notion of causality is — lato sensu — not plainly descriptive. The sub-thesis of this section is that even causation is tied to evaluative elements.

This section is split into *two* parts: in Section 4.2.1, I shall give an account of the three most discussed contributions to the rela-

---
13 *For how is the concept of game bounded? What still count as a game, and what no longer does? Can you say where the boundaries are? No. You can draw some, for there aren't any drawn yet* (Wittgenstein, 2009, §68).
14 I chose to limit my discussion to legal responsibility because it is more structured and this lets me avoid all those clumsy *Gedankenexperimente*. I am aware that this choice belittles the philosophical import of my argument, but I hope that if the reader accepts this argument with regard to legal responsibility, he can think of an analogous strategy for moral responsibility.

tionship between causation and responsibility (legal and moral) in the last 50 years: H.Kelsen's *Society and Nature* (1948), Hart and Honoré's *Causation in the Law* (1959) and finally M. Moore's *Causation and Responsibility* (2009).

In Section 4.2.2, I shall defend the thesis that causation, at least in law and morals, is fundamentally non-descriptive.

4.2.1 A Bird's Eye View

4.2.1.1 *Kelsen:* Kausalität und Zurechnung

Hans Kelsen (1886 – 1973), one of the major legal philosophers of the twentieth century, engaged with the problem of causation and responsibility in several works (cf. Kelsen, 1939, 1943, 1960, 1973a).[15]

This section is roughly split in *two*: in the *first* part, I shall account for Kelsen's understanding of imputation (that is the principle, analogous but distinct from causation, we use to ascribe responsibility in normative domains); in the *second*, I shall show how Kelsen argues that causality is not a given, but a cultural category of modern societies — and therefore causality pertains, as imputation does, to a normative, and not descriptive, sphere.

ZURECHNUNG   For Kelsen, the principle we apply when we consider human society as a normative order (in law, morals, sociology, politics) is not causality [*Kausalität*] but "may be called imputation [*Zurechnung*] (Kelsen, 1967, p. 76)."

A rule of law [*Rechts-Satz*] (different from the legal norm [*Rechts-Norm*]) connects two elements, "precisely like a law of nature (p. 77)": "If an individual commits a crime, he ought to punished (p. 76)".[16] But the connection between effect and cause in the law of nature and the connection expressed in the

---

15 A note of caution: I really dislike the translation of *Zurechnung* as imputation, but use it nonetheless so as not to confound the anglophone reader. I warn Italian readers that the once-common Italian translation of 'Zurechnung' as "contrappasso" seems to me even worse.

16 "Wenn ein Mensch ein Verbrechen begeht, soll eine Strafe über ihn verhängt werden (Kelsen, 1960, p. 80)."

rule of law are "entirely different (from causality)". "The rule of law [*Rechts-Satz*] does not say, as the law of nature does: when A is, "is" B; but: when A is, B "ought" to be [*sein soll*], even though B perhaps actually is not (p. 77)."[17]

And why is there this difference? Because "the connection described by the rule of law is brought about by a legal authority (by a legal norm [*Rechts-Norm*] created by an act of will), whereas the connection of cause and effect is independent from such human interference."

As for the relationship between imputation and responsibility [*Verantwortung*]:

> that an individual is responsible [*zurechnungsfähig*] for his behavior means that he may be punished for this behavior; and that he is irresponsible [*unzurechnungsfähig*], or not responsible, means that he, for the same behavior — because he is a minor or insane — may not be punished. That means [...] that the behavior is or is not a condition for punishment; that punishment is or is not *imputed* to the behavior (p. 81).[18]

And again,

> Imputation [*Zurechnung*] merely consists in this connection between delict and sanction. Imputation expresses itself in the concept of responsibility [*Verantwortung*] [...]. [T]he sanction is imputed to the delict, but the sanction is not "effected by" (is not "caused by") the delict. The science of law does not aim at a causal explanation [...] it is not the principle of

---

17 "Im Rechtssatz wird nicht, wie im Naturgesetz, ausgesagt, daß, wenn A ist, B ist, sondern, daß, wenn A ist, B sein soll, auch wenn B vielleichl tatsächlich nicht ist (Kelsen, 1960, p. 80)."
18 "Zurechnungsfähig ist, wer wegen seines Verhaltens bestraft, das heißt: dafür zur Verantwortung gezogen werden kann, während unzurechnungsfähig jener ist, der wegen eines gleichen Verhaltens — etwa weil er unmündig oder geisteskrank ist — nicht bestraft, das heißt: dafür nicht zur Verantwortung gezogen werden kann (Kelsen, 1960, p. 85)."

causality which is employed, but [...] imputation (p. 81).[19]

KAUSALITÄT   For a good half of *Society and Nature*,[20] based on evidence from anthropology and conceptual analysis, Kelsen argues that the principle of causality to explain natural events is "the achievement of a relatively advanced civilization (RR, p. 82)."[21]

Primitive men were likely to explain natural phenomena in terms of imputation:

> condition and consequence are not connected according to the principle of causality [...]. If an event was regarded as harmful, it was interpreted as a punishment for bad behavior; if beneficial, as a reward for good behavior. Misfortune (poor harvest, defeat in war, illness, death) were imputed, as punishment, to the wrong behavior of group members [...] (p. 82-3).[22]

---

19 "Das heißt aber, daß die Zurechnung in gar nichts anderem als in dieser Verknüpfung von Unrecht und Unrechtsfolge besteht. [...] Die Zurechnung, die in dem Begriff der Zurechnungsfähigkeit zum Ausdruck kommt, ist die Verknüpfung eines bestimmten Verhaltens, nämlich des Unrechts, mit einer Unrechtsfolge. Daher kann man sagen: die Unrechtsfolge wird dem Unrecht zugerechnet, sie wird aber nicht durch das Unrecht — als ihre Ursache — bewirkt. Daß die Rechtswissenschaft durchaus nicht auf eine kausale Erklärung der Rechtsphänomene: Unrecht und Unrechtsfolge, abzielt, ist selbverständlich. In den Rechtssätzen, mit denen sie diese Phänomene beschreibt, wendet sie nicht das Prinzip der Kausalität, sondern ein Prinzip an, das man — wie diese Analyse zeigt — als Zurechnung bezeichnen darf (Kelsen, 1960, p. 85-6)."

20 Kelsen, 1943 but also in Kelsen, 1939, 1973a. For critical remarks, see also Stockhammer, 1970 and Paulson, 2004.

21 "Dieses Prinzip ist die Errungenschaft einer verhältnismäßig vorgeschrittenen Zivilisation (Kelsen, 1960, p. 86)."

22 "In dieser Grundregel sind Bedingung und Folge miteinander nicht nach dem Grundsatz der Kausalität. [...] Wenn ein Ereignis als Übel empfunden wird, wird es als Strafe für ein schlechtes Verhalten, ein Unrecht, wenn es als Wohltat empfunden wird, als Belohnung für ein gutes Verhalten gedeutet. Mit anderen Worten: Unglück, das heißt nachteilige Ereignisse, wie schlechte Ernte, erfolglose Jagd, Niederlage im Krieg, Krankheit, Tod, werden, als

Theirs was not a causal, it was a normative interpretation of nature. Animism might be a striking factor to account for the matter: if things had a soul, then they would behave toward men like men treated each other: according to the principle of retribution. In consequence, "the concept of nature as an order of elements connected together according to the principle of causality, cannot be formed in the thinking of primitive men (p. 83)."[23]

Nature is part of society, and the primitive man does not distinguish, Kelsen tells us, natural as causal and society as normative: "nature as a causal order was created by science only after [mankind] liberated itself from animism. The instrument of this liberation is the principle of causality (p. 84)."

The "natural" question from the reader might now be: So what? Now comes the best bit! In fact, Kelsen argues that the principle of causality has its origin in retribution (imputation):

> It is significant that the Greek word for cause, 'αἰτία', originally meant guilt: the cause is "guilty" of the effect, is responsible for the effect; the effect is imputed to the cause in the same way that the punishment is imputed to the delict. [...] The decisive step [...] consists in men becoming aware that the relations between things [...] are independent of a human or superhuman will, or [...] not determined by norms (p. 84-5).[24]

Strafe, dem normwidrigen Verhalten der Mitglieder der Gruppe, vorteilhafte Ereignisse, wie gute Ernte, erfolgreiche Jagd, Sieg im Krieg, Gesundheit, langes Leben, werden, als Belohnung, dem normgemäßen Verhalten der Mitglieder der Gruppe zugerechnet (Kelsen, 1960, p. 87)."

23 "Folglich kann es im Bewußtsein des Primitiven so etwas wie Natur im Sinne moderner Wissenschaft, eine Ordnung von Elementen, die nach dem Prinzip der Kausalität miteinander verknüpft werden, überhaupt nicht geben (Kelsen, 1960, p. 88)."

24 "Es ist höchst bezeichnend, daß das griechische Wort für Ursache: 'αἰτία', ursprünglich soviel wie Schuld bedeutet: die Ursache ist schuld an der Wirkung, ist verantwortlich für die Wirkung, die Wirkung wird der Ursache so zugerechnet wie die Strafe dem Unrecht. [...] Der entscheidende Schritt in diesem Übergang von einer normativen zu einer kausalen Deutung der

And now, from *Society and Nature* (SN):

> The transformation of the notion of causality, the last step of which is the replacement of absolute necessity by simple statistical probability, is correctly considered "revolutionary" in scientific thinking. Its significance lies in the fact that the notion of causality was stripped of its most important element, with which it was still burdened as the heir of the principle of retribution: Ἀνάγκη. This is necessity with which Δίκη, the goddess of retribution, punishes evildoers and at the same time keeps nature in its prescribed course (p. 262).

Admittedly, Kelsen — in the quoted passages — does not care about causation, but about our knowledge and interpretation of natural events as causal. Even if he was non-committal about causation, it is quite clear that he did not believe causation to be a given, either naturally, factually, descriptively (as a noumenon, one might say with reference to Kelsen's neokantianism) or otherwise (as a scheme of the intellect, epistemological category and so on).[25]

Quite on the contrary, the principle of causation (probabilistic or otherwise) is used by hard sciences to describe nature, whereas the principle of imputation is used by normative sciences (namely law and morals) to study society *qua* normative body, an entity governed by human-made norms.[26]

But in the end, causation and imputation are severed (at least from an epistemological point of view): there is no evidence to

---

Natur, vom Prinzip der Zurechnung zum Prinzip der Kausalität, besteht darin, daß sich der Mensch bewußt wird, daß die Beziehungen zwischen den Dingen — zum Unterschied von Beziehungen zwischen den Menschen — unabhängig von einem menschichen oder übermenschlichen Willen oder, was auf dasselbe hinausläuft, nicht von Normen bestimmt sind (Kelsen, 1960, p. 88-9)."

[25] This is slightly surprising, given Kelsen's usual depiction as a neokantian and Kant's description of causation as one of intellect's category.

[26] This is not to say that society is not part of nature, or that causation is not at work in society. Social sciences — sociology, economics — study society as governed by causal laws.

affirm that for Kelsen imputation stemmed from causation (nor the other way round), or that the two need to be necessarily connected. Thus, imputation (and thence responsibility) is not necessarily allocated on a causal basis: it may well be, but this is not necessarily the case.

This conclusion flows well with the rest of Kelsen's pure theory of law: once we have the *principle* of imputation, it is for the actual laws to fill it with practical criteria. There is no need for responsibility to be based on causality.

We shall shortly see that not all legal theorists were of the same opinion.

4.2.1.2 *Hart and Honoré:* Causation in the Law

Published in 1959, Hart's and Honoré's (hereafter HH) monumental study *Causation in the Law* sought to found (normative) principles for attributing moral and legal responsibility on the (descriptive) principle of causation.

The principles for moral and legal responsibility are not "inventions of the law" but rather are "common-sense principles of causation" that are "part of the ordinary man's stock of general notions" and based on questions of fact "similar to the conventional view of the law's use of other highly general notions such as those of temporal or spatial location" (Hart and Honoré, 1959, pp. 91-2). And again,

> [W]henever we are concerned with [...] assessing responsibility [...] we employ a set of concepts restricting in various ways what counts as a consequence. These restrictions colour *all* our thinking in causal terms; when we find them in the law we are not finding something invented by or peculiar to the law, though of course it is for the law to say when and how far it will use them and, where they are vague, to supplement them (p. 70).

HH were concerned with the concept of causation commonly used by ordinary people (and therefore — for them — reflected in law *via* ordinary language)[27] rather than those used by philosophers or physicists (cf. pp. xxxiii-xxxiv, 1-3).

In an extreme synthesis and taking into account the three points (1–3) I highlighted above, HH's argument can be summarized in the following way:

(1) Legal responsibility (the criteria for) is justified if it tracks (the criteria for) moral responsibility.[28]

(2) Causation is a necessary condition for moral responsibility.[29]

(3) This causation is the concept commonly used by ordinary men in speech.

Now, what is this "ordinary speech" causation? It is useful to split HH's reasoning about causation into three separate points.

(i) HH started with a counterfactual concept of cause: cause must be at least a necessary condition for its effect.[30] (They later

---

[27] The work was in fact implicitly and explicitly influenced by the then-fashionable linguistic analysis, as Honoré himself acknowledges in the preface of the second edition.

[28] Needless to say, they need not be coincident: "we must bear in mind the many factors which must differentiate moral from legal responsibility in spite of their partial correspondence. The law is not only not bound to follow the patterns of moral attribution of responsibility, but, even when it does, it must take into account, in a way in which the private moral judgment need not and does not, the general social consequences which are attached to its judgments of responsibility [...]. [T]he fact that the individuals have a type of [causal] connection with harm which is adequate for moral censure or claims for compensation is only one of the factors which the law must consider (p. 66)."

[29] And then cf. with legal responsibility: "to say that someone is responsible for some harm means that in accordance with legal rules [...] it is at least permissible, if not mandatory, to [...] punish or exact compensation from him [...]. [D]*oing or causing harm* constitutes not only the most usual but the primary type of ground for holding persons responsible in [this] sense." (p. 65, emphasis added).

[30] Note that (i) is the classic doctrine of *condicio sine qua non*, endorsed, for instance, by the Italian penal code, Art. 40.1: " Nessuno può essere punito per un fatto preveduto dalla legge come reato, se l'evento dannoso o pericoloso, da cui dipende la esistenza del reato, non è conseguenza della sua azione od omissione."

dropped this position to endorse a more nuanced one; see *infra* for discussion.)

(ii) But then, not *all* necessary conditions of w are *causes* of w. Only two kinds of necessary conditions can be causes: (ii.a) voluntary human actions and (ii.b) coincidences or "abnormal conjunctions of natural events (p. 103)". All other necessary conditions for a w to obtain are merely "background conditions".[31]

(iii) So you have initial necessary conditions *and* the final event they cause. Yet, *intervening causes* (defined again as voluntary human actions and coincidences) can intervene and break the causal chain — more, they annihilate preceding causes and begin a new causal chain.

Finally, HH came up with a sort of standardized test, according to which:

> (HH test:) "A 'causally relevant factor' need merely be 'necessary just in the sense that it is one of the set of conditions jointly sufficient for the production of the consequence: it is necessary because it is required to complete this set' (p. 112)."

The test put forward by HH was refined and popularized by Wright 1988 as the NESS test; since then, it has become the *de facto* test for causation — at least in US courts.[32]

Unfortunately, the HH test is a *petitio principii*: it is not a test for causation, it is a stipulative meaning of it. Their explanation explained nothing, because it assumed a definition of the explanandum.

LINGUISTIC ANALYSIS   First, linguistic analysis (the method chose by HH to tackle the issue of causation) does not exhaust

---

31 Again, HH's (ii) is mirrored in Italian jurisprudence with the doctrines of "causalità adeguata", that excludes extraordinary events, and "causalità umana".

32 Here, it is a proper formulation of Wright's NESS test. I shall not discuss it here.
   NESS test: "a condition contributed to some consequence IFF it was *necessary* for the sufficiency of a set of existing antecedent conditions that was *sufficient* for the occurrence of that consequence (Wright, 2003, p. 1141)."

empirical and conceptual aspects of the problems. It is thus a dubious method to investigate such a complex task.

WHICH EVENT IS A CAUSE? Since we have seen that not all necessary conditions (for the sufficiency of the set) are causes, why is that the case? Because what can be a cause is not natural or descriptive, but depends on the aim we have to ascribe an action to that agent, and is therefore the evaluative part of the process.

Involuntary human actions, for instance, cannot be causes in HH's view. I suggest this is the case because the fact we hold someone (morally or legally) causally responsible is not only a purely descriptive act, but it is mediated by the aims and purposes of the law — or of a certain kind of law tracking its underlying morality. Let me explain: if it is considered "immoral" to punish involuntary actions, it would thence also be illegal, even if involuntary human actions can perfectly be (natural) causes of events.

As HH admit, what is a "*voluntary*[33] human action", "abnormal" and therefore a "cause" depends on the interests and purposes of the person making the causal statement (pp. 35-7, 62), and that "[i]n relation to human conduct [...] the notion of what is 'natural' is strongly influenced by moral and legal standards of proper conduct (p. 183)."[34]

WHICH CAUSE IS RELEVANT? Once we have a list of causes for our event, we still need to choose which is relevant. Think of a so-called overdetermination case. A fire, deliberately started by John, reached Rachel's house and was about to burn it down. Suddenly, a violent earthquake made the house collapse.

Now, both events were independently sufficient to destroy the house. There's an important difference though: while the fire

---

[33] For the problem of voluntariness, intention, justifications and excuses, see *supra* in Chapter 3, passim.
[34] For a similar, striking position on the relationship between law and moral of Hart the positivist, see Section 2.2.3; for a general critique of this position, see Section 3.2.

was lit by John with the purpose of destroying Rachel's house (and let's take that for granted), the earthquake was a natural, "extraordinary" event.

According to HH's test, both the fire and the earthquake are causal relevant factors, because each was independently necessary for the sufficiency of the set of factors that destroyed Rachel's house.

Now, is John to pay for reparation, even if the event that destroyed Rachel's house was the earthquake? It seems we must choose which cause is relevant for our purposes. If we adopt a mere chronological criterion, the earthquake was the most recent event and therefore causally responsible, perhaps. But again, this sort of relevance decision seems based not on purely arbitrary factors, but at least on evaluative premises.

As for "intervening causes", HH simply invented — it seems to me — a new, queer entity (the intervening cause) in order to account for difficult legal counterexamples otherwise almost impossible to explain in a metaphysically-robust theory. In more than one way, they made up that sort of "legal fiction" that Hart's great inspirer, J. Bentham, so radically criticized.[35]

In the end, HH overlapped and conflated the issue of natural causation with the issue of responsibility-attribution. They failed to see that the attribution of responsibility can be noncausal, and therefore that natural causation *and* the attribution of responsibility cannot be accounted for in the same (causal) way.[36] Natural causation and responsibility are different — though not unrelated — "things".[37]

---

35 See Bentham, 1996 and Hart, 1982.
36 For a parallel reading of HH, cf. Wright, 2008: "they insisted that the principles of attributable responsibility should be treated as causal rather than noncausal principles. They seem to assume that in order to avoid ad hoc, policy-driven determinations of attributable responsibility, the principles of attributable responsibility (beyond the basic natural causation principle) must be 'causal' principles" (p. 177).
37 The classical debate in (at least common) law was dominated by minimalists works (holding that the criteria for the attribution of responsibility are not objective nor causal) such as Posner, 1972, 1973 and maximalists (there are

4.2.1.3 *Moore:* Causation and Responsibility

I shall examine now the position of Micheal S. Moore, expressed in particular in his latest book, *Causation and Responsibility*. Apart from his independently important and sustained contribution to the field of legal and moral philosophy in general, I think considering his stance would benefit my argumentation, because he takes a side quite opposite to mine — although I will be directly concerned only with small portions of his huge book.

I said opposite, because Moore has a number of theses contrasting mine. He thinks, for instance, that legal responsibility should closely track *moral* responsibility,[38] and that moral responsibility is based on *natural*, empirical properties such as causation, which is necessary for it and purely descriptive.[39]

I shall now quote two brief passages and then try to formalize and dismantle his argument.

> "The metaethical postulate is that moral responsibility [...] supervenes on natural properties like causation, intention, and the like. The postulate of legal theory is that legal liability (in torts and criminal law) falls only on those who are morally responsible (M. S. Moore, 2009, p. vii — cf. also M. S. Moore, 1997)."

In other words,

> [A]ll law, on my view of it, must be based on policy [...]. This policy would be to attach legal liability to morally blameworthy actions. It is morality, not legal policy, that tells us that actions that cause harm are more blameworthy than those that merely attempt or risk such harm. It is metaphysics, not legal policy, that tells us when an action *causes* a certain harm (M. S. Moore, 2009, p.230).

---

factual causal criteria for attributing responsibility) cf. for instance Epstein, 1973.
38 I rejected this thesis back in Chapter 3.2.1.
39 For a position different from both mine and Moore's, see Stapleton, 2008, 2009: for her, the notion of cause in legal settings, must be "untainted by normative controversies".

Moore's complex and rich book, *Responsibility and Causation*, is devoted to showing that

(i) moral responsibility depends (necessarily but partially) on causation, and since

(ii.a) criminal liability (and *lato sensu* criminal law) is based on moral responsibility, and since

(ii.b) criminal liability (and *lato sensu* criminal law) *ought to* be based on moral responsibility, then

(iii) criminal liability substantially depends on causation and

(iv) criminal liability ought to depend (ie it is justified in depending) on causation.

I do not think Moore's reasoning sound, and I reject both conclusion (iii) and (iv), for three main reasons. First, I have shown in Chapter 3.2.1 that both premises (ii.a) and (ii.b) are false or to be rejected. Second, I shall argue (*infra* at Accomplice Liability) that premise (i) is false too: responsibility in general is not *necessarily* based on causation — even if it may be contingently based on causation. Third, I am going to argue that Moore's understanding of causation (in law and morals) as naturalistically justified is fundamentally wrong — cf. *infra* in Section 4.2.2.

To compare with HH's argument, here is the Moorean version:

(1) Legal responsibility (the criteria for) is justified if it tracks moral responsibility (the criteria for).

(2) Causation is a necessary condition for moral responsibility.[40]

(3) *This causation is NOT the concept commonly used by ordinary men in speech. A careful metaphysical theory of causation is needed to justify moral and legal doctrines.*

---

[40] "[A]bsence of causation *eliminates* responsibility (by licensing consequentialist justifications), rather than merely reducing it (when justifications are not in issue) (p. 77)."

Moore rejects both HH's claim that we must content ourselves with the *use* of 'cause' in ordinary speech (but alas, that was the philosophical agenda of the 50s); and their analysis of "intervening causes" (those — for HH — ultimately relevant for law and morality) as metaphysically unfounded and unjustified, especially because — by resting on common, "stipulative" use of what counts as a cause, of what 'cause' means — such an approach would cut off any possible scientifically-informed investigation on the nature of causation.

Moore's aim, then, is to provide us with a convincing theory about causation *tout court* and causation *in the law*, starting from the role of causation for moral responsibility and moral blameworthiness. The whole point of the discussion is to root our responsibility practices in something naturalistic, descriptive and scientifically based, justified as causation.[41]

But responsibility in general is not based necessarily on causation. As a matter of fact, there are several phenomena we want to call 'responsibility' that are not causal-based, as my argument *ex differentia* showed in Section 4.1.

Now, for Moore it is quite the contrary: all responsibilities must be causal. Therefore, he has almost no choice: either his theory is factually disproved, or those non-causal responsibilities (vicarious responsibility, accomplice liability) must not be considered proper cases of responsibility. The latter is precisely his strategy.

The next paragraph is devoted to showing how Moore ignores the facts (the reality of accomplice, non-causal liability) to fit his theory (no liability/responsibility without causation).

ACCOMPLICE LIABILITY   The key test of the notion of causation, both in the law and in metaphysics, is to account for accomplice liability. Obviously, an accomplice is a person who presumably helps or instigates the wrongdoer to bring about the crime, but

---

41 "The nature of causation — what causation is — is a matter of fact, inviting theoretical speculation". Causation is "a real relationship in the world" — cf. M. S. Moore, 2009, passim.

the extent to which the accomplice's contribution is a *causal* contribution is open to question.

It is plausible this instigation require both an *actus reus* and a *mens rea* to be considered accomplice liability.[42] Let alone the *actus reus* requirement, is *mens rea* limited to *knowledge* (of possible consequences) or does it possibly require *purpose* (the purpose of helping the future wrongdoer)? And must there be an *intention* to merely help the future wrongdoer, or intention to bring about the criminal offence, directly or indirectly *via* the wrongdoer? Unfortunately, Moore limits his discussion only to the *actus reus* requirement.

Moore seeks to abandon the accomplice liability doctrine. Why? I try to summarize (and alas simplify a little bit) his argument here.

(i) The attribution of responsibility (here, liability) must be strictly causal.[43]

(ii) An accomplice has a causal role only in HH's *intervening cause* sense.

(iii) HH's idea of intervening causes is metaphysically unfounded and should be abandoned.

(iv) The role of an accomplice cannot be causal (in regard to the offence) in any sound metaphysical sense. Therefore,

(v) There must be no accomplice liability.

But accomplice liability is a perfectly accepted form of (at least legal) responsibility, and since there are great difficulties to interpret accomplice liability in causal terms, it seems advisable to forgo the causal requirement, as I maintained *supra*.

CAUSATION IN LAW (AND MORALS)   In the last part of his book, Moore finally tackles the "beast": the metaphysical notion of cause (causality). His analysis is roughly split in two: (a) an

---

42 As many criminal statuses do — cf. Model Penal Code.
43 *Vide supra* for my account of Moore's justification of this argument.

analysis of causal relata and (b) an analysis of the causal relation. In other words, to account for what causation is ("counterfactual dependence, nomic sufficiency, probabilistic dependence, regular concurrence, something else or nothing at all (p.327)") is quite different (yet related) to account for what entities causation links ("events, aspects of events, facts, negative events (p. 327)").

(A) CAUSAL RELATA: A DEONTIC FALLACY   As for (a): causal relata, we might start to notice a crack in his mechanism. He loosely argues for a distinction between metaphysics and the law. In metaphysics, the true causal relata are "fine-grained" things: states-of-affairs. Instead,

> [t]he relation most *desirable* for use in law is different: (coarse-grained) events are the relata on which legal liability *should* turn, recognizing that such relata will be *constructions* based on the *true* relata of the causal relations, which are states of affairs (p. ix, emphasis added).

Now, let me just put forward *two* informal objections:

First, he commits a robust deontic fallacy:[44] the fact that something is desirable or should obtain (for instance, responsibility must be based on causation), determines our thinking that the world *is* as it should be (that responsibility is based on causation, all other non-causal forms of responsibility do not exist).

Second, from the basic descriptive level we creep into the domain of the normative. He said that we need an objective, descriptive account of the metaphysics of causation and causal relata (as fine-grained states-of-affairs) and then he changes his mind and builds up new causal relata especially for the law, as the above quotation shows. Why? Because this relation is "most desirable for use in law". Those two different theories do not seem either equivalent or interchangeable. He simply appears to pick the most convenient, regardless of which is true.

---

44 For which see Faroldi, 2012a. A deontic fallacy is deriving in some way an "is" from an "ought", for instance by acknowledging the reality of something not as it is, but how it should be.

(B) THE NATURE OF CAUSATION   As for (b): the nature of causation (see pp. x-xi and part IV), things continue to be muddled. Moore identifies law's causal theory as counterfactual dependence.[45] For the law, counterfactual dependence (roughly, the thesis that c is a cause of offense y iff y would not have occurred if c had not occurred) is both necessary and sufficient for causation.

Moore adopts a *twofold* (and almost inconsistent) strategy: *first*, he provides us with a series of reasons and arguments *against* both the sufficiency and the necessity of counterfactual dependence for causation (citing, among others, the existence of *non-causal counterfactuals*, the need to consider omissions as causes, overdetermination etc.): counterfactual dependence and causation are not the same thing; but *second*, he confidently argues that counterfactual dependence *is* a legal and moral "desert-determiner independent of causation (p. 426)." This is to say that blameworthiness (and *mutatis mutandis* liability) depends not (only) on causation but (also?) on counterfactual dependence. How and when? Moore presents us with counterintuitive cases, such as symmetrical and asymmetrical overdetermination (see Sartorio, 2012) and blameworthiness for omissions and preventions — cases hardly accountable for in terms of non-counterfactual causation. There, counterfactual dependence occurs without causation, and Moore wants to assign liability without causation.

---

45 I cannot go into detail about counterfactual dependence here. In sum, this view descends from this much quoted passage in Hume, 1902, p. 87: *First definition*: "We may define a cause to be an object followed by another, and where all the objects, similar to the first, are followed by objects similar to the second." *Second definition*: "Or, in other words where, *if the first object had not been, the second never had existed*" (emphasis added for the definition of counterfactual dependence). Please note that in this quoted passage, Hume equated a *regularist* and a *counterfactual* (in italics) view of causation: these views are *not* extensionally equivalent. This equation is problematic, as for instance notes Beebee, 2013. For a general interpretation of causality and responsibility in Hume, see P. Russell, 1995 and P. Russell, 2008. Counterfactual dependence has been recently questioned widely in philosophy in general and ethics in particular following Frankfurt, 1969, who argued for a non-counterfactual-based attribution of responsibility.

For this last part on causation and counterfactual dependence, I shall adopt the so-called charity principle in reading Moore's theory. Above, we have seen that Moore's idea is that causation is necessary for responsibility (liability). Then, we saw how desert is often determinable only by using a criterion of counterfactual dependence; but we have seen how — according to Moore — counterfactual dependence neither is, nor implies, causation.

Now, I would *prima facie* say that there is a non-sequitur in Moore's argumentation. But on a more charitable reading, we might try to apply the familiar, legal distinction between conviction and sentence. In this way, causation is necessary for conviction (ie, the attribution of responsibility/liability); counterfactual dependence determines instead the (severity of the) sentence — even if I cannot say to what extent counterfactual dependence would be either sufficient or necessary for the sentence.

But in the end, I think Moore's arguments are simply untenable. Just one example. We have seen that

(a) he considers causation necessary for responsibility/liability;

(b) he repeatedly states that "omissions cannot be causes (p. 444)"

(c) he thinks that there must be liability for omissions (pp. 444ff.)

And these three premises are simply inconsistent. If (b) holds, than we must discard either (a), so that causation is not necessary for responsibility/liability, or (c), that is, we cannot attribute liability for omissions, since (b) they cannot be causes.

I do not think Moore's reasoning sound, and I have rejected both conclusion (iii) (that liability necessarily depends on causation) and (iv) (that liability must depend on causation), for *three* main reasons.

First, I have shown in Chapter 3.2.1 that both premises (ii.a) and (ii.b) are false or to be rejected.

Second, I have argued (*supra* in Section 4.1) that premise (i) is false too: responsibility in general is not *necessarily* based on causation — even if it may be contingently based on causation.

Third, in this last part, I have argued that Moore's reasoning is at least inconsistent, as the case of omissions shows.

The next section, 4.2.2, is devoted to showing that Moore's (and not only his) understanding of causation (in law and morals) as naturalistically justified is fundamentally wrong. This is my second argument, *ex causatione*.

4.2.2 Causation as Normative

The scope of this subsection is to hold the following thesis. Even if causation were jointly necessary *and* sufficient to determine responsibility,[46] this would *not* show that responsibility is non-normative, that is, grounded in something ultimately descriptive.[47]

The general, common argument can be summarized as follows:

- (i) causation is necessary for responsibility;

- (ii) causation is descriptive, objective, or non-normative (because it is scientifically provable, etc.); therefore

- (iii) (at least causal-) responsibility is necessarily descriptive, objective, or non-normative.

I will reject the conclusion. My strategy is twofold: tackle both premise (ii), showing that causation is not descriptive, objective, or non-normative and premise (i), showing that causation is not necessary for responsibility, adapting my argument from Chapter 3.2.1.

---

[46] Alternative formulation: if causation were the sole criterion to assign responsibility, ...

[47] For both subjective and objective limitations, I shall not be concerned here with a critique of the general, metaphysical notion of "causation". This section's title might also be read as "Moral and Legal Causation as Normative".

4.2.2.1   *(i) Causation is not necessary*

As for (i), causation is apparently not necessary for responsibility, whether we distinguish responsibility from liability (to punishment or blame) or not.

I put forward *two* arguments to sustain my thesis: that of (i.a) vicarious responsibility and that of (i.b) consequentialism.

(I.A) VICARIOUS RESPONSIBILITY   Vicarious responsibility in law (and morals too) consists in ascribing responsibility/liability for an action someone else committed (employer/employee, parent/children). The relationship according to which liability is attributed is not causal.

We have *two* ways out of this impasse: *first*, to disown vicarious responsibility as an actual form of responsibility (because it is not causal-based) — but this would be question-begging; *second*, we may acknowledge that there are forms of responsibility *de facto* non causal. I have expanded a little bit on this problem in Section 4.1.

(I.B) RESPONSIBILITY FOR CONSEQUENTIALISTS   In a strict consequentialist view, one can do away with causation — exactly as with desert: what matters is not (only) past deeds, but what happens next. If the state-of-affairs justifies placing responsibility (or blame, or punishment) on someone completely unrelated to the action in question, an act-consequentialist is *prima facie* compelled to accept the fact that causation is not necessarily linked to responsibility (although it might contingently be). And since (act-)consequentialism is a legitimate (even if not necessarily true or correct) moral theory that can account for responsibility, then it is not even a conceptual truth that responsibility is necessarily based on causation, but this would eventually depend on the (meta-)normative theory of values one endorses (his *Wertanschauung*).

4.2.2.2 *(ii) Causation in law and morals is* not *descriptive*

I shall put forward *three* arguments, that, even conceding premise (i) for the argument's sake, I think summarize the problems with premise (ii), ie considering causation (in law) descriptive: *first*, the problem of remoteness; *second*, what I call the "causal sorites"; *third*, the heterogeneity of actions with regard to omissions.

REGRESSUS AD INFINITUM/REMOTENESS This problem is pretty familiar (also) to lawyers: how far should one go before causes become irrelevant? Several acts are jointly necessary for an action to happen, and these acts can be remote. Now, are these remote acts (still necessary for further necessary things to obtain) of *legal relevance* for the action in question?[48]

Take a murder. If the killer's mother and father had not met, this particular homicide would not have occurred, because — it seems, on an intuitive reading — this particular killer would not have existed (and so on, back in time).

It seems that from a purely descriptive point of view, the encounter of the killer's mother and father is a necessary condition for the killer's being there (and eventually committing the murder): so it should be considered a cause, or at least part of the relevant causal chain. In a counterfactual analysis, if the killer's mother and father had not met, then this killer would not have existed and this homicide would not have been committed.

Now, the law (and morals) is usually not interested in this kind of "causal" chains. Instead, judges and lawyers are more concerned with a specifically *legal* cause, called also proximate, that is "near and immediate, or directly traceable, or foreseeable (Feinberg and Coleman, p.603)". The legal or proximate cause is called also *cause-in-fact*.

Now, it seems very hard to justify such a *choice* on purely descriptive grounds. The only *real* difference I can think of in the murder example is that of a temporal factor — but still this does not clearly point out why more recent or more remote causes

---

48 Here, I am using 'act', 'action' and 'event' in a non-technical way.

are to be preferred or discarded without a choice already made on our part.

Please keep in mind that this argument has a specific diachronic dimension.

THE CAUSAL SORITES PARADOX   A lesser problem — quite distinct from the "regressus ad infinitum" — is the causal version of the Sorite paradox: not how far back in time we should go to pick the relevant cause, but *how much* our cause has contributed to (say) the offense. Let's grant that causation is *metaphysically primitive* (ie not reducible to other physical things or forces). Still, it is plausible that causation is a 'scalar relation' (M. S. Moore, 2009, p. 105) and therefore a matter of degree.[49]

This might be a problem with accomplice liability, if we, counterintuitively, admit that the accomplice has had a causal (albeit maybe non-physical) role in the offence.

It is for the law (or for morals) to "draw the line": to decide whether a certain amount of contribution is going to count as a cause or not. And it is apparent that this line is not descriptively fixed or scientifically discoverable but always based on some sort of evaluation.

Please note that the "causal sorites" is quite different from the "regressus ad infinitum": the former is a *synchronic* problem, while the latter is *diachronic*.

ACTIONS VS. OMISSIONS   A notion of responsibility necessarily requiring a descriptive conception of causation has a problem with omissions. In fact, whereas omissions are of some importance at least for criminal responsibility, descriptive criteria for causation cannot easily track the intuitive distinction between actions and omissions. Either omissions cannot cause anything (and one cannot be responsible for an omission, contra the evidence from criminal law), or—in order to give responsibility for omissions—omissions are causes: this either makes them coincide with actions, or escalates into counterintuitive conclusions

---

49 For the general problem of vagueness, see at least Williamson, 1994 and Luzzati, 1990.

(for example, that roughly the whole humanity should be held responsible for the effects of any omission whatsoever).

Consider two situations where a person dies. Now, let's stipulate that situation (a), where a robber shoots a passerby, may be prima facie described as "killing"; another situation (b), where nourishment for a terminally ill patient isn't provided, may be described as "letting die". Do (a) and (b) differ? Moral philosophers do not agree on this problem, so let's keep our discussion to the legal domain. It seems that they may be considered different, for instance in the distinction between active and passive *euthanasia* or in radically different charges you can incur: to pick an example from Italian criminal law, (a) would possibly get you a sentence for "omicidio volontario" [approximately: murder] (up to 21 years in prison), (b) for "omissione di soccorso" [approximately: duty to rescue] (1 year sentence or a 2.500-euro fine).[50]

If (a) and (b) were two different things (as criminal law seems to recognize), then a possible grounding would be identifying (a) — killing — with an action, and (b) — letting die — with an omission: actions would be causes, whereas omissions would not. On these grounds killing could be punished because someone actively caused it — in a legal (moral) framework where causation is necessary for responsibility. Given that, it is easy to see why in (a), murder, one is responsible. But (b), letting die, is rather puzzling. Either omissions are causes, and then there should be no difference in responsibility between (a) and (b), because the effects are the same; or omissions are not causes, and so no responsibility is warranted.[51]

Carolina Sartorio (for instance cf. Sartorio, 2009 and Sartorio, 2012) argues that accepting this distinction between causal action and non-causal omission is an untenable position, because it is metaphysically unfounded and because it would force us to accept absurd consequences (the familiar "Queen of England's

---

50 The Italian penal code (Art. 40.2) states (stipulates, prescribes?) that omissions *are* (to be considered? count as?) causes: "[...] Non impedire un evento, che si ha l'obbligo giuridico di impedire, equivale a cagionarlo."
51 I thank Fabio Bacchini for discussion on this point.

problem" in terms of omissions: if my gardener had watered my plants, they wouldn't have died; therefore, the Queen of England is *responsible* for my plants' death, because, had she watered my plants, they wouldn't have died). In fact, it is not clear on what grounds we would count something as an action or as an omission: if it is independently sufficient to bring about the desired state-of-affairs? If it is pragmatically *salient*?

On a philosophically accurate account, it seems that an independent, "descriptive" view of causation cannot convincingly account for the traditional (and legally relevant!) distinction between killing and letting die, or more generally between action and omissions. The law "treats omissions both as causes and yet not as causes (M. S. Moore, 2009, p. 82)."

If we considered responsible someone for an omission, then (without further qualifications based on specific roles or requirements) we should consider responsible all those who haven't done that action, because the descriptive criteria are the same —and literally all those imputable according to the the relevant criteria (age, (in)sanity, and so on). This suggests that descriptive criteria aren't enough for responsibility, which needs non-descriptive elements to discriminate between finer alternatives.

I have argued that causation is neither necessary for responsibility, nor convincingly descriptive. I have suggested that, although based on physical, empirical evidence, both law and morals need to draw a line based on evaluative considerations.

To sum up, I have shown how there are non-causal forms of responsibility and how causal facts alone are not sufficient to have a complete theory of responsibility. Empirical research might tell us where to look to find causes, but it will not indicate which causes are relevant in order to ascribe responsibility — or, in other words, where to draw the line.

The general thesis of this work is that responsibility is fundamentally normative. In this chapter I provided two major arguments.

In the two preceding sections, I argued that there cannot be a common metaphysical, true real basis of our practice of attributing responsibility. In section Section 4.1, I held an argument "from difference", that is, that not all forms of responsibility are based on causation.

In Section 4.2, I adopted an argument "from causality". I hope to have disproven the claim that responsibility is ultimately descriptive because it is fundamentally rooted in causality, and causality is descriptive. My strategy was *twofold*. *First*, I have shown that there are significant and independent non-causal forms of responsibility that cannot be reduced to causal responsibility; *second*, I have shown that the very notion of causality (in law and morals) is — *lato sensu* — normative, or at least non plainly descriptive.

In the next chapter, I shall provide a third and final argument, an argument "from negation".

Part III

The Language of Responsibility: Semantics and Pragmatics

5 | ASCRIPTION OF RESPONSIBILITY

5.1 *Two* Paradigms: Ascription *vs.* Description, Ascription *vs.* Prescription

    5.1.1 *First* Paradigm: Ascription *vs.* Description in Hart

    5.1.2 *Second* Paradigm: Ascription *vs.* Prescription in Kelsen

    5.1.3 Ascription, Responsibility, Imputation

    5.1.4 Ascription and Thetic States-of-Affairs

5.2 Phenomenology of Responsibility Judgments

    5.2.1 Attribution of Responsibility (Accusations)

    5.2.2 Denial of Responsibility (Excuses, Absolutions)

    5.2.3 Ascription *vs.* Description of Responsibility

    5.2.4 FIRST Argument: Axiological Evaluation

    5.2.5 SECOND Argument: Normative Relationships

    5.2.6 THIRD Argument: Discretionality

5.3 FOURTH Argument: Denial of Responsibility

    5.3.1 Negation, Negations

    5.3.2 Normative Negation

    5.3.3 Denial of Responsibility, Formalized

5.4 The Relevance of Context: Pragmatics and Normativity

Der Begriff der Handlung an sich selbst enthält schon ein Gesetz für mich.
The concept of action already contains in itself a law for me.
Immanuel Kant, *Grundlegung zur Metaphysik der Sitten.*

El universo es fluido y cambiante, el lenguaje, rígido.
Jorge Luis Borges

In this chapter, I consider the pragmatics of responsibility, and in particular all those acts (linguistic or not linguistic) connected with responsibility such as accusing, excusing, offering justifications and so on. These I provisionally label responsibility judgments.

The thesis of this chapter is that judgments of responsibility are normative.

In Section 5.1, I consider *ascription*, contrasting it with *description* (Section 5.1.1) and with *prescription* (Section 5.1.2).

In Section 5.2, I consider ascriptions of *responsibility*, putting forward a fourfold distinction between *rhetic* and *thetic* ascription of responsibility, and between *rhetic* and *thetic* denial of responsibility.

I then present *four* arguments to maintain that ascriptions of responsibility are normative.

In Section 5.2.3, I put forward *three* arguments: the *first* from axiological evaluation; the *second* from normative relationships; the *third* from discretionality.

In Section 5.3.2, there is my *fourth* three-step argument *ex negatione* (from negation), using negation as a test to discriminate a *normative* from a *non-normative* linguistic entity.

In Section 5.3.2, *first*, I try to set up a minimal model for the negation of normative sentences, starting out with sentences usually accepted as normative, such as (valid) orders or commands. I extend this analysis both to (a) evaluative or axiological judgments (*A is good; B is morally wrong*); and to (b) sentences pragmatically normative, but without semantic or syntactic clues of their normative character.

Second, I contrast *two* sorts of negation: negation of *normative* sentences and negation of *descriptive* sentences, pointing out where they differ. My provisional hypothesis is that *internal* negation and *external* negation work in opposite ways for descriptive sentences and normative sentences. (i) In descriptive sentences internal negation inverts their (truth) value;[1] whereas (ii) in normative sentences it is external negation that changes their (normative) value, by rejecting their presupposition of normativity.

Third, in Section 5.3.3, I consider denials of responsibility. I show that negation of responsibility judgments falls under case (ii). It is only external negation that inverts the value of responsibility judgments, thus showing that responsibility judgments should be considered non-descriptive and normative-like.

So my argument runs as follows:

- (i) External negation inverts the value of a sentence if and only if this sentence is not descriptive;

- (ii) External negation of responsibility judgments does invert their value; Therefore,

- (iii) Responsibility judgments are not descriptive.

At the end of this chapter I consider *three* apparently possible objections to my argument: *first*, I have begged the question in the definition of responsibility judgments; *second*, all I have shown is that external negation inverts the value of sentences if they are not descriptive, but this tells nothing about the exact nature of those sentences; *third*, that these features of negation hold for other modalities, so there is nothing special about normativity.

---

1 Of course the value inversion occurs only in classical two-valued logic. In multivalued logics, it assigns its complement. This observation applies every time I mention truth-values.

5.1 TWO PARADIGMS: ASCRIPTION *VS.* DESCRIPTION, ASCRIPTION *VS.* PRESCRIPTION

A possible (and common) account of speech acts is in term of *descriptions* (usually considered apophantic, truth-apt) and *prescriptions* (such as commands, usually considered anapophantic, truth-*in*apt).

Are *description* and *prescription* jointly exhaustive of *all* speech acts? It doesn't seem the case. To use but a few examples, what kind of discourse (or acts) are prayers,[2] or insults? *First*, both prayers and insults don't describe anything at all[3] and they don't seem to be true or, respectively, false. *Second*, they apparently don't prescribe anything either.

Thus, *description* and *prescription* do not jointly cover all possible cases of linguistic acts.

My concern in this work is, however, on responsibility. Is/are the act(s) of attributing responsibility (such as, for one, accusations) either descriptive *vel* prescriptive, only descriptive, only prescriptive or is there a *quartum quid*, so that they are neither descriptive, nor prescriptive?

In the following sections I shall introduce *two* paradigms, where ascription is opposed to something else:

- in Section 5.1.1, ascription *vs.* description, I shall introduce Hart's thesis that ascription is not reducible to description;

- in Section 5.1.2, ascription *vs.* prescription, Kelsen's distinction between ascriptive *primary* rules and *prescriptive* secondary rules.

---

2 There are striking analogies between religious language and normative language I cannot develop here.
3 This is not to say that from a prayer or an insult one cannot abduce some information, of course.

5.1.1 First Paradigm: Ascription vs. Description in Hart

Hart, 1948 maintained two theses: (i) attributing responsibility (and rights) is an *ascriptive* act; (ii) ascription is not reducible to description.

5.1.1.1 First Thesis: Attribution of Responsibility Is an Ascription

Hart's first thesis is that sentences usually considered to attribute responsibility to someone for something, sentences such as "you hit her", "I did it" are *ascriptive*.[4]

> The sentences "I did it", "you did it","he did it" are, I suggest, primarily utterances with which we *confess* or *admit* liability, make accusations, or *ascribe* responsibility (p. 187).

Again:

> [S]entences of the form "He did it" have been traditionally regarded as primarily descriptive whereas their principal function is what I venture to call *ascriptive*, being quite literally to ascribe responsibility for actions much as the principal function of sentences of the form "This is his" is to ascribe rights in property (p. 171).

5.1.1.2 Second Thesis: Ascription Is Not Reducible to Description

Hart's second thesis is that while *ascriptive* sentences have an informative content, they are not reducible to *descriptive* ones.

> Nor, I suggest, can the difference between *His body moved in violent contact with anothers* [sic] and "He did

---

4 For Hart, 1948, ascription is ascription of *actions*. Hart will retract his theses after criticisms in Geach, 1960 and Pitcher, 1960 to move towards an ascription of liability, for instance in the postscript of Hart, 2008. For a critical reconstruction of his positions and his critics, see Silvi, 2004a, §3 and Bazzoni, 2012, §1. What concerns us here, however, is the focus on ascription as a peculiar act.

> it" (*e.g.*, "He hit her") be explained without reference to the non-descriptive use of sentences by which liabilities or responsibility are ascribed.
>
> What is wrong [...] is identifying the meaning of a non-descriptive utterance ascribing responsibility in stronger or weaker form, with the factual circumstances which support or are good reasons for the ascription (p. 189).

And again:

> [S]entences of the form "He did it" have been traditionally regarded as primarily descriptive whereas their principal function is what I venture to call *ascriptive*, being quite literally to ascribe responsibility for actions much as the principal function of sentences of the form "This is his" is to ascribe rights in property (p. 171).

Hart puts forward several arguments to back up his theses, arguments having to do with similarities with ascriptions of rights or properties and the *defeasibility* of the concept of action — cf. Hart, 1948, pp. 189–194.[5]

Very interesting evidence of the fact that ascriptive sentences are *not* descriptive is the following: when we retract ascriptive sentences, we don't do it because they are *factually* false, but because they were wrong or we were unjustified in asserting them:

> if, on investigating the facts, it appears that [...] our first judgment has to be qualified, [...] it is important to notice that it is not withdrawn as a false statement

---

5 In brief, a concept is defeasible if there are no fixed necessary and sufficient conditions to define it. Hart's original paper identifies at least two examples of defeasible concepts: contracts (in common law) and human actions. Reasoning is defeasible when rationally compelling but not deductively valid. On defeasible reasoning, see at least Koons, 2013. On defeasibility in the legal domain, a good survey is in Ferrer Beltrán and Ratti, 2012.

of fact or as a false inference that some essential mental event had occurred necessary for the truth of the sentence "He did it." Our ascription of responsibility is no longer justified in the light of the new circumstances of which we have notice. So we must judge again: *not describe again* (p.193).

5.1.2 Second Paradigm: Ascription *vs.* Prescription in Kelsen

In this section, I shall address in turn these two theses of Kelsen's: (i) a distinction between *primary* and *secondary* norms; (ii) the ascriptive character of primary norms contrasted with prescriptive secondary norms.

5.1.2.1 *First Distinction: Primary vs. Secondary Norms*

Primary norms, for Kelsen, attach a sanction [*Sanktion*] to a behavior. *Secondary* norms *prescribe* [*gebieten*] the opposite behavior to that sanctioned by primary norms.

> Schon in einem anderen Zusammenhange wurde darauf hingewiesen, daß, wenn eine Norm ein bestimmtes Verhalten gebietet und eine zweite Norm für den Fall der Nichtbefolgung der ersten eine Sanktion statuiert, beide miteinander wesentlich verbunden sind Kelsen, 1960, p. 55.[6]

An example:

> (i) One shall not steal; (ii) if somebody steal, he shall be punished. [...] If at all existent, the first norm is contained in the second, which is the only genuine legal norm. [...] the first norm, which demand the omission of the delict, is dependent upon the second norm, which stipulates the sanction. We may express

---

[6] It was pointed out earlier that: if one norm commands a certain behavior and a second norm stipulates a sanction as reaction against nonobservance, the two norms are tied to each other (Kelsen, 1967, p. 54).

this dependence by *designating the second norm as the* primary *norm, and the first norm as the* secondary *norm* (Kelsen, 1949/2006, p. 61).

Moreover,

> Enthält eine Rechtsordnung, etwa ein von dem Parlament beschlossenes Gesetz, eine Norm, die ein bestimmtes Verhalten vorschreibt, und eine andere Norm, die an die Nichtbefolgung der ersten eine Sanktion knüpft, *ist die erste keine selbständige Norm, sondern mit der zweiten wesentlich verbunden*; sie bestimmt nur — negativ — die Bedingung, an die die zweite die Sanktion knüpft; und wenn die zweite positiv die Bedingung bestimmt, an die sie die Sanktion knüpft, ist die erste vom Standpunkt legislativer Technik überflüssig (Kelsen, 1960, p. 55, *emphasis* added).[7]

5.1.2.2 Second Distinction: Ascriptive Primary Norms vs. Prescriptive Secondary Norms

But *primary* norms are not prescriptive, they are *ascriptive*, because they attach [*knüpfen*] (ascribe, impute) something to something else (in this case: a sanction to a behavior).

Only *secondary* norms *prescribe* [*schreiben vor*] a certain behavior [*Verhalten*].[8]

Ascriptive primary norms are then contrasted with *prescriptive* secondary norms — prescriptive secondary norms that are disposable (literally: superfluous [*überflüssig*]).

---

7 If a legal order, such as a statute passed by parliament, contains one norm that prescribes a certain behavior and a second norm that attaches a sanction to the nonobservance of the first, then the first norm is not an independent norm, but fundamentally tied to the second; the first norm merely designates — negatively — the condition under which the second stipulates the sanction; and if the second one positively designates the condition under which it stipulates the sanction, then the first one is superfluous from the point of view of legislative technique (Kelsen, 1967, p. 55).
8 It is interesting to point out that Kelsen's primary norms became Hart's *secondary* rules in Hart, 2012.

> Enthält eine Rechtsordnung, etwa ein von dem Parlament beschlossenes Gesetz, *eine Norm, die ein bestimmtes Verhalten vorschreibt, und eine andere Norm, die an die Nichtbefolgung der ersten eine Sanktion knüpft,* ist die erste keine selbständige Norm, sondern mit der zweiten wesentlich verbunden; sie bestimmt nur — negativ — die Bedingung, an die die zweite die Sanktion knüpft; und wenn die zweite positiv die Bedingung bestimmt, an die sie die Sanktion knüpft, ist die erste vom Standpunkt legislativer Technik überflüssig (Kelsen, 1960, p. 55, *emphasis* added).[9]

(Interestingly, Kelsen uses 'it designates' [*bestimmt*] for prescriptive norms and again 'knüpft' ("it ties, it stipulates") for ascriptive primary norms.)

Thus the law can be characterized as a coercive order even though not all norms are prescriptions. To sum up:

> Aus dem Gesagten ergibt sich, daß eine Rechtsordnung, obgleich keineswegs alle ihre Normen Zwangsakte statuieren, dennoch als Zwangsordnung insofern gekennzeichnet werden kann, als alle Normen, die nicht selbst einen Zwangsakt statuieren und daher nicht gebieten, sondern zur Setzung von Normen ermächtigen oder positiv erlauben, unselbständige Normen sind, da sie nur in Verbindung mit einer einen Zwangsakt statuierenden Norm gelten. Aber auch nicht alle einen Zwangsakt statuierenden Normen, sondern nur jene, die den Zwangsakt als Reaktion gegen ein bestimmtes menschliches Verhalten, und das heißt als

---

9 If a legal order, such as a statute passed by parliament, contains one norm that prescribes a certain behavior and a second norm that attaches a sanction to the nonobservance of the first, then the first norm is not an independent norm, but fundamentally tied to the second; the first norm merely designates [*bestimmt*] — negatively — the condition under which the second stipulates [*knüpft*] the sanction; and if the second one positively designates [*bestimmt*] the condition under which it stipulates [*knüpft*] the sanction, then the first one is superfluous from the point of view of legislative technique (Kelsen, 1967, p. 55).

Sanktion statuieren, gebieten ein bestimmtes, nämlich das gegenteilige Verhalten. Daher hat das Recht auch aus diesem Grunde nicht ausschließlich gebietenden oder imperativischen Charakter (Kelsen, 1960, p. 59).[10]

5.1.3 Ascription, Responsibility, Imputation

Ascription and responsibility have multiple connections: beyond being ascribed, responsibility is conceptually and historically linked to *Zurechnung* or imputation.[11]

As I pointed out above in Chapter 4.2.1.1, primary norms are characteristic of what Kelsen calls '*Zurechnung*' ["imputation"]. *Zurechnung* is — according to Kelsen — the paradigmatic example of the normative (as opposed to *Kausalität* [causality] in the natural domain).

But '*Zurechnung*' started out as a purely *descriptive* term, as the etymology from *rechnen* ("to count", "to com*pute*") suggests (cf. Polish '*rachunek*'). A similar evolution had the term 'imputation' [*imputatio*] from 'puto', 'putare' ("to count").[12])

The underlying idea is akin to Latin 'redde rationem', It. 'fare i conti', an idea that I see in Engl. 'ac*count*ability' — the idea of

---

10 It follows that a legal order may be characterized as a coercive order, even though not all its norms stipulate coercive acts; because norms that do not themselves stipulate coercive acts (and hence do not command, but authorize the creation of norms or positively permit a definite behavior) are dependent norms, valid only in connection with norms, that *do* stipulate coercive acts. Again, not all norms that stipulate a coercive act but only those that stipulate the coercive act as a reaction against a certain behavior (that is, as a sanction), command a specific, namely the opposite, behavior. This, therefore, is another reason why the law does not have exclusively a commanding or imperative character (Kelsen, 1967, p. 58).

11 At least according to Ricœur, 1994 and Fonnesu, 2013. Both works suggest that imputation was the conceptual (and real) *ancêtre* of responsibility and work their way through modern philosophy, at least starting from Pufendorf, 1672/1934. For a useful history of the concept, see Nüssel, 2011; for etymology, see Köbler, 1995.

12 "'Imputare' [est] nativa significatione terminus arithmeticus" Thomasius, 1718/1979.

a record on which to write or to *a-scribe* (Lat: *ad*-scribere, Germ: *zuschreiben*) everyone's (moral or legal) "bill".

This moral record (the ledger) is that which is involved in a contemporary conception of responsibility also called "ledger view" (see previous discussion in Chapter 1.3.1.1).

5.1.4 Ascription and Thetic Acts

We have seen contrasted *ascription, description,* and *prescription,* and we have seen that they do not jointly exhaust the whole domain of speech acts.

Anyhow, we can heuristically (and quite naively) characterize them in the following (defeasible) way with a provisional definition: descriptions *say* something; prescriptions *rule* on something; ascriptions *produce* something, or *alter* the "normative status quo", for instance by conferring or claiming rights, or advancing accusations.

It is quite natural, at this point, to note a striking parallelism between ascriptions and *thetic performative* acts,[13] that is, acts producing some kind of entity.[14]

Thetic performative verbs (see at least Conte, 1995a,b, 2001b) are a subset of *performative* verbs. But what is the relationship between ascriptions and thetic performative verbs? Two questions come to mind:

1. Are ascriptions reducible to (thetic) performative acts? In other words, is any ascription done by using a thetic performative verb?

---

13 It must be noted that my use of 'thetic' is quite different from that of Czesław Znamierowski [Warszaw, 1888 — Poznań, 1967], probably the first proponent of the word in modern times. In Znamierowski, 1924, for instance, he contrasts psycho-physic acts with thetic acts [*akty tetyczne*]: the latter possess a conventional significance and depend on norms. For a threefold concept of theticity in Znamierowski, see Di Lucia, 2013a.

14 For 'thetic' and thetic acts [*atti thetici, actes thétiques, akty tetyczne*], I point the reader to the etymology of Greek 'θῆσις' and 'τίθημι' from Proto-Indoeuropean *dhē ("to pose", "porre"). Cf. Latin '*fa*-cere' and 'cre-*do*', German '*tun*', English '(to) *do*', Polish '*sąd*', and so on.

2. Are all (thetic) performative utterances ascriptions?

These *two* questions have *one* answer: no.

Firstly, not every ascription is (reducible to) a (thetic) performative utterance, because if performative utterances require (a) a specific verb; and (b) the first person (singular), present tense, then all ascriptions — in order to be reducible to performative verbs — need to have a specific verb. But there is *no* specific verb to ascribe responsibility: in fact, there are ascriptions of responsibility done neither with a specific verb ('It's your fault') nor in the first person, present tense ('It was him'). Most ascriptions of responsibility are not reducible to performative utterances.[15]

Secondly, not every (thetic) performative utterance is an ascription. I shall show this with *three exempla contraria* (three counterexamples) of thetic performative utterances that are *not* ascriptions.

1. The *first* exemplum contrarium against the thesis that all thetic performative utterances are ascriptions: thetic performative utterances done with the verbs 'to forgive' and 'perdonare'. According to Conte, 1995b, 'perdonare' is a thetic performative verb. But saying 'ti perdono', 'I forgive you', while being a thetic performative utterance, is not at all an ascription, because it does not ascribe a status or impute to *x* the consequence(s) *y*.[16] At most it — with a neologism prompted by Amedeo G. Conte — *ab*-scribes it.

2. The *second* exemplum contrarium against the thesis that all thetic performative utterances are ascriptions: thetic performative utterances done with the verb 'abrogare' (while 'abrogazione' in English is 'derogation', 'abrogare' is 'to abrogate', 'to repeal'). According to Conte, 1995b, 'abrogare' is a thetic performative verb: 'abrogare' is not *saying* that a norm is invalid, but is *making* it invalid.[17]

---

15 The verb 'responsabilizzare' it is *not* used to ascribe responsibility. The verb 'colpevolizzare' is *not* used to accuse. Neither 'responsabilizzare' nor 'colpevolizzare' are performative verbs.
16 For an analysis of forgiveness, see Silvi, 2004b.
17 On this point, see also Kelsen, 1973b.

3. The *third* exemplum contrarium against the thesis that all thetic performative utterances are ascriptions: thetic performative utterances done with the verb 'scommettere' ('to bet'). According to Conte, 1995b, 'scommettere' is a thetic performative verb: saying 'io scommetto' is making a bet. But making a bet is — in my view — not an ascription at all, because there is no phenomenon akin to those involved in ascriptions, ie changing in normative status or claims.

Thirdly, the preceding reasons, if true, shed light on another fact: that *theticity* transcends *performativity*, because there are thetic states-of-affairs[18] that come into being *not* through (thetic) performative utterances, but through non-performative ascriptions (such as ascriptions of responsibility).[19]

These remarks need immediately to stand corrected: at most they show that *theticity* trascends *explicit* performativity. But *explicit* performativity doesn't exhaust performative phenomena. An informal donation need not be done by uttering: "I give it to you", but can be done also by saying: "Eccoti" "Here you are", or even *non*-linguistically.

For these phenomena I propose the phrase: '*implicit performativity*'.

The next section will explore the theticity of responsibility ascriptions.

5.2 PHENOMENOLOGY OF RESPONSIBILITY JUDGMENTS

In this section, I shall discuss different kinds of ascriptions because of the different concepts of responsibility (see my taxonomy) that can be ascribed.

In particular, I shall put forward *two* distinctions: one, in the positive, between mere *rhetic* description and *thetic* ascription of

---

18 Such as "aitiological" states-of-affairs, for instance.
19 On this point, see also Lorini, 2000, §4.

responsibility; the other, in the negative, between *rhetic* denial and *thetic* negation of responsibility.

5.2.1   Attribution of Responsibility (Accusation)

In this subsection, I put forward a difference between *descriptions* of responsibility and *ascriptions* of responsibility.

Responsibility is — in this respect — akin to what Amedeo Giovanni Conte calls *'deontic status'*: like deontic status, responsibility admits both to a descriptive and a non-descriptive utterance.

In Section 5.2.1.1, I tackle the mere *description* of responsibility; in Section 5.2.1.2, I confront with *ascriptions* of responsibility.

I contextually offer a modest semantic analysis of some English verbs: 'to credit', 'to praise', 'to accuse', 'to blame', 'to condemn'; and of an Italian verb: 'criticare'.

5.2.1.1   *Rhetic Affirmation of Responsibility (Credit, Praise)*

There is a rhetic affirmation of responsibility when an utterance is used to (theoretically) describe that someone is responsible for something — without moving any accusation or holding any judgment of value.

Rhetic affirmations of responsibility presuppose responsibility and merely describe it. One paraphrase could be: 'say responsible' as in: 'a lightning was responsible for the blackout'.

'TO CREDIT'   A possible rhetic affirmation of responsibility seems the use of the English verb 'to credit' (in at least one of its possible meanings). As a matter of fact, the utterance, 'He is credited with writing more than a hundred peer-reviewed papers' has two presuppositions: (i) the fact in question has really happened (factive presupposition — cf. Kiparsky and Kiparsky, 1971); (ii) this fact is axiologically positive (axiological presupposition), but it merely describes the responsibility for it.

'TO PRAISE' The English verb 'to praise', instead, presupposes the responsibility for an act and *says* that it is (axiologically) good. (Example: 'She praised me for giving the talk'.)

5.2.1.2 *Thetic Ascription of Responsibility: Accusations*

In sharp contrast with *rhetic* affirmations of responsibility (cf. the preceding section) there are *thetic* ascriptions of responsibility.

Possible *thetic* ascriptions of responsibility are *accusations* [French: *accusation*, German: *Anklage, Anschuldigung, Beschuldigung*, Italian: *accusa*, Polish: *obwinienie, oskarżenie*].

That accusations are linked to responsibility is quite apparent (though not definitive) even for linguistic reasons: in at least three languages (Italian: 'accusa', French and English: 'accusation') the word for accusation is linked to 'cause'; in at least three words of two languages (German: 'An*schuld*igung', 'Be*schuld*igung'; Polish: 'ob*wini*enie') 'accusation' is linked to the word 'fault' [German: '*Schuld*'; Polish: '*wina*'].[20] Both cause and fault are usually considered fundamental for responsibility.[21]

That accusations are thetic (and not merely rhetic) ascriptions of responsibility is pointed out by several clues. At least one way of accusing (using the verb 'to accuse') makes up a thetic performative utterance, as for instance Conte, 1977 maintains.

Another (indirect) piece of linguistic evidence is obtained by contrasting verbs such as 'colpevolizzare' vs. 'incolpare' ('colpevolizzare' means merely saying things to make one feel culpable, and it is thus *rhetic*; whereas 'incolpare' means constituting one culpable, and it is thus *thetic*) and 'criminalizzare' vs. 'incriminare' ('criminalizzare' means roughly saying things to make something appear criminal, and it is thus *rhetic*; whereas 'incriminare' means formally accusing someone of a crime, and it is thus *thetic*).

If using 'to accuse' in 'I accuse you' is one possible way to accuse, and if using 'to accuse' in 'I accuse you' is a thetic usage,

---
20 For a linguistic analysis of fault, guilt and related concepts, see Conte, 2001a.
21 In the Introduction, I noted that the Greek 'αἰτία' means both "guilt" and (secondarily) "cause".

then accusations moved through 'to accuse' in 'I accuse you' are thetic ascriptions of responsibility.

Of course one can raise accusations without using 'to accuse' (for instance one can accuse uttering 'it was you!') but either these are different kinds of accusations or — for the identity of indiscernibles — if accusations (raised through 'I accuse you') are thetic acts, then each and every accusation — if it is a true accusation, whatever the way it is raised — must keep its thetic character.[22]

Charles J. Fillmore (Fillmore, 1969) denies that 'to accuse' is a thetic verb. According to Fillmore, saying 'I accuse you' is to *say responsible*, and not *make* responsible. Quite on the contrary, one says 'I accuse you' in order to *make* an accusation, to accuse, to produce a state-of-affairs, not (only) to describe that an accusation is there.

'CRITICARE'   From accusations differ critiques [Italian: *'critiche'*, plural of *'critica'*], in particular those raised with the verb 'criticare'.

While an accusation thetically poses responsibility (which may factually be non-existent), a critique presupposes responsibility and shouts the wrongness of the presupposed act. 'Criticare', moreover, is not even a performative verb (cf. Conte, 2001b, p.973).

'TO CONDEMN'   From accusations differ condemnations or sentences [Italian: *'condanna'*].

Among the different meanings of the Italian verb 'condannare' and the English verb 'to condemn', *two* are outstanding for my investigation: *first*, a *rhetic* meaning (expressing censure or disapproval: 'The UN *condemns* the riots in Syria'); *second*, a *thetic* meaning (take a sentence: 'Questa corte *condanna* l'imputato a 13 anni di reclusione').

The latter sense (the thetic one) is not, however, a thetic ascription of responsibility: in fact, a condemnation [*condanna*] does

---

22 Of course using 'to accuse' is neither sufficient nor necessary to result in an accusation.

not give a responsibility (which is presupposed), but a punishment.[23]

Blame differs from accusations, and 'to accuse' differs from 'to blame'.[24]

5.2.2 Denial of Responsibility (Excuses, Absolutions)

5.2.2.1 *Rhetic Denials: Excuses and Justifications*

EXCUSES   A possible rhetic negation of responsibility[25] may be considered an *excuse*.

With 'excuse' I do not refer to the linguistic act of excusing oneself (uttering, for instance, 'Excuse me'). The verb 'scusarsi', for instance, is a *factive* performative verb: it presupposes the truth (the occurrence, the obtaining) of the fact for which one is excused, and the utterance of the verb 'scusarsi' constitutes the offer of excuses.[26]

---

23 Even in a predictive (consequentialist) conception of responsibility (responsibility as punishability) it is possible to distinguish punishability from punishment. Common law distinguishes *conviction*, ie an ascription of culpability pronounced by a jury, and *sentence*, ie the attribution of punishment (like a life-sentence, usually given by a judge).
24 For an excellent inquiry on the presuppositions and the semantics of 'to blame', see Fillmore, 1969; for a comparison between 'accusare' and 'biasimare', see Conte, 2001b, p. 973.
25 With 'negation of responsibility' I mean — for the purposes of this chapter — the denial of the fact that someone is responsible in a given circumstance, not denial of the very possibility of responsibility *tout court*, as for instance G. Strawson, 1994, 2009 and Waller, 2011 maintain.
26 Devoto distiguished *two* different words (in Italian) for 'excuse': one singular ('scusa'), one plural ('scuse'): "Che cosa è la scusa? Propongo "giustificazione pretestuosa, non necessariamente formulata in cattiva fede". Esempio: "La scusa era futile. Avrebbe avuto il tempo di fare le due cose, terminare la lettera e mettere ordine sulla scrivania. Come si definiscono le scuse? Propongo "dichiarazione che deplora un torto fatto ad altri per inavvertenza, motivo grave o forza maggiore. Esempio: "Per mantenere l'ordine, non poté guardare tanto per il sottile: i primi li ricevette, gli altri li lasciò fuori. A questi fece pervenire le sue scuse e le sue scuse erano sincere (Devoto, 1968)."

With 'excuses' I shall hereby refer to what John Langshaw Austin called 'excuses' and contrasted with 'justifications':[27]

> In the one defense [justification], briefly, we accept responsibility but deny that it was bad: in the other [excuse], we admit that it was bad but don't accept full, or even any, responsibility (Austin, 1956).

In excuses, in particular,

> it is not quite fair or correct to say baldly "X *did A*". We may say it isn't fair just to say X did it; perhaps he was under somebody's influence, or was nudged. Or, it isn't fair to say baldly he *did* A; it may have been partly accidental, or an unintentional slip. Or, it isn't fair to say he did simply *A* – he was really doing something quite different and A was only incidental, or he was looking at the whole thing quite differently (Austin, 1956).

I argue that the excuses-giving linguistic act is a *rhetic negation* of responsibility for the following *two* reasons:

first, excuses are *denial* of responsibility because, in giving excuses, a person contests or opposes a previously ascribed responsibility, by rejecting constitutive elements of the accusation: for instance, by denying having committed anything. He simply denies that the previous ascription of responsibility is sound.

Second, excuses are *rhetic* (and not thetic) negations (denials) of responsibility because they do not seek to cancel or nullify responsibility, because they assume that there is *no* responsibility whatsoever. Absence of responsibility is constitutive of excuses: if there were responsibility, they would not be excuses but — at most — justifications. Excuses do not presuppose responsibility, but only ascription of responsibility.[28]

---

[27] At least for the purposes of this work. I'm aware that this use, though quite well-known in analytic philosophy, is not universally accepted.

[28] As I noted with accusations, not all excuses are pled using a verb like 'to excuse' or 'scusare'; in an analogous fashion, it is not only the use of 'to excuse' or 'scusare' that can make an excuse.

JUSTIFICATIONS   Justifications, instead, are not at all negations of responsibility — *a fortiori* they cannot be either *rhetic*, or *thetic* negation of responsibility. Justifications aren't negations of responsibility because justifications presuppose responsibility: justifications affirm responsibility, but deny it is responsibility for something bad. (A paradigmatic example seems to me "self defense": *a* admits to having killed *b*, but *b* was assaulting him with a knife, for instance.)[29]

5.2.2.2 *Thetic Denial: Legal* vs. *Religious Absolution*

ACQUITTAL (LEGAL ABSOLUTION) [FREISPRUCH]   *Thetic* negations of responsibility are acquittal or *legal* absolution (German: *Freispruch*; Dutch: *vrijspraak*; Norwegian: *frikjenning*; Danish: *frifindelse*; Swedish: *frikännande*; French: *acquittement*; Polish: *uniewinnienie*).

The judge presupposes the preceding ascription of responsibility as true and poses it as non-true in that legal proceeding, *in* and *for* that convention. Acquittal has *two* presuppositions: (i) the preceding ascription of responsibility and, jointly, (ii) the absence of responsibility.[30]

---

29 With 'justification' I don't mean what in Italian jurisprudence is called 'causa di giustificazione' (ie. legittima difesa, consenso dell'avente diritto, adempimento di un dovere, uso delle armi da parte della polizia, stato di necessità, esercizio di un diritto). Those "cause di giustificazione", along with other classes (such as "cause di non-punibilità") make what some call 'scriminanti' or 'discriminanti'. I thank Emil Mazzoleni for an enlightening conversation.

30 The fact that acquittal has certain realizations in a given legal system seems to me purely contingent. For instance, all six types of acquittal in Art. 529 of Italian Penal Code are *thetic* negation of responsibility, because they dissolve the preceding ascription of responsibility. Those six types are: acquittal because: (i) il fatto non sussiste; (ii) l'imputato non ha commesso il fatto; (iii) il fatto non costituisce reato; (iv) il fatto non è previsto dalla legge come reato; (v) il reato è stato commesso da persona non imputabile; (vi) il reato è stato commesso da persona non punibile. Of course, these six do not exhaust all possible forms of acquittal. In particular, there are also "la sentenza di non doversi procedere del giudice per l'indagine preliminare" and "la sentenza di non luogo a procedere del giudice per l'udienza preliminare".

RELIGIOUS ABSOLUTION [ABSOLUTION]   Quite on the contrary, religious (not: legal) absolution (legal absolution in German: *Freispruch*) as a sacrament (German: *Absolution, Sündennachlaß*; Dutch: *absolutie*; Norwegian: *absolusjon*; Danish: *syndsforladelse*; Swedish: *absolution*; French: *absolution*; Polish: *rozgrzeszenie, absolucja*) *a fortiori* is not a *thetic* negation of responsibility, because it is not a negation of responsibility at all.

Religious absolution not only presupposes responsibility but also requires responsibility to be completed, that is to release the penitent from his sins (absolution cancels one's sins, not one's responsibility or punishment for them.)[31]

5.2.3 Ascription vs. Description of Responsibility

In this section, I shall argue that responsibility judgments are normative when used ascriptively.

I shall now put forward *three* considerations.

First, not every ascription is a judgment of responsibility. In other words, not every ascription is concerned with responsibility. Questions of responsibility arise when we have a special interest or aim to pursue, when a situation deviates from the norm or the standard, when we want to understand more, as Feinberg, 1965 points out.

Second, the very same sentence can be used to ascribe responsibility or to describe, but when used descriptively that sentence is not describing responsibility, but is doing something else.

Third, judgments of responsibility are such only when they are used to ascribe responsibility.[32]

---

31 I think my point is confirmed by the practice of "plenary indulgence". Among the requisites of plenary indulgence stands some act (say, a pilgrimage) and, necessarily, formal penance. If religious absolution were — alone — sufficient condition of the removal of every possible punishment, then all other required acts for that indulgence would be useless (for plenary indulgence). From this reasoning I abduce that religious absolution "cancels" sins, but not the responsibility thereof — responsibility connected to some form of punishment untouched by religious absolution. Many thanks to don Paolo Pelosi for discussion on this point.

32 For a similar opinion, see Feinberg, 1965 and Feinberg, 1970.

For argument's sake, let's admit two possible uses of responsibility judgments: *descriptive* and *ascriptive*.[33] For ascriptive responsibility judgments there is no conceptual problem. Let us then turn to *descriptive* responsibility judgments.

Can responsibility be an object of description? Or can it only be ascribed?[34] *Prima facie*, it seems possible to utter a responsibility judgment only to *inform* that someone is responsible of something.

Now, descriptive judgments may be either

(i) *independent* from ascriptive judgments (*ascription-independent*); or

(ii) *dependent* on ascriptive judgments (*ascription-dependent*).

In case (i), descriptive judgments of responsibility are *independent* of ascriptive judgments. This seems to imply that they (a) can be true or false and (b) there are "truthmakers", ie something in the world that "makes" these judgments true or, respectively, false.[35] This presupposes that responsibility is objective, that is, an object that, as such, is independent from human practices.

In case (ii), descriptive judgments of responsibility are *dependent* on ascriptive judgments. I see two possibilities:

(ii.i) Ascriptive judgments are (temporally) *prior* to descriptive judgments, and therefore descriptive judgments are used to describe the historical fact that an ascriptive judgment has previously taken place.

(ii.ii) Ascriptive judgments are logically prior: an (apophantic) responsibility judgment can be uttered to inform only if it is used at the same time to also ascribe responsibility.

---

33 Is it possible to consider ascriptions of responsibility as *prescriptive*? I leave this question open here.
34 There seems to be a striking parallelism with the question *Sollsatz* vs. *Sollnorm* in Kelsen.
35 On truthmakers, see at least Mulligan, Simons, and Smith, 1984; Rodríguez-Pereyra, 2006 and MacBride, 2013.

In both cases (ii.i) and (ii.ii) it seems that a descriptive (apophantic) responsibility judgment (if it exists) must presuppose an ascriptive (thetic) responsibility judgment.

Thus, when I use the phrase 'descriptive responsibility judgment' I shall mean that they always presuppose an ascriptive judgment.

The very same sentence, for instance 'Juan is responsible for robbing the bank', may be *pragmatically polyvalent* [*mehrdeutig*]:[36] it can be used in *three* ways:

1. to (brutely) *state* a brute fact (that something has happened — for instance that Juan got a thousand euros);

2. to (institutionally) *describe* an institutional fact (a state-of-affairs — for instance the fact that Juan has been so-and-so sentenced);

3. to (thetically) *ascribe* responsibility (for instance to accuse Juan of robbing the bank).[37]

5.2.3.1 *Metapragmatics of Responsibility*

The thesis that ascription is normative-like presupposes that there is only *one* possible *kind* of ascription. But this presupposition is false. It is false for *two* reasons: *first*, I have already shown that there are at least *two* (heterogeneous) concepts of ascription: that considered by Hart (ascription of an action or responsibility or rights), and that considered by Kelsen (ascription of sanctions

---

36 On semantic ambiguity *vs.* pragmatic ambivalence, see Conte, 2007a.
37 Some brief words of justification. *First*, I shall be content to investigate *linguistic* entities. I am well aware that some accusation is advanced or some excuse pled *without* any words being spoken. Mine shall be a linguistic analysis, even though I hope that my conclusion will shed some light on the phenomenon of responsibility judgments in general. *Second*, since there is no shared consensus either on what responsibility is or on what responsibility judgments are, I feel confident in making use of a certain degree of arbitrariness. As a matter of fact, we need at least a *prima facie* distinction between responsibility judgments and other kinds of judgments. There is no conceptual reason precluding my analysis from being extended further, given the right premises.

to conducts). And since *ab esse ad posse valet consequentia*, if there are two concepts of ascription, then there can be two concepts of ascription. But for argument's sake let's assume that this first reason is false, and only one is the *true* ascription. But *second*, Feinberg acutely showed that even this kind of ascription (ie. ascription of responsibility) is not a simple concept, but that there are at least *two* different concepts of ascription of responsibility.[38]

They do not differ because of the possible object of ascription (say, several different concepts of responsibility, such as liability-responsibility or causal responsibility), but they differ in nature.

In order to correctly judge the nature of a responsibility judgment, I shall put forward *three* considerations.

First, we should grasp *what kind* of entity we are talking about in a given responsibility judgment. *Two* entities that can be ascribed are (i) *actions*; (ii) *responsibilities*.[39]

Second, even ascriptions of responsibility depend on the particular concept of responsibility we are considering. In Part 1, I distinguished several concepts of responsibility, and many of these can be ascribed by different speech acts.

A causal judgment *on* responsibility ('Hitler was responsible for WWII') may be considered akin to descriptive judgments, whereas judgments *of* responsibility ('It's your fault') may be considered ascriptions.

Third, a good cue (or a *prima facie heuristic* criterion) to distinguish between *descriptive* and *ascriptive* judgments of (one concept of) responsibility is the verbal *tense*. Descriptive judgments of responsibility usually are in the *past* tense, whereas ascriptive judgments of responsibility usually are in the *present* tense.

I shall now put forward *three* arguments to back up my thesis that responsibility judgments are normative.

---

38 For instance in Feinberg, 1965.
39 Hart, 1948 for one, when talking of ascriptions, meant ascription of actions (cf. Silvi, 2004a, §3); Hart's critic, Pitcher, (Pitcher, 1960) meant censurability; Feinberg, 1965 distinguished ascription of actions from ascriptions of liability; Hart, 2008 had in mind ascription of punibility.

5.2.4 FIRST Argument: Axiological Evaluation

First, then, there is some sort of *evaluation* involved in responsibility judgments: whether the *judicata* was good or bad, right or wrong, or even if it fell under a given rubric.

5.2.5 SECOND Argument: Normative Relationships

Second, it follows from my definition above that in responsibility judgments there are at least a *judge* and and a *judgee* (of course these may coincide, as Nagel, 1986 points out), and — as it turns out — those positions (even if temporary) in society are surely constituted by relationships established by (social, moral or legal) norms, such as roles (a teacher evaluating or scolding his pupil) or duties.

5.2.6 THIRD Argument: Discretionality

Third, responsibility judgments are discretionary, because they always involve a choice or a decision, rather than a discovery. Choice we find in the selection of the object of imputation (simple action *vs.* complex state-of-affairs; causal responsibility *vs.* censurability) and in the breadth and depth of the selection.

I believe that these *three* reasons (evaluations, normative relationships and discretionality), although not decisive, may back up my working hypothesis of responsibility judgments as normative.

If we then — provisionally, but not without justification (cf. for instance Nagel, 1986; Scanlon, 1998) — consider responsibility judgments akin to normative judgments — for one, moral judgments such as 'Abortion is wrong' — we can start to see many problems arising.

In fact, normative (and *a fortiori* moral) judgments have usually been considered anapophantic, truth-*in*apt, in other words: not true or false.

But if responsibility judgments cannot be true or false, and if negation acts on the truth-value of a sentence, how can responsibility judgments be negated? And since it seems they *are* being negated, what is it that is negated, if not their truth?

I shall tackle these problems in the next section, in Section 5.3.2.

5.3 FOURTH ARGUMENT: DENIAL OF RE-SPONSIBILITY

This section has a narrow focus, inasmuch as it is centered on a particular test-case: norm negation.

The logical status of normative language has long been of interest. In modern times, the question about a possible logic of norms, following the birth of modern logic from Frege on, began seriously with Grue-Sørensen, 1939; Jørgensen, 1938a,b, 1969 and has had pundits such as Rand, 1939, 1962, Hofstadter and McKinsey, 1939, Ross, 1941, Rudziński, 1947, and many others.[40]

The first question usually asked is about the truth-aptness of normative language. Can imperatives be true or false? Is the sentence "Abortion is wrong" true or false? Or right, perhaps?

In general, what does it mean for normative language to be true or false? If we limit our investigation to imperatives, it turns out that there have been quite a lot of answers. With selected exceptions, scholars usually deny that imperatives are truth-apt.[41]

---

40 For instance cf. Sorainen, 1939 (for which see Faroldi, 2013b). In general, for the origin of the logic of norms, see Lorini, 2001, 2013. The birth of *deontic* logic is usually traced back to Mally, 1926, although "true" deontic logic starts with Wright, 1951, Kalinowski, 1953 and Oskar Becker.

41 Here it is a partial list of predicates analogous (or homologous) to truth considered holding for norms:
(i) *accountable*: Hamblin, 1987, pp. 20, 91-2;
(ii) *adempiuta* [adempimento = *Vollführung*]: Rand, 1939; Geach, 1958, p. 58;
(iii) *appropriate* [appropriata]: Castañeda, 1960a, pp. 35-43, Castañeda, 1963, p. 278; Kaufmann, 2012, p. 2; Wright, 1968, p. 154;
(iv) *assented to*: Bhat, 1983, pp. 451, 460; Espersen, 1967, pp. 67-8; Gardiner, 1955, pp. 23-9; Gauthier, 1963, pp. 63-4; Hare, 1952, pp. 19-20; Wright, 1968, p. 154;

(v) *effettuata* (le azioni prescritte) [effettuazione = *Ausführung*]: Rand, 1939;
(vi) *authoritative* [autorevole]: Hall, 1952, pp. 120-1; cf. Oppenheim, 1944, pp. 152-3;
(vii) *binding* [vincolante]: Dubislav, 1937, pp. 341-2; Lang, 1960, 1962; Prior, 1971, pp. 65-9; Ross, 1968, p. 81; Wedeking, 1969, pp. 20, 93;
(viii) *correct* [corretta, *richtig*]: Bohnert, 1945, p. 314; Castañeda, 1960a, p. 36; Gensler, 1990, p. 194; Grue-Sørensen, 1939, p. 197; Ramírez, 2003, pp. 151, 189, 284;
(ix) *in force* [vigente, in vigore, *in Kraft*]: Espersen, 1967, pp. 68-9; Hamblin, 1987, p. 169; Lemmon, 1965, pp. 52-3; Rudziński, 1947 (*obowiązywanie*); Sosa, 1964, pp. 70-1, Sosa, 1967, pp. 60-2; van Fraassen, 1973, p. 15; Wright, 1968, p. 154; Wedeking, 1969, p. 93; Zellner, 1971, p. 49;
(x) *fondata* [fondatezza = *Begründung*]: Moritz, 1941, p. 240;
(xi) *justified* [giustificata]: Castañeda, 1960a, pp. 35-43, Castañeda, 1960b, pp. 170-3, Castañeda, 1963, p. 278, Castañeda, 1974, §4; Dubislav, 1937, pp. 341-2; Espersen, 1967, p. 78; Frey, 1957, pp. 457-8; Gauthier, 1963, p. 63; Grue-Sørensen, 1939, p. 197; Hofstadter and McKinsey, 1939, p. 455; Jørgensen, 1938a, p. 289; Kaufmann, 2012, p. 2; Nielsen 1966: 239; Sosa, 1967, p. 60; Wilder, 1980, pp. 246-7; Zellner, 1971, pp. 49–51;
(xii) *legitimate* [legittima]: Broad, 1950, p. 63; Castañeda, 1975, pp. 121-2; Hall, 1947, p. 341, Hall, 1952, p. 115; Wedeking, 1969, pp. 93, 136–41; Raz 1977: 83;
(xiii) *obeyed* [obbedita]: Adler, 1980, pp. 26, 74; Fisher, 1962b, p. 198, Fisher, 1962a, p. 232; Grant, 1968, p. 195; Hamblin, 1987, p. 26; Jørgensen, 1938a, p. 289, Jørgensen, 1938b, p. 10; Lemmon, 1965, pp. 52-3; Prior, 1949, pp. 71-2, Prior, 1971, pp. 71-2; Sosa, 1964, pp. 41–54; P. F. Strawson, 1950, pp. 141-2; Wright, 1968, p. 154; B. A. O. Williams, 1963, p. 30; Zellner, 1971, pp. 83–97;
(xiv) *orthonomica*: Conte, personal communication.
(xv) *orthopractic*: Castañeda, 1960a, p. 37; Wedeking, 1969, p. 107; Zellner, 1971, p. 49;
(xvi) *orthotic*: Castañeda, 1974, Castañeda, 1975, pp. 121-2;
(xvii) *proper*: Keene 1966: 60;
(xviii) *required*: Johanson, 1988, pp. 8, 13, Johanson, 1996, p. 128, Johanson, 2000, p. 247;
(xix) *satisfied* [soddisfatta]: Beardsley, 1944, p. 178; Bergström, 1962, pp. 29–30; Clarke 1985: 100; Espersen, 1967, p. 72; Frey, 1957, 450–1; Grant, 1968, pp. 189–90; Hamblin, 1987, 139–40; Hansen, 2001, p. 207; Hare, 1972, pp. 62–3; Harrison, 1991, pp. 105-6; Hofstadter and McKinsey, 1939, p. 447; Milo, 1976, p. 15; Ross, 1941, p. 60; Sosa, 1964, pp. 65-6, 76, Sosa, 1966, 225–6, Sosa, 1967, pp. 59-60, Sosa, 1970, p. 216; Weinberger, 1958, pp. 29-30; Zellner, 1971, pp. 52-3;
(xx) *słuszny* [giustezza = *słuszność*]: Sztykgold, 1936;
(xxi) *operante* [operanza]: Conte, pc.;
(xxii) *valente* [valenza]: Conte, pc..

Let's go into the detail. If imperatives cannot be true or false — as general consensus has it — can imperatives (and normative language in general) be negated? Can they be subject to inferences and arguments?[42] Since it seems that in fact imperatives *are* negated, what does this negation mean? Is the same negation used in indicative language? Is it analogous? Or is it of a different kind altogether?

An investigation — not even theoretical — but merely historical of the most common stances in regard to a logic of imperatives (and of normative language at large) exceeds not only the physical limits of this work but also the capacities of its author.

(xxiii) *valid* [valida, *gültig*]: Alchourrón and Martino, 1990, pp. 47, 55; Bergström, 1962, p. 30; Bobbio, 1958, §2; Espersen, 1967, p. 67; Grue-Sørensen, 1939, pp. 196-7; Kelsen, 1960, pp. 9-10, Kelsen, 1979, pp. 22, 39-40; Nino, 1978; Prior, 1949, pp. 71-6; Ross, 1941, pp. 58–60, Ross, 1968, pp. 49, 177–80; Weinberger, 1957, 109 n.14, 124-5, Weinberger, 1958, p. 4; Wedgwood, 2007;

(xxiv) *vera* [true, vrai, wahr]: Borchardt, 1979; Conte, 1995a; Gibbons, 1960, p. 118; Ho, 1969, p. 232; Kalinowski, 1964, 1967; Kanger, 1971, p. 55; Kaufmann, 2012, p. 2; Langford, 1968, p. 332; Leonard, 1959, pp. 172, 184-5; Lewis, 1969, p. 150, Lewis, 1983, p. 224, Lewis, 2000, pp. 24-5; Lewis and Lewis, 1975, pp. 52-4; Scanlon, 2014, §5; Sorainen, 1939, pp. 203-4; Sosa, 1970, pp. 215-16.

(xxv) *usata/utilizzata/impiegata*: Conte, *Nomotropismo*, nomotropía;

(xxvi) *warranted* (garantita; garantitezza = *warrantedness*) Prior, 1968.

(xxvii) *doable* [fattibile]: Wright, 1991, 1999.

(xxviii) *giusta* [giustizia]: Bobbio, 1958, §2;

(xxix) *efficace*: Bobbio, 1958, §2;

(xxx) *osservata* [osservanza]: Conte, pc.;

(xxxi) *applied* [applicata]: Ross, 1968, p. 81;

(xxxii) *followed* [seguita]: Ross, 1968, p. 81;

(xxxiii) *complied with*: Ross, 1968, p. 82.

(xxxiv) *fulfilled*: Wittgenstein, 2009, §§451, 458. For help with this list I extend special thanks to P. Vranas, Amedeo Giovanni Conte, and Guglielmo Feis; see also Vranas, 2008, 2011, 2012; Lorini, 2001; McNamara, 2010 and Unwin, 1999, 2001.

42 This has been traditionally known, after Ross, 1941, 1968, as Jørgensen's dilemma (in particular following Jørgensen, 1938a,b, for a recent account of which see Marturano, 2012). As a problem for expressivism that — at least in Blackburn's and Gibbard's versions (Blackburn, 1984, 1998 and Gibbard, 1990, 2003) — considers normative judgments as truth-*in*apt, this question is known as the Frege-Geach problem (cf. Geach, 1965, Unwin, 1999, 2001, Schroeder, 2008a,b, Schroeder, 2008c, Charlow, 2014 and Hom and Schwartz, 2013).

For these reasons, I shall content myself with a more modest, yet I hope provocative, analysis of norm negation.

Norm negation is a fair theme, I think, because of the following advantages:

- It lets us appreciate the "multidimensionality" of normative language: not every norm is a normative sentence, nor normative sentences exhaust the normative domain.
- In the case of linguistic norms, norm-negation compels us to consider their truth-aptness, in order to refute or accept it.
- In the case of non-linguistic norms, norm-negation forces us to ponder what happens when the normative entity we are negating it is not a sentence.

In general, norm negation provides us with a field test for general theories of normativity.

This chapter aims at clarifying the various kinds of negation in logic and natural language (in Section 5.3.1). It then advances an interpretation of normative negation (Section 5.3.2) and considers how this model might shed light on responsibility judgments and in particular on negative responsibility judgments (Section 5.3.3).

5.3.1 Negation, Negations

I shall now briefly introduce some concepts I use in this chapter, without even trying to pretend to master the whole topic.[43]

5.3.1.1 *Negation, Denial, Rejection*

For the purposes of this chapter, I shall adopt the now common distinction among *negation*, *denial* and *rejection*.[44] While these

---

43 For an engaging yet theory-driven introduction to negation, see Horn, 1989.
44 For a survey on the matter, see Ripley, 2011. The paper even discusses some theories about the respective relationships among *negation*, *denial* and *rejection*.

definitions are apodictically stated, nothing significant for my arguments relies on them.

Very roughly, *negation* [*negazione*] acts on *contents*. For instance, '*un*happy' is the *negation* of 'happy'.⁴⁵

Denial [*diniego*] is, instead, an *act*. It can be either a linguistic act, or a non-linguistic act (for instance: shaking one's head).

Rejection [*rifiuto*] is, instead, a mental *attitude*, for instance, that of one who refuses to accept the death of a relative.⁴⁶

5.3.1.2 *Internal* vs. *External Negation*

Due to a felicitous intuition in B. Russell, 1905,⁴⁷ the well-known sentence:

(1) The King of France is *not* bald

can be given two readings, usually paraphrased as follows:⁴⁸

(1a) INTERNAL: The King of France is *not*-bald (is *un*-bald);

---

45 We got 'un', in English, from a reconstructed *en-, from Proto-Indoeuropean *n- (probably zero grade of *ne-), prefix usually found in most Indo-European tongues, for instance: Old Armenian: (an-); Armenian: (an-); Proto-Celtic: *an-; Old Irish: an-, é-; Irish: an-, éa-; Breton: an-; Welsh: an-; Proto-Germanic: *un-; Old English: un-; English: un-;; Old Saxon: un-; Old Dutch: un-; Dutch: on-; Old High German: un-; German: un-; Old Norse: ú-, ó-; Icelandic: ó-; Faroese: ó-; Swedish: o-; Danish: u-; Norwegian: u-; Gothic: (un-); Ancient Greek: (an-), (ne-), (a-); English: a-; French: a-; Kurdish: na, ne, no, na-, ne-, me-, ni-; Middle Persian: (an-); Latin: in-, ne-, nasalized i-; English: in-; French: in-; Portuguese: in-, im- before p, b and m; Sanskrit: (a-); Proto-Slavic: ne-, ni-; Czech: ne-, ni-; Polish: nie-; Russian: (nje-); Slovak: ne-, ni-.
From Proto-Indoeuropean *ne- we got: Proto-Celtic: *n; Old Irish: ní; Irish: ní; Welsh: ni; Germanic: *ne, *ni; Sanskrit: (na); Middle Persian: (n); Persian: (nê), (na); Kurdish: na, ne, no, na-, ne-, me-, ni-; Latin: ne; Slavic: *ne. Cf. at least Brückner, 1957; Pokorny, 1994; Vasmer, 1958.
46 On rejection, see Gomolińska, 1998; Incurvati and Smith, 2010; T. Smiley, 1996; Tamminga, 1994.
47 As far as I am aware, Frege (for instance in Frege, 1918–9) did not notice this phenomenon or shunned it.
48 For instance by Horn, 1989, §6.

(1b) EXTERNAL: It is *not* the case (true)[49] that the King of France is bald.

The former (1a) is usually read as an example of *internal* negation; whereas the latter (1b) is usually read as an example of *external* negation.[50]

In propositional logic internal negation and external negation are equivalent, that is, they both equally invert the logical value of a given sentence.[51]

So, for instance:

(2) Maria is a brunette

changes its truth-value both in (2a) and (2b), examples of internal negation and external negation, respectively:

(2a) INTERNAL: Maria is *not* a brunette;

(2b) EXTERNAL: It is *not* the case (true) that Maria is a brunette.

Please keep this point in mind because it will come in handy *infra* in Section 5.3.2, when we shall see that internal negation and external negation are not equivalent in normative sentences.[52]

---

49 'True' was proposed by Karttunen and Peters, 1979.
50 Horn, 1989, §6 questions the use of 'true' and underlines how *no* known natural language employs two distinct negative operators corresponding directly to internal and external negation, even if a given language employs two (or more) negative operators, for instance (former: *declarative* negation; latter: *emphatic* negation): Ancient Greek: 'ou' *vs.* 'mē'; Modern Greek: 'den' *vs.* 'me'; Hungarian: 'nem' *vs.* 'ne'; Latin: 'non' *vs.* 'nē'; Irish: 'nach' *vs.* 'gan'; Sanskrit: 'na' *vs.* 'mā'. There is another 'un-' in English which is not a negative operator, but it is analogous to German 'ent-' as in 'un-fold', 'ent-falten'. See Horn's interesting list of languages with distinct negative operators on p. 366.
51 But please keep in mind that *duplex negatio affirmat* only in propositional logic and some natural languages, for instance contemporary standard English. Both in Old and Middle English, along with contemporary languages such as Italian, Portuguese and many others, *duplex negatio n e g a t*.
52 This point was also noticed by St. Anselm of Canterbury: "dicimus etiam nos "non debere peccare" pro "debere non peccare". Non enim omnis, qui facit, quod non debet, peccat, si proprie consideretur." Cf. Schmitt, 1936, p. 36. (The extended passage is quoted and translated in Appendix A. For an

5.3.1.3 *Metalinguistic Negation*

Metalinguistic negation is defined[53] as a formally negative utterance used to object to a previous utterance on any grounds (even of intonations, assertability, and so on).

Here is an example of metalinguistic negation:

(3) John didn't *manage* to pass his viva — it was quite easy for him. (Emphasis signals stressed intonation here.)

(4) Ben is meeting a man this evening. No, he's not — he's meeting his brother.

Interestingly, Dummett, 1973, p. 330 points out that there cannot be a "proper" negation of a conditional (material? He does not say) in natural language but only an objection to its assertability.

So one does not object to the truth of a sentence, but to its (felicitous, appropriate) assertability.

Another interesting feature of metalinguistic negation is its inability to be incorporated prefixally:

(5) The King of France is not happy (*unhappy) — in fact, there isn't any king of France.[54]

Sometimes natural languages may be able to discriminate a descriptive from a metalinguistic use. German and Russian, for instance, modify the slot of the negative particle:[55]

(6a) Er besuchte uns gestern nicht. [He did not visit us yesterday]
(6b) Er besuchte uns nicht gestern, sondern … [He visited us not yesterday, but…]

---

interesting survey of modal logics in Anselm, see Henry, 1953 and Uckelman, 2007, 2009.
53 For instance by Horn, 1985, 1989.
54 Horn, 1989, p. 392.
55 Cf. Horn, 1989, p. 438-9

(7a) On etogo ne delal — [He didn't do that]
he-NOM that-GEN not did

(7b) Ne on eto delal — [It wasn't he who did that]
not he-NOM that-ACC did

5.3.1.4 Illocutionary or Neustic Negation

Introduced as neustic negation by Hare (Hare, 1952, p. 21 Hare, 1989, p. 35) and later called 'illocutionary negation' (originally by Searle, cf. Peetz, 1979; Searle and Vanderveken, 1985), it should apply to what expresses illocutive force in a sentence or the neustic.

Here is an example:
(8) I promise to come.
(9a) I promise not to come.
(9b) I don't promise to come.

According to Searle, (9a) is simply a propositional (or internal) negation, whereas (9b) is an example of illocutionary negation: one denies the very linguistic act, not its content. (9a) and (9b) are not equivalent.

Illocutionary negation, if it exists, seems non-truth conditional. Is it assimilable to metalinguistic negation? As Moeschler, 2010 maintains, not always: in fact metalinguistic negation need not be expressed linguistically, whereas illocutionary negation is necessarily linguistic.

Some doubts about the very existence of illocutionary (or neustic) negation are expressed by Cohen, 1964; Garner, 1971; Hoche, 1995 and Moeschler, 2010.

Hoche, 1995 has proposed a very interesting reading of illocutionary negation not as external or metalinguistic negation (ie, a negation of the whole speech-act), but simply as an internal negation.

According to him,
(10) It is not the case (that) I promise to come
is not equivalent to (9b).

But (9b) must be read not as the internal negation of the coming, but as the negation of promise (as in not-promise):
(9b) I don't *promise* to come.

(9b) would be — at most — the negation of a preceding speech-act, rather the negation of that very speech-act produced by uttering (9b).

5.3.1.5 *To Sum Up*

First, there is *logical negation*. Logical negation is a logical operator (for instance: '$\neg$') which is unambiguous: it always inverts the truth-value of a given sentence p.[56] Moreover, internal (logical) negation and external (logical) negation are functionally equivalent.[57]

Second, there is *natural negation*, ie negation in natural languages. As we have seen *supra*, negation in natural languages is much more complex a phenomenon than logical negation. *Firstly*, it may be pragmatically ambiguous (as Horn, 1989, Ch. 6 and Speranza and Horn, 2010 masterly argued); *secondly*, other than descriptive negation, natural negation can be realized externally or metalinguistically, and it is not the case that it always be used to act on the truth of a given sentence; *thirdly*, non-descriptive negation cannot always be semantically analyzed in terms of external or metalinguistic negation, because there are pragmatic phenomena (intonation, phonetics, etc.) involved: external or metalinguistic negation can be realized implicitly, without fixed semantic features ('it is not the case that', 'it is not true that', etc.). *Fourthly*, not all (negated) sentences in natural language are truth-functional, but they may be commands, prayers, wishes or insults.

---

[56] In many-valued logics, it assigns p's truth-value complement.
[57] Of course I am referring here to classical propositional logic. Intuitionistic logics do not accept the equivalence of internal and external negation, nor the law of double negation: $\neg\neg B \neq B$. Cf. for instance Heyting, 1930 Brouwer, 1907 (1975), Gentzen, 1934/5.

Third, natural negation, for instance via metalinguistic negation, can be used not only to invert the truth-value of a sentence, but also to reject or question its assertability.

5.3.2 Normative Negation

The last section was devoted to analyzing different kinds of negation in logic and natural languages.

In this section, I try to give an account of normative negation. I maintain that it can be differentiated from non-normative negation because normative negation cancels (at least) one of its presuppositions, whereas non-normative negation preserves the presuppositions of the negated sentence.

I have argued elsewhere that is not possible to have distinct species of negation for descriptive and normative language, but only different realizations of a single attitude.[58] I therefore propose to extend the model we have sketched in the preceding sections to normative language.

We have seen that logical negation, although unambiguous, is quite limited. Natural negation is instead a complex phe-

---

[58] In particular, see Faroldi, 2012b. There, I maintained that norm denial is a diapraxical act. Diapraxical is an act or an event that is done or obtains only through another act or event. (The concept of diapraxia has been defined and explained in Conte, 2012.) Take chess for instance. There is no specific move for a "check". A check is *another* move (let's say, a pawn advancing, for one) that counts as the act of check. The diapraxical act (the check) supervenes on the other moves, given their specific nature and the context of playing. In a similar way, I maintain that denying norms is a diapraxical act, that is, an act that supervenes another, more common, act and depends on the very nature of the negated entities (i.e. their normativity) and the context. To negate a norm, one does not need a *peculiar* kind of negation: given negation and the very nature of what is negated (normative entities), one gets that particular act we have called "norm negation". This is shown, I suppose, from a fact and a theoretical principle of intellectual economy. *First*, we have seen that even with simple acts such a internal and external negation (done by the usual means such as 'not') the results one gets are pretty different if the negated entity is normative. *Second*, it would be costly (and unjustified, I think) to admit another kind of negation specific to normative linguistic entities. Ockham's razor suggests that we do not multiply items beyond necessity.

nomenon, it does not always act on truth-values and it can be pragmatically ambiguous, divided among at least internal and external or metalinguistic negation.

Moreover, following Horn, 1989, Ch.6, Grice, Dummett and Geach, we have noticed that at least metalinguistic negation is a formally negative utterance used to object to a previous utterance on any grounds, especially its assertability.

I propose to extend this model also to normative language. To stick to a logical level, even Ross, 1968, Ch.s 31-2 noticed that while external and internal negation are functionally equivalent in propositional logic, internal negation and external negation differ quite radically in deontic logic: the fact you are under an obligation not to teach deontic logic ($O\neg\delta$), for instance, is quite different from the fact you are not under an obligation to teach deontic logic ($\neg O\delta$).

In an analogous fashion, I maintain that internal normative negation keeps the sentence binding or, so to speak, normative, only to invert its deonticity: from obligatory to forbidden, and so on.[59] (Please note that I am not forced to assign normative sentences truth-aptness, because truth does not tell us the whole story even when (non-normative) natural language is concerned.)

External or metalinguistic negation is a rejection of the assertability (*lato sensu*) of a *prima facie*, allegedly normative sentence. Specifically, though, rejection of the assertability of a normative sentence is (implicity, I maintain) not a normative judgment, but a judgment on its normativity (or bindingness, or you name it). If a speaker feels[60] a given (non-normative) proposition unassertable, he rejects it metalinguistically; if he feels a given (*prima facie* normative) proposition not binding or not nor-

---

59 I am well aware that not all normative sentences (or propositions) are in deontic terms. This was only an example to illustrate the general principle I want to bring forth.
60 Please note that 'to feel' here is used generally and has no intended reference to emotivism or expressivism.

mative, he rejects it metalinguistically or externally, canceling its presupposition of normativity.[61]

Consider the following normative sentence:

(1) Abortion is wrong

and its *prima facie* negation:

(2) Abortion is not wrong.

Both are moral (normative) judgments, and share — among others — the following presupposition:

(0) Abortion can be an object of a genuine moral judgment.

Now consider external negation of (1):[62]

(3) It is not the case that abortion is wrong.

Now, while (2) is still a normative judgment, (3) seems a judgment on the normativity of (1).

(3) cancels (1)'s and (2)'s presupposition (0), because it simply rejects that abortion can be object of (that) moral judgment.

Let's now make a comparison with internal and external negation of non-normative sentences.

Let's consider

(4) He stopped beating his wife

its internal negation:

(5) He didn't stop beating his wife

and its external negation:

(6) It's not true that he stopped beating his wife.

Neither (5) nor (6) modify the ("factive") presuppositions of (4) such as that he has a wife and that he used to beat her.

Since — as we have seen — not every instance of external or metalinguistic negation is analyzable with distinct semantic features, I assume a paraphrase in terms of external negation will account for the phenomenon, at least for our present purposes.

Considering the problem with normative negation only from the point of view of truth is quite limited, because truth does not

---

61 I am using this as a sort of a term of art, in order to make a general point without supporting a substantive theory of normativity either in terms of reasons (cf. for instance Scanlon, 2014; Skorupski, 2010), good (cf. Thomson, 2008) or oughts.

62 Of course it can also be realized metalinguistically.

tell the whole story even in non-normative negation, as I pointed out in the case of metalinguistic negation. This turns out to be a plus, because normative sentences are usually not considered truth-apt.[63]

In this section, I contrasted descriptive and normative sentences by considering negation. I showed that normative negation, usually realized externally or metalinguistically, cancels its presupposition(s) of normativity.

The next section applies this conclusion to judgments of responsibility, showing that their structure with respect to negation is akin to normative sentences.

5.3.3 Denial of Responsibility, Formalized

In the last section, I contrasted descriptive and normative sentences by considering negation. I showed that normative negation, usually realized externally or metalinguistically, cancels its presupposition(s) of normativity.

---

[63] And consequently one may maintain that (a) what you negate is not their truth; or that (b) norms cannot be negated. (a) was the position of the very first philosopher known to have written on this topic: Jerzy Sztykgold. In Sztykgold, 1936, he argued that you cannot negate the truth of norms, but only their righteousness [righteousness, giustezza = *słuszność*] in terms of non-righteousness [non-righteousness, non-giustezza = *niesłuszność*]. Righteousness and unrighteousness are, for Sztykgold, the strict *análogon* of truth and falseness. (For Sztykgold's positions, see appendix D.)
(b) was instead the position of Karel Engliš (Engliš, 1947), according to which:
(i) logical operations are possible only for "descriptive judgments" [*soudy*];
(ii) negation [*popření*] is a logical operation;
(iii) norms [*normy*] and postulates [*postuláty*], although sentential, are not "descriptive judgments";
and therefore
(iv) logical operations don't apply to norms and postulates.
In particular:
(v) norms cannot be negated.
Of course Engliš' argument shows — at most, if premise (i) holds — that negation *as* a logical operator doesn't apply to norms. But negation is not exclusively a logical operator. Negation exists outside logic, in natural language, with different characteristics.

5.3 FOURTH ARGUMENT: DENIAL OF RESPONSIBILITY

In this section, I apply these results to judgments of responsibility, in order to provide a fourth and final argument to the thesis that responsibility judgments are normative, and namely an argument "from negation". I shall show that when one denies responsibility, what happens is (a) what happens when one denies normative statements; (b) what happens is the case *only* when normative entities are concerned. This might show that judgments of responsibility are normative.[64]

Here is a more schematic version of my fourth argument:

1. When you deny a responsibility judgment, what happens (what obtains) is a cancelation of its presuppositions;

2. Canceling of presuppositions obtains only when normative judgments are negated;

3. Therefore, responsibility judgements are normative judgments.

Let's begin. I shall use negation as a test to isolate a normative entity. We have seen back in Section 5.3.2 that negation of descriptive and normative entities differs in at least one substantial point: internal and external negation work in opposite ways.

Here is an example for descriptive statements:

Internal negation (1) "John isn't tall'

vs.

External negation (2) "It's not the case that John is tall"

Now, let's take a normative statement (for simplicity's sake, I shall consider an imperative):

Internal negation $O(\neg W)$ (3): "Don't shut the window!" (that is: "Shut not the window").

---

[64] This is by no means the standard theory. When judgments of responsibility are kept separate from responsibility or concepts of responsibility, they are usually considered *non*-normative; for example, judgments of responsibility are considered *explanatory* by Björnsson and Persson, 2012, forthcoming. Anderson, 2011, Sect.3.1 considers responsibility judgments to be normative, even though he does not provide any arguments for this thesis.

Note that (3) and its "positive"
(3a) Shut the window
share a presupposition of normativity.
Now, (3a)'s external negation:

External negation ¬O(W) (4a) "I do not accept that is the case of shutting the window"/ (4b) "I do not accept the command 'Shut the window'"/ (4c) "I don't care".[65]

instead, rejects (cancels) the presupposition of normativity that both (3) and (3a) shared.

As I explained in Section 5.3.1, for descriptive sentences it is *internal* negation that might change their truth-value (from truth to false and viceversa); vice versa, for normative (imperative, in this case) sentences, it is *external* negation that changes their normativity-value, by rejecting the presupposition of normativity.

Now, let's apply this test to responsibility.

Internal negation (5) "He is not responsible for killing A, because..."

vs.

External negation (6) "It is not the case that he is responsible for killing A, because..."/

Now, if (5) stands to (1) as (6) stands to (2), we can confidently conclude that (5) and (6) are statements analogous to (1) and (2), that is, non-normative.

Quite on the contrary, if (5) stands to (3) as (6) stands to (4), we can confidently conclude that (5) and (6) are statements analogous to (3) and (4), that is, broadly normative.

It turns out, unfortunately, that you cannot really tell if (5) — internal negation of responsibility — tells us something of significance, for the very simple reason that its interpretation requires

---

[65] Of course, I am aware these are only some possible paraphrases — there might be many more. The most important fact is that internal and external negation can consistently be kept separable.

5.3 FOURTH ARGUMENT: DENIAL OF RESPONSIBILITY

an understanding of responsibility. If you think responsibility is an objective state-of-affairs, that can be somehow empirically ascertained, then you would interpret (5) as a descriptive statement, whose truth-value is to be checked against the world; and vice versa.

Therefore, let's turn to (6) to seek some clarification of the matter.

My hypothesis is that a statement such as (5) stands for a justification; while (6) stands for an excuse. I take advantage of the paradigm excuse *vs.* justification developed in Austin, 1956.

With a justification, I maintain, we remain in the domain of the normative: we accept A, and even add some *reasons* for it. The presupposition of normativity is kept.

Quite on the contrary, an excuse, in a way, suspends what was going on; it makes "normativity freeze" because it refers to conditions other than the very act A, conditions that (by definition) rule out responsibility (duress, infancy, mental incapacity, maybe psychopathy for moral responsibility). The presupposition of normativity is canceled.

In the words of Austin:

> [i]n the one defence [= justification], briefly, we accept responsibility but deny that it was bad: in the other [= excuse], we admit that it was bad but don't accept full, or even any, responsibility (Austin, 1956).

> it is not quite fair or correct to say baldly "X did A". We may say it isn't fair just to say X did it; perhaps he was under somebody's influence, or was nudged. Or, it isn't fair to say baldly he *did* A; it may have been partly accidental, or an unintentional slip. Or, it isn't fair to say he did simply *A* – he was really doing something quite different and A was only incidental, or he was looking at the whole thing quite differently (Austin, 1956, p.2).

I am going to illustrate the difference between justification and excuses. As usual, I ask the reader to imagine two fictional criminal cases (both involve a death), and to abstract from particular legal systems in order to focus on the general point.

In the first, let's call it WIFE, a man comes back home and sees an intruder trying to rape or kill his wife. By chance, there is the intruder's loaded gun at hand. The man picks it up, aims and finally shoots the intruder down — killing him. In court, he admits the murder and puts forward his reasons. His lawyer says: "Look, *he is* not *responsible* for the killing, because that was self-defense: he was trying to defend and save his own wife." This is a *justification*: you admit your deed (there are all the relevant required elements: *actus reus*, *mens rea*, volition, intention, knowledge and so on to make that killing a murder) but you have a (good) reason for your action.

In the second, let's call it MAD, a mentally-ill man escapes from a psychiatric hospital, manages to get a gun, and shoots down a random passer-by. His lawyer says: "Look, he is *not* responsible for the killing, because *it is* not *the case he is* (= *can be*) *responsible at all*: he is mad (under duress, in infancy...)." This is an *excuse*: you may admit the deed, but it was done without the relevant required conditions: without *mens rea*, for instance, or without those capacities required for a death or a killing to be a murder.

To sum up, with a justification you deny your responsibility for that deed *qua* a particular action (but you admit, nonetheless, that you are under the domain of responsibility, that you can be responsible); with an excuse you deny your responsibility tout court, you deny that you are under the very domain of responsibility.

The lawyer's sentence in WIFE: "*he is* not *responsible* for the killing" is comparable to (3): "Don't shut the window" and (5): "He was not responsible", inasmuch as they are internal negations.

On the contrary, the lawyer's sentence in MAD: "*it is* not *the case he is* (= *can be*) *responsible at all*" seems to me analogous to (4): "It is not the case you order me to shut the window" and (6): "It is not the case that he is responsible for A, because..."

As (3) conserved the imperative nature of the sentence, so WIFE conserved the domain of responsibility. As (4) instead went outside the domain of the imperative, to make a non-imperative claim, in the same way MAD appealed to a condition — in a way a non-normative, even factual condition — to be excluded from the domain of responsibility.

This linguistic evidence is consistent with the conceptual arguments I put forward earlier in this section: while justifications aren't at all denial of responsibility because they presuppose responsibility, excuses are in fact denial of responsibility, because they reject it.

With justifications and excuses, negation of responsibility coincides both with a linguistic act (denial) and a mental state (rejection).

We suggested that

- (i) when we deny responsibility, we have (at least) two cases: internal negation (which stands for a justification) and external negation (standing for an excuse). Then, we have seen that

- (ii) internal negations of responsibility do not exit the domain of responsibility (they presuppose responsibility); whereas external negations do (they reject the presupposition of responsibility). But this was exactly what happened with normative sentences (as I showed in Section 5.3.2): internal negation keeps the sentence normative (it keeps the presupposition of normativity), whereas external negation rejects it (it cancels the presupposition of normativity).

If we suppose that this kind of negation is at work only with non-descriptive (and namely, normative statements), we can therefore conclude that

- (iii) since judgments denying responsibility are structurally akin to normative sentences, responsibility judgments are akin to normative sentences.

5.3.3.1 Caveats & Assumptions

Now, some caveats. I have limited my discussion to the word (and the concept) of responsibility in the proper, fuller sense. I am very aware that there may be pragmatic ways to express a responsibility judgment without mentioning the word 'responsibility' or any related. I am also aware that we may get indicative (or descriptive) sentences (to express/ascribe responsibility).

Last but not least, my argument makes the following assumption: there are only two kinds of language relevant to our investigation here: descriptive and normative language. This may not be the case: there are several other language domains I am not considering: prayers, exclamations, insults, whose "status" with regard to negation is unclear. Therefore, it might be the case that the different ways negation works (in descriptive and normative domains) is not exclusive: negation might work in prayers as in normativity, and the second premise of my argument would be factually undermined. Assuming the *prima facie* evidence I discussed as conclusive might be too strong, and other interpretations are certainly possible depending on substantive theories of normativity, modality, and responsibility. But even if in general this argument does not prove to be conceptually unassailable, I think it is still very telling.

5.3.3.2 Objections

There are *two* apparently possible objections to my argument: *first*, I have begged the question in the definition of responsibility judgments; *second*, all I have shown is that external negation inverts the value of sentences if they are not descriptive, but this tells nothing about the exact nature of those sentences; *third*, these features of negation may be shared by other kinds of modality, so there is not special about normativity.

To the *first* objection, I put forward a twofold reply: *first*, there is no shared consensus either on what responsibility is or on what responsibility judgments are: a degree of arbitrariness is needed anyway; *second*, there is no conceptual reason precluding my analysis to be extended further, given the right premises.

To the *second* objection, I reply that I have at least shown that responsibility judgments are not descriptive; nonetheless I believe a linguistic test such as mine cannot exhaust the richness of human practices – in other words, normativity is not a sheer linguistic notion.

To the *third* objection, I reply that, examples with "oughts" notwithstanding, it is not clear whether normativity is a modality or not (it may be a property, for one). Moreover, other modalities may be normative as well (recently Skorupski, 2010 so argued for necessity, the *a priori*, and other modalities), and thus these features of negation shouldn't come as a surprise.

This last consideration leads me to the next section, where I recap my arguments and point to future directions of research.

5.4 THE RELEVANCE OF CONTEXT: PRAGMATICS AND NORMATIVITY

In this chapter, I analyzed ascriptions as judgments of responsibility. What stands out in my analysis is (i) the relevance of context; (ii) the normative nature of ascriptions as judgments of responsibility.

But they are interrelated.

In case (i) (Section 5.2), ascriptions of responsibility are considered as *acts* (*sub specie actus*). The normative nature of ascriptions of responsibility as acts emerges from the context, in the continuous and multidimensional interplay between facts, perceptions, interpretation and policy.

In case (ii) (Section 5.3.2), ascriptions of responsibility are considered as *sentences* (*sub specie dicti*). The normative nature of ascriptions of responsibility as acts emerges from their negation. But we can grasp that their negation is a negation of normative entities because it is realized metalinguistically, that is, at the pragmatic level, where context rules.

Both normativity and responsibility transcend the boundaries of our language.

6 | THE NORMATIVITY OF CONTEXT

"No olvidemos el Goofus Bird, pájaro que construye el nido al revés y vuela para atrás, porque no le importa adónde va, sino dónde estuvo."
Jorge Luis Borges

In this work (*The Normative Structure of Responsibility*), I have argued for *two* theses: *first*, that responsibility is normative; *second*, that responsibility should be normative.

I tried to show that we can reach a better understanding of responsibility through pragmatics — both through an analysis of pragmatics and a pragmatic analysis, that is, paying attention to context (utterances, speakers, situations) and to contextual considerations (policies, normative systems).

Recall I have distinguished between *two* senses of normativity: axiological and nomophoric. I have also distinguished responsibility in *praxical* responsibility (ie responsibility for human actions) and *non-praxical* responsibility (ie responsibility not for human actions).

If responsibility is praxical, then responsibility is *normative* in the nomophoric sense: responsibility for actions (a) is attributed because of rules (explicit or implicit, legal, moral, reasons-derived or otherwise); and, moreover, (b) the concept of action is not descriptive.[1]

If responsibility is non-praxical, then responsibility is *normative* in the axiological sense: responsibility for things other than actions depends on standards of evaluation and presupposes a system of (moral) values, as the case of causation shows. Although I did not consider explicitly the reasons approach to normativity, it shouldn't pose problems to my arguments. If reasons

---

[1] I have not given evidence for this claim in my work, but see at least Hart, 1948, Feinberg, 1965, 1970, Wilson and Shpall, 2012. For a partially contrary view, see Geach, 1960.

theorists are right about the basicness of reasons, then there are reductions (or non-reductive analyses, maybe) of nomophoric and axiological concepts to reasons, and my point should generalize.

I do not know yet whether these conclusions may shed some light on different phenomena, such as the difference between morals and the law, or whether they admit a modular approach, that is, they can serve well and can be integrated with different normative theories (cf. Vargas, 2013, p. 185).

My dichotomy may not complete and responsibility may not be captured completely by it, but I hope to have shown (or started to show) that conceptual analysis coupled with pragmatics and attentions to contexts may reveal more, not only on responsibility but on normativity itself. But what normativity is I am still asking:

> *V'è sempre, nel piú profondo del nostro io, una risposta che ci assilla, e questa risposta è la domanda stessa.*
>
> Daniel-Robs, *Nocturnes*, 1956.[2]

---

[2] Daniel-Robs is the nom-de-plume of Henri Petiot [Épinal, 1901 — Chambéry, 1965]. The original work is Daniel-Rops, 1956. The Italian translation by Franca de Angelis is in Daniel-Rops, 1958.

Appendices

Appendix A: Anselm's "Debēre" (from Lambeth's Fragments)

Appendix B: Rudziński's *"Z logiki norm"*: a Fragment

Appendix C: Sorainen's *"Der Modus und die Logik"*: a Fragment

Appendix D: Sztykgold's *"Negacja normy"*

I include here four (partial) works relevant to chapter §5. These works are hard to find or not available in English.

A | ANSELM'S "DEBĒRE"

St. Anselm of Canterbury [Aosta, 1033 or 1034 – Canterbury, 1109] in what are now known as *Lambeth's Fragments*, dealt with internal and external negation of deontic operators. I shall quote a brief passage from Schmitt, 1936, p. 36. The English translation from Latin is mine.

[...] *dicimus nos* 'non debēre peccare' *pro* 'debēre non peccare'. *Non enim omnis, qui facit, quod non debet, peccat.* [...] *Sicut dicimus* 'non facere esse' *pro* 'facere non esse': *ita dicimus* 'non debēre facere' *pro* 'debēre non facere'; *et ideo, ubi est* 'debēre non peccare', *dicitur pro eo* 'non debēre peccare'. *Quod in tantum obtinuit usus, ut non aliud intelligatur, quam* 'debēre non peccare'.

We say *'non debēre peccare'* for *'debēre non peccare'*. Indeed, not everyone who does what he ought not [*qui facit quod non debet*], sins. [...]

As we say *'non facere esse'* for *'facere non esse'*, likewise we say *'non debēre facere'* for *'debēre non facere'*; and, in a similar fashion, for *'debēre non peccare'* we say *'non debēre peccare'*.

In our use, when we say *'non debēre peccare'* we mean *'debēre non peccare'*.

B | RUDZIŃSKI'S "Z LOGIKI NORM": A FRAGMENT

Aleksander Witold Rudziński, born Witold Steinberg [Kraków, 4.3. 1900 — New York, 1989], was a Polish scholar and diplomat. He earned his PhD in philosophy and law at the Jagellonian University and taught philosophy of law there and in Łódź, before emigrating to the US and becoming a professor at Columbia University.[1]

Some of his personal papers and pictures are collected in the "The Aleksander and Anna Rudziński Collection", The New York Public Library, New York.

Here I report and translate some excerpts from his Rudziński, 1947, p. 9. The translation from Polish is mine, although due thanks go to Amedeo Giovanni Conte and Katarzyna Nowicka, and to Edoardo Fittipaldi for bringing this work to my attention.

PRAWDA I FAŁSZ NA TERENIE NORMATYWNYM

Czy obowiązywanie *lub nieobowiązywanie normy jest analogiczną cechą do* prawdy *lub fałszu sądów?*

Musiałoby być wówczas relacją.

I tak jest istotnie.

1. *Prawda jest, mówiąc całkiem z grubsza, relacją sądu do rzeczywistości (faktów), a*

2. *obowiązywanie [jest] relacją normy do osób (adresatów).*

---
[1] For more biographical information, see his obituary on *The New York Times*: Pace, 1989.

TRUTH AND FALSENESS AT THE NORMA-
TIVE LEVEL

Is *validity* [*obowiązywanie*] (or, respectively, invalidity [*nieobowiązywanie*]) of a norm [*norma*] the analogon [*analogiczna cecha*] of the *truth* [*prawda*] (or, respectively, falseness [*fałsz*]) of judgments [*sąd* = judgment]?

If so, there would be a relation [*relacja*] between *validity* and *truth* (or, respectively, between invalidity and falseness).

And that is the case.

1. Truth [*prawda*] is a relation [*relacja*] of the judgment [*sąd*] to the reality (of facts) [*rzeczywistość (faktów)*].

2. Validity [*obowiązywanie*] is a relation of a norm [*norma*] to persons [person = *osoba*], to addressees [addressee = *adresat*].

C | SORAINEN'S "DER MODUS UND DIE LOGIK": A FRAGMENT

Kalle Sorainen, *Der Modus und die Logik* [Verbal Mood and Logic], "Theoria", 5 (1939), pp. 202–204. English translation by Federico L. G. Faroldi.[1]

1. Sorainen's Question

Eine interessante Frage ist es auch, warum gerade der modus indicativus, wie Professor Jørgensen meint, eine unabweisliche Voraussetzung falscher und wahrer Urteile ist.

An interesting question is the following: Why only the indicative mood (as Jørgensen believes) is an indispensable prerequisite [*unabweisliche Voraussetzung*] of true or false judgments [*falscher und wahrer Urteile*]?

2. Sorainen's Answer

Ein Imperativ kann auch als wahr oder falsch betrachtet werden, je nachdem derselbe in Übereinstimmung mit seinem Grundwert steht.

---

[1] The full text and translation of Sorainen, 1939 is archived at https://dl.dropboxusercontent.com/u/7646829/Sorainen39ita.pdf. A brief note on the author and his work can be found in Faroldi, 2013b.

Also an imperative can be considered true [*wahr*] (or, respectively, *un*-true, false [*falsch*]), when it is (or, respectively, it isn't) in accordance with [*Übereinstimmung*] its fundamental value [*Grundwert*].

D | SZTYKGOLD'S "NEGACJA NORMY"

Jerzy Sztykgold, *Negacja normy* [Norm Negation], "Przegląd filozoficzny", 39 (1936), pp. 492-494 (Sztykgold, 1936). Partial English translation by Federico L. G. Faroldi. Due thanks to Katarzyna Nowicka.

I.1

Normatywne teorje prawa pragną być teorjami zdań, wyrażających powinność[,] a nie być logiką formalną.

Szukają specyficznych metod i w rezultacie nie wychodzą poza te poszukiwania i definicje prawa.

Psychologiczna teorja etyki nie zajmuje się normami.

Nikt nie zebrał dotąd tez logiki formalnej mających zastosowanie do norm, nikt nie ustalił warunków równoważności norm. Psychologiści nie wiedzą nawet, czy pewnemu przeżyciu etyczemu odpowiada na ekranie naszej mowy jedno tylko sformułowanie treści tego przeżycia, czy też kilka równoważnych sobie norm.

Nie wiedzą także, czy i odwrotnie dla każdego sformułowania treści normatywnej istnieje odpowiednik w postaci odrębnego specyficznego przeżycia etycznego, czy też istnieją treści normatywne, których psychika nasza nie aktualizuje w specyficzny dla sądów etycznych sposób.

Normative theories of law wish to be theories of duty-expounding sentences [duty-expounding sentence = *zdanie wyrażające powinność*], rather than a formal logic.

Normative theories of law aim to specific methods; therefore they do not stretch these boundaries beyond it nor beyond legal definitions.

The psychological theory of ethics is not concerned with norms [norm = *norma*].

Until now, no one has tried to apply formal logic to norms, no one has tried to establish conditions of equivalence [equivalence = *równoważność*] for norms.

Psychologists do not know whether — in our language — a moral emotion [moral emotion = *przeżycie etyczne*] is correlated with only one formulation [formulation = *sformułowanie*] of its (semantic) content [(semantic) content = *treść*] or there are several equivalent norms.

They do not even know whether, vice versa, for every formulation of a normative content [normative content = *treść normatywna*] there is a relatum through a specific moral emotion, or there are normative contents that our mind does not actualize [actualize = *aktualizować*] specifically for moral judgments [moral judgment = *sąd etyczny*].

2

Zarówno normatywna, jak i psychologiczna teorja prawa zamuje się wyłącznie sądami (logicznemi wzgl. psychologicznemi), wyrażającemi prawa i obowiązki, zaś w definicjach prawa te sądy, w których stwierdzamy brak prawa lub brak obowiązku. Tezy tych teoryj są jednak prawdziwe także i w stosunku do tych ostatnich.

Both the normative theory of law and the psychological theory of law deal only with (logical or psychological) judgments [judgment = *sąd*] expounding rights [right = *prawo*] and duties [duty = *obowiązek*]; in their definition of law those theories do not take into account those judgments affirming the nonsubsistency [nonsubsistency = *brak*] of a right or, respectively, a duty.

The theses of these theories are nonetheless applicable even to negative judgments.

3

Należy ustalić, które tezy logistyki, tej skrystalizowanej już nauki o wyrażeniach, mają zastosowanie do zdań, wyrażających (i) uprawnienia i (ii) obowiązki, (iii) brak praw i (iv) brak obowiązków.

One must determine which theses of formal logic, as a crystallized science about linguistic expressions [linguistic expression = *wyrażenie*], can be applied to sentences expressing:

(i) rights [*uprawnienie* = right, entitlement],

(ii) duties [*obowiązek* = duty],

(iii) non-existence of rights [*brak praw*],

(iv) non-existence of duties [*brak obowiązków*].

II.1

Do norm mają zastosowanie kryterja słuszność i niesłuszność, odpowiadające ściśle kryterjom prawdy i fałszu.
  Wszystkie tezy rachunku zdań mają zatem zastosowanie także i do norm. [...]

Criteria of rightness [rightness = *słuszność*] and non-rightness [non-rightness = *niesłuszność*] apply to norms. These two criteria stands strictly for those of truth [truth = *prawda*] and falseness [falseness = *fałsz*].

All those theses of logical calculus, therefore, apply also to norms. [...]

IV.1

Nie można stworzyć adekwatnej logistycznej "czystej teorji prawa", lecz można wypowiadać sądy logistyczne, mające znaczenie dla teorji prawa.

It is not possible to build a proper logical "pure theory of law"; however, it is possible to formulate logical judgments relevant for a theory of law.

2

Dla psychologicznej teorii etyki wynika z powyższych rozważań, że dla pewnego przeżycia etycznego istnieją przynajmniej dwie równoważne sobie projekcje — sformułowania w świecie mowy, że zatem doszukiwanie się odrębnego i specyficznego przeżycia dla każdej normy, którą sobie możemy pomyśleć, jest metodycznym błędem i nie może dać zadawalających wyników.

From what I said above, it follows a relevant consequence for a psychological theory of ethics.

For a given moral emotion, there are at *least two* equivalent projections [projection = *projekcja*] in the language-world (two equivalent linguistic formulations).

Thus, it is methodologically erroneous to look for only one specific moral emotion for every conceivable norm.

In the bibliography backreferences point to the pages where the works are cited.

BIBLIOGRAPHY

Adkins, William Arthur
    1960 *Merit and Responsibility: a Study in Greek Values*, Oxford University Press, Oxford. (Cited on p. 4.)

Adler, Melvin J.
    1980 *A Pragmatic Logic For Commands*, John Benjamins, Amsterdam. (Cited on p. 165.)

Adshead, Gwen
    1996 "Commentary on "Psychopathy, Other-Regarding Moral Beliefs, and Responsibility," *Philosophy, Psychiatry, and Psychology*, 3, 4, pp. 279–281. (Cited on p. 79.)
    2003 "Measuring Moral Identities: Psychopaths and Responsibility," *Philosophy, Psychiatry, and Psychology*, 10, 2, pp. 185–187. (Cited on p. 79.)

Alchourrón, Carlos Eduardo and Antonio A. Martino
    1990 "Logic without Truth," *Ratio Juris*, 3, pp. 46–67. (Cited on p. 166.)

Alexander, Larry
    2011 "Criminal and Moral Responsibility and the Libet Experiments," in *Conscious Will and Responsibility*, ed. by Benjamin Libet, Walter Sinnott-Armstrong, and Lynn Nadel, Oxford University Press, Oxford. (Cited on p. 82.)

Alexander, Larry, Kimberly K. Ferzan, and Stephen J. Morse
    2009 *Crime and Culpability: A Theory of Criminal Law*, Cambridge University Press, Cambridge. (Cited on p. 75.)

Anderson, Scott
    2011 "Coercion," in *The Stanford Encyclopedia of Philosophy*, ed. by Edward N. Zalta, Winter 2011. (Cited on p. 177.)

Anselm of Canterbury
    1936 "Lambeth's Fragments," in *Ein neues unvollendetes Werk des hl. Anselm von Canterbury*, ed. by Franciscus Saverius Schmitt, Aschendorff, Münster i W. (Cited on pp. 169, 191.)

Arendt, Johanna
  1987 "Collective Responsibility," in *Amor mundi*, ed. by James Bernhauer, M. Nijhoff, Dordrecht. (Cited on p. 108.)

Aristotle [Aristotélēs]
  Ethica Nicomachea. (Cited on p. 20.)

Aspinwall, L. G., T. R. Brown, and J. Tabery
  2012 "The Double-Edged Sword: Does Biomechanism Increase or Decrease Judges' Sentencing of Psychopaths?" *Science*, 337, 6096, pp. 846–849. (Cited on p. 83.)

Atlas, Jay David
  1977 "Negation, Ambiguity, and Presupposition," *Linguistics and Philosophy*, 1, 3, pp. 321–336. (Cited on p. 13.)

Austin, John Langshaw
  1956 "A Plea for Excuses: The Presidential Address," in *Proceedings of the Aristotelian Society*, 57, pp. 1–30. (Cited on pp. 20, 84, 157, 179.)
  1966 "Three Ways of Spilling Ink," *The Philosophical Review*, 75, 4, pp. 427–440. (Cited on p. 84.)

Azzoni, Giampaolo M.
  1988 *Il concetto di condizione nella tipologia delle regole*, CEDAM, Padova. (Cited on pp. vii, 18, 19.)
  2004 "Religioni aziendali," *Sociologia del diritto*, 31, 2, pp. 181–212. (Cited on p. 110.)
  2012 "Etica e comunicazione della Corporate Social Responsibility," in *Relazioni pubbliche e Corporate Communication. La gestione dei servizi specializzati*, ed. by Emanuele Invernizzi and Stefania Romenti, 2, McGraw-Hill, Milan, pp. 29–66. (Cited on p. 110.)

Bacon, Francis
  1630 *The Elements of the Common Law of England.* (Cited on p. 103.)

Balasubramanian, P.
  1984 *The Concept of Presupposition: A Study*, Radhakrishnan Institute for Advanced Study in Philosophy, University of Madras, Madras. (Cited on p. 13.)

Bayertz, Kurt
  1995 "Eine kurze Geschichte der Herkunft der Verantwortung," *Verantwortung: Prinzip oder problem*, pp. 3–71. (Cited on p. 26.)

Bazzoni, Mattia
  2012 *Moral Responsibility: the Contemporary Debate*, MA thesis, University of Pavia. (Cited on pp. 63, 144.)

Beardsley, Elizabeth Lane
    1944 "Imperative Sentences in Relation to Indicatives," *The Philosophical Review*, 53, pp. 175–185. (Cited on p. 165.)

Beaver, David I. and Bart Geurts
    2011 "Presupposition," in *The Stanford Encyclopedia of Philosophy*, ed. by Edward N. Zalta, Summer 2011. (Cited on p. 13.)

Beebee, Helen
    2013 "Hume's Two Definitions: The Procedural Interpretation," *Hume Studies*, 37, 2, pp. 243–274. (Cited on pp. vii, 127.)

Beebee, Helen, Christopher Hitchcock, and Peter Menzies
    2009 *The Oxford Handbook of Causation*, Oxford University Press, Oxford. (Cited on pp. 103, 234, 238.)

Beekes, Robert S. P.
    2009 *Etymological Dictionary of Greek*, Brill, Leiden. (Cited on pp. 3, 4.)

Benjamin, Martin
    1976 "Can Moral Responsibility Be Collective and Nondistributive?" *Social Theory and Practice*, 4, 1, pp. 93–106. (Cited on p. 108.)
    1998 "Why Blame the Organization? A Pragmatic Analysis of Collective Moral Responsibility," *Teaching Philosophy*, 21, 2, pp. 201–204. (Cited on p. 108.)

Bentham, Jeremy
    1996 *An Introduction to the Principles of Morals and Legislation (Collected Works of Jeremy Bentham)*, Clarendon Press, Oxford. (Cited on p. 121.)

Benveniste, Émile
    1969 *Le Vocabulaire des institutions indo-européennes*, Éditions de Minuit, Paris. (Cited on p. 3.)

Bergström, Lars
    1962 *Imperatives and Ethics: A Study of the Logic of Imperatives and of the Relation Between Imperatives and Moral Judgments*, Stockholm University, Stockholm. (Cited on pp. 165, 166.)

Bhat, P. R.
    1983 "Hare on Imperative Logic and Inference," *Indian Philosophical Quarterly*, 10, pp. 449–463. (Cited on p. 164.)

Björnsson, Gunnar and Karl Persson
    2012 "The Explanatory Component of Moral Responsibility," *Noûs*, 46, 2, pp. 326–354. (Cited on pp. 2, 77, 177.)

Björnsson, Gunnar and Karl Persson
- forthcoming "A Unified Empirical Account of Responsibility Judgments," *Philosophy and Phenomenological Research*. (Cited on pp. 2, 177.)

Blackburn, Simon
- 1984 *Spreading the Word*, Clarendon Press, Oxford. (Cited on p. 166.)
- 1998 *Ruling Passions*, Oxford University Press, Oxford. (Cited on pp. vii, 166.)

Bobbio, Norberto
- 1958 *Teoria della norma giuridica*, Giappichelli, Torino. (Cited on p. 166.)

Bobzien, Susanne
- 2006 "Moral Responsibility and Moral Development in Epicurus," in *The Virtuous Life in Greek Ethics*, Cambridge University Press, Cambridge. (Cited on p. 108.)

Bohnert, Herbert Gaylord
- 1945 "The Semiotic Status of Commands," *Philosophy of Science*, 12, pp. 302–315. (Cited on p. 165.)

Bok, Hilary
- 1998 *Freedom and Responsibility*, Princeton University Press, Princeton. (Cited on p. 77.)
- 2002 "Wallace's Normative Approach to Moral Responsibility," *Philosophy and Phenomenological Research*, 64, 3, pp. 682–686. (Cited on p. 77.)

Borchardt, Edward
- 1979 "The Semantics of Imperatives," *Logique et Analyse*, 22, pp. 191–205. (Cited on p. 166.)

Borges, Jorge Luis
- 1989 *Obras Completas*, Emecé editores, Buenos Aires. (Cited on pp. 41, 141, 185.)

Braham, Matthew and Martin van Hees
- 2012 "An Anatomy of Moral Responsibility," *Mind*, 121, 483, pp. 601–634. (Cited on pp. 77, 108.)

Braude, Stephen E.
- 1996 "Multiple Personality Disorder and Moral Responsibility," *Philosophy, Psychiatry, and Psychology*, 3, 1, pp. 37–54. (Cited on p. 79.)

Broad, Charlie Dunbar
- 1950 "Imperatives, Categorical & Hypothetical," *The Philosopher*, 2, pp. 62–75. (Cited on p. 165.)

Brouwer, Luitzen Egbertus Jan

1907 (1975) "On the Foundations of Mathematics," in *Collected Works*, 1, North-Holland, pp. 11–101. (Cited on p. 172.)

Brown, Vivienne

2006 "Choice, Moral Responsibility and Alternative Possibilities," *Ethical Theory and Moral Practice*, 9, 3, pp. 265–288. (Cited on p. 77.)

Brückner, Alexander

1957 *Słownik etymologiczny języka polskiego*, Wiedza Powszechna, Warszawa. (Cited on p. 168.)

Bruckner, Donald W.

2007 "Rational Responsibility for Preferences and Moral Responsibility for Character Traits," *Journal of Philosophical Research*, 32, pp. 191–209. (Cited on p. 77.)

Burns, J. M. and R. H. Swerdlow

2003 "Right Orbitogrontal Tumor with Pedophilia Symptom and Constructional Apraxia Sign," *Archives of Neurology*, 60, pp. 437–440. (Cited on p. 94.)

Burrington, Dale E.

1999 "Blameworthiness," *Journal of Philosophical Research*, 24, pp. 505–527. (Cited on p. 77.)

Byrd, Jeremy

2007 "Moral Responsibility and Omissions," *Philosophical Quarterly*, 57, 226, pp. 56–67. (Cited on p. 77.)

2010 "Agnosticism About Moral Responsibility," *Canadian Journal of Philosophy*, 40, 3, pp. 411–432. (Cited on p. 77.)

Callender, John S.

2010 *Free Will and Responsibility. A Guide for Practitioners*, Oxford University Press, Oxford. (Cited on p. 79.)

Campbell, Joseph Keim

2008 "New Essays on the Metaphysics of Moral Responsibility," *Journal of Ethics*, 12, 3/4, pp. 193–201. (Cited on p. 77.)

Carcaterra, Gaetano

1974 *Le norme costitutive*, Giuffrè, Milan. (Cited on p. 18.)

Carston, Robyn

1998 "Negation, 'Presupposition' and the Semantics/Pragmatics Distinction," *Journal of Linguistics*, 34, pp. 309–350. (Cited on p. 13.)

Caruso, Gregg

forthcoming *Exploring the Illusion of Free Will and Moral Responsibility*, Lexington Books, Lanham (Maryland). (Cited on pp. 78, 79, 108.)

Cashmore, A.R.

2010 "The Lucretian Swerve: The Biological Basis of Human Behavior and the Criminal Justice System," *Proceedings of the National Academy of Sciences*, 107, 10, pp. 4499–4504. (Cited on p. 42.)

Castañeda, Héctor-Neri

1960a "Imperative Reasonings," *Philosophy and Phenomenological Research*, 21, pp. 21–49. (Cited on pp. 164, 165.)

1960b "Outline of a Theory on the General Logical Structure of the Language of Action," *Theoria*, 26, pp. 151–182. (Cited on p. 165.)

1963 "Imperatives, Decisions, and "Oughts": A Logico-Metaphysical Investigation," in *Morality and the Language of Conduct*, ed. by Héctor-Neri Castañeda and G. Nakhnikian, Wayne State University Press, Detroit, pp. 219–299. (Cited on pp. 164, 165.)

1974 *The Structure of Morality*, Charles C. Thomas, Springfield, IL. (Cited on p. 165.)

1975 *Thinking and Doing: The Philosophical Foundations of Institutions*, Reidel, Dordrecht. (Cited on p. 165.)

Chan, David K.

2000 "Intention and Responsibility in Double Effect Cases," *Ethical Theory and Moral Practice*, 3, 4, pp. 405–434. (Cited on p. 78.)

Charlow, Nate

2014 "The Problem with the Frege–Geach Problem," *Philosophical Studies*, 167, 3, pp. 635–665. (Cited on p. 166.)

Ciocchetti, Christopher

2003a "Some Thoughts on Diverse Psychopathic Offenders and Legal Responsibility," *Philosophy, Psychiatry, and Psychology*, 10, 2, pp. 195–198. (Cited on p. 79.)

2003b "The Responsibility of the Psychopathic Offender," *Philosophy, Psychiatry, and Psychology*, 10, 2, pp. 175–183. (Cited on p. 79.)

Ciurria, Michelle

2012 "Situationism, Moral Responsibility and Blame," *Philosophia*, pp. 1–12. (Cited on p. 78.)

Clarke, Randolph

1997 "Responsibility and the Moral Sentiments," *Philosophy and Phenomenological Research*, 57, 1, pp. 230–232. (Cited on p. 78.)

Coates, D. Justin and Philip Swenson

forthcoming "Reasons-Responsiveness and Degrees of Responsibility," *Philosophical Studies*. (Cited on p. 78.)

Cobb, John B. Jr

1959 "The Philosophic Grounds of Moral Responsibility: A Comment on Matson and Niebuhr," *Journal of Philosophy*, 56, 14, pp. 619–621. (Cited on p. 78.)

Cohen, L. Jonathan

1964 "Do Illocutionary Forces Exist?" *The Philosophical Quarterly*, 14, pp. 118–137. (Cited on p. 171.)

Colloca, Stefano

2013 (ed. by)*The Truth of Value/The Value of Truth*, LED, Milano. (Cited on pp. vii, 91.)

Compton, E.S.

2010 "Not guilty by reason of neuroimaging: the need for cautionary jury instructions for neuroscience evidence in criminal trials," *Vand. J. Ent. & Tech. L.*, 12, pp. 333–947. (Cited on p. 83.)

Conte, Amedeo Giovanni

1977 "Aspekte der Semantik der deontischen Sprache," in *Deontische Logik und Semantik*, ed. by Amedeo Giovanni Conte, Risto Hilpinen, and Georg Henrik von Wright, Athenaion, Wiesbaden, pp. 59–73. (Cited on p. 154.)

1995a "Minima deontica," in *Filosofia del linguaggio normativo II, 1982-1994*. Giappichelli, Torino, pp. 355–407. (Cited on pp. 150, 166.)

1995b "Performativo *vs*. normativo," in *Filosofia del linguaggio normativo II*, Giappichelli, Turin, pp. 589–607. (Cited on pp. 150–152.)

1995c "Regola costitutiva in Wittgenstein," in *Filosofia del linguaggio normativo I*, 2nd ed., Giappichelli, Turin. (Cited on pp. 17, 87.)

2001a "Il linguaggio della colpa e del peccato: colpa peccato verità," in *Filosofia del linguaggio normativo III*, Giappichelli, Turin, pp. 987–1000. (Cited on pp. 57, 154.)

2001b "Il linguaggio dell'atto," in *Filosofia del linguaggio normativo III*, Giappichelli, Turin, pp. 947–986. (Cited on pp. 16, 150, 155, 156.)

2007a "Due specie di ambiguità nel linguaggio normativo. Ambiguità semantica *vs*. ambivalenza pragmatica," in *Ricerche di filosofia del diritto*, ed. by Lorenzo Passerini Glazel, Giappichelli, Turin. (Cited on p. 161.)

2007b "Norma: cinque referenti," in *Ricerche di filosofia del diritto*, ed. by Lorenzo Passerini Glazel, Giappichelli, Turin, pp. 27–35. (Cited on pp. 15, 30.)

Conte, Amedeo Giovanni

2007c "Regola eidetico-costitutiva *vs.* regola anankastico-costitutiva," in *Ricerche di filosofia del diritto*, ed. by Lorenzo Passerini Glazel, Giappichelli, Turin, pp. 48–68. (Cited on pp. 17, 88.)

2008 "Normativismo," in *Enciclopedia filosofica Bompiani*, ed. by Virgilio Melchiorre, Bompiani, Milano. (Cited on pp. 15, 30.)

2011 *Sociologia filosofica del diritto*, Giappichelli, Torino. (Cited on p. 91.)

2012 "Diapraxía," in *Ontologia del normativo. Studi per Gaetano Carcaterra*, ed. by Daniele M. Cananzi and Roberto Righi, I, Giuffrè, Milan, pp. 419–424. (Cited on p. 173.)

2013a *Adelaster. Il nome del vero*, forthcoming. (Cited on p. viii.)

2013b "Benedetto da Norcia. Impossibilia," *Rivista Internazionale di Filosofia del Diritto*, 90. (Cited on pp. 15, 30.)

Copp, David

1997 "Defending the Principle of Alternate Possibilities: Blameworthiness and Moral Responsibility," *Noûs*, 31, 4, pp. 441–456. (Cited on p. 78.)

Corlett, J. Angelo

2001 "Collective Moral Responsibility," *Journal of Social Philosophy*, 32, 4, pp. 573–584. (Cited on p. 108.)

Daniel-Rops, [Henri Petiot]

1956 *Nocturnes*, Grasset, Paris. (Cited on p. 186.)

1958 *Notturni*, Centro Internazionale del Libro, Firenze. (Cited on p. 186.)

Das, Ramon

2002 "Suffering and Moral Responsibility," *Australasian Journal of Philosophy*, 80, 2, pp. 240–241. (Cited on p. 78.)

De Brigard, Felipe, Eric Mandelbaum, and David Ripley

2009 "Responsibility and the Brain Sciences," *Ethical Theory and Moral Practice*, 12, 5. (Cited on pp. 78, 79.)

de Haan, Jacob Israël

1912 "Nieuwe Rechtstaalphilosophie," *Rechtsgeleerd Magazin*, 31, pp. 480–522. (Cited on p. 5.)

1916 *Rechtskundige significa en hare toepassing op de begrippen: 'aansprakelijk', 'verantwoordelijk' 'toerekeningsvatbaar'*, [Dissertatie]. (Cited on p. 5.)

1919 "Rechtkundige Significa," *Rechtsgeleerd Magazin*, 38, pp. 429–538. (Cited on p. 5.)

Denaro, Pietro
- 2012 "Moral Harm and Moral Responsibility: A Defence of Ascriptivism," *Ratio Juris*, 25, 2, pp. 149–179. (Cited on pp. 77, 78.)

Devlin, Patrick
- 1965 *The Enforcement of Morals*, Oxford University Press, Oxford. (Cited on p. 43.)

Devoto, Giacomo
- 1968 "La scusa e le scuse," *Corriere della Sera*, 93, 273, p. 3. (Cited on p. 156.)

Di Lucia, Paolo
- 2013a "Impossibilità nel gioco e nel diritto," ms. (Cited on pp. vii, 150.)
- 2013b "Responsabilità pragmatica," in *Davanti a Dio e davanti agli uomini*, ed. by Natascia Marchei, Daniela Milani, and Jlia Pasquali Cerioli. (Cited on pp. 5, 13, 16.)

Di Lucia, Paolo and Guglielmo Feis
- 2013 "Assuming Norms," Seminario di Sant'Alberto di Butrio. (Cited on p. 79.)

Dodig-Crnkovic, Gordana and Daniel Persson
- 2008 "Sharing Moral Responsibility with Robots: A Pragmatic Approach," in *Frontiers in Artificial Intelligence and Applications*, IOS Press, Amsterdam. (Cited on p. 78.)

Downie, R. S.
- 1964 "Social Roles And Moral Responsibility," *Philosophy*, 39, 147, pp. 29–. (Cited on p. 78.)

Dubbink, Wim and Jeffery Smith
- 2011 "A Political Account of Corporate Moral Responsibility," *Ethical Theory and Moral Practice*, 14, 2, pp. 223–246. (Cited on p. 109.)

Dubislav, Walter
- 1937 "Zur Unbegründbarkeit der Forderungssätze," *Theoria*, 3, pp. 330–342. (Cited on p. 165.)

Duff, Antony
- 2008 "Responsibility and Liability in Criminal Law," in *The Legacy of H.L.A. Hart*, ed. by M. Kramer *et al.*, Oxford University Press, Oxford. (Cited on pp. 15, 58, 91, 106.)
- 2009 *Answering for Crime*, Responsibility and Liability in the Criminal Law, Hart Publishing, Oxford. (Cited on pp. 15, 58, 92, 106.)

Dummett, Michael A. E.
- 1973 *Frege: Philosophy of Language*, Duckworth. (Cited on p. 170.)

Dworkin, Gerald
- 2011 "The Limits of the Criminal Law," in *The Oxford Handbook of Philosophy of Criminal Law*, ed. by John Deigh and David Dolinko, Oxford University Press, Oxford, pp. 3–16. (Cited on p. 75.)

Edwards, Craig
- 2009 "Changing Functions, Moral Responsibility, and Mental Illness," *Philosophy, Psychiatry, and Psychology*, 16, 1, pp. 105–107. (Cited on p. 79.)

Elliott, Carl
- 1991 "Moral Responsibility, Psychiatric Disorders and Duress," *Journal of Applied Philosophy*, 8, 1, pp. 45–56. (Cited on p. 79.)
- 1992 "Diagnosing Blame: Responsibility and the Psychopath," *Journal of Medicine and Philosophy*, 17, 2, pp. 199–214. (Cited on p. 80.)

Engliš, Karel
- 1947 "Postulát a norma nejsou soudy," *Časopis pro právní a státní vědu* XXVIII, pp. 95–113. (Cited on p. 176.)

Epstein, R.A.
- 1973 "A Theory of Strict Liability," *The Journal of Legal Studies*, 2, 1, pp. 151–204. (Cited on p. 122.)

Eshleman, Andrew
- 2009 "Moral Responsibility," in *The Stanford Encyclopedia of Philosophy*, ed. by Edward N. Zalta, Winter 2009. (Cited on p. 77.)

Espersen, Jon
- 1967 "The Logic of Imperatives," *Danish Yearbook of Philosophy*, 4, pp. 57–112. (Cited on pp. 164–166.)

Faraci, David and David Shoemaker
- 2010 "Insanity, Deep Selves, and Moral Responsibility: The Case of JoJo," *Review of Philosophy and Psychology*, 1, 3, pp. 319–332. (Cited on p. 80.)

Faroldi, Federico L. G.
- 2012a "Fallacia deontica. From "ought" to "is"," *Rivista Internazionale di Filosofia del Diritto*, 89, 3, pp. 413–418. (Cited on p. 126.)
- 2012b *Negazione di norme*, Seminario filosofico internazionale di Sant'Alberto di Butrio, Pavia. (Cited on p. 173.)
- 2013a "Hart e la responsabilità oggettiva," ms. (Cited on p. 107.)

2013b   "Verità d'imperativi in Kalle Sorainen," *Rivista Internazionale di Filosofia del Diritto*, 90, 1, pp. 93–98. (Cited on pp. 164, 195, 197.)

2014a   "Denial of Responsibility and Normative Negation," in *Deontic Modalities in Natural Language*, ed. by Fabrizio Cariani *et al.*, Springer, Heidelberg. (Cited on p. vii.)

2014b   "Responsibility Regardless of Causation," in *New Advances in Causation, Agency and Moral Responsibility*, ed. by Fabio Bacchini, Massimo Dell'Utri, and Stefano Caputo, Cambridge Scholars, Newcastle upon Tyne. (Cited on p. vii.)

Feinberg, Joel

1965   "Action and Responsibility," in *Philosophy in America*, ed. by Max Black, Allen & Unwin, London, pp. 134–160. (Cited on pp. 104, 159, 162, 185.)

1968   "Collective Responsibility," *Journal of Philosophy*, 65, pp. 674–688. (Cited on p. 108.)

1970   *Doing & Deserving: Essays in the Theory of Responsibility*, Princeton University Press, Princeton. (Cited on pp. 24, 25, 49, 53, 83, 104, 159, 185.)

1990   *Harmless Wrongdoing*, 4, Oxford University Press, USA. (Cited on pp. 49, 75, 78.)

Ferrer Beltrán, Jordi and Giovanni Battista Ratti

2012   (ed. by)*The Logic of Legal Requirements: Essays on Defeasibility*, Oxford University Press, Oxford. (Cited on p. 145.)

Ferzan, Kimberly K.

2008   "Living on the Edge: The Margins of Legal Personhood: Foreword," *Rutgers L. Rev.*, 39, pp. 237–459. (Cited on p. 75.)

Fields, Lloyd

1996   "Psychopathy, Other-Regarding Moral Beliefs, and Responsibility," *Philosophy, Psychiatry, and Psychology*, 3, 4, pp. 261–277. (Cited on p. 80.)

Fillmore, Charles J.

1969   "Verbs of Judging: an Exercise in Semantic Description," *Research on Language & Social Interaction*, 1, 1, pp. 91–117. (Cited on pp. 155, 156.)

Fingarette, Herbert

1955   "Psychoanalytic Perspectives on Moral Guilt and Responsibility: A Re-Evaluation," *Philosophy and Phenomenological Research*, 16, 1, pp. 18–36. (Cited on p. 80.)

Finlay, Stephen
- 2010 "Recent Work on Normativity," *Analysis*, 70, 2, pp. 331–346. (Cited on pp. 15, 30.)

Finnis, John
- 1991 "Intention and Side Effects," in *Liability and Responsibility: Essays in Law and Morals*, ed. by R. G. Frey and C. W. Morris, Cambridge University Press Cambridge, Cambridge. (Cited on p. 60.)

Fischer, John Martin
- 1986 *Moral Responsibility*, Cornell University Press, Ithaca. (Cited on p. 78.)
- 1999a "Recent Work on Moral Responsibility," *Ethics*, 110, 1, pp. 93–139. (Cited on p. 78.)
- 1999b "The Value of Moral Responsibility," *The Proceedings of the Twentieth World Congress of Philosophy*, 1, pp. 129–140. (Cited on p. 78.)
- 2006 *My Way: Essays on Moral Responsibility*, Oxford University Press, Ox. (Cited on pp. 78, 108.)
- 2012 *Deep Control: A Theory of Moral Responsibility*, Oxford University Press, Oxford. (Cited on p. 108.)

Fischer, John Martin and Mark Ravizza
- 1993 *Perspectives on Moral Responsibility*, Cornell University Press, Ithaca. (Cited on pp. 77, 78.)
- 1998a "Morally Responsible People Without Freedom," in *Responsibility and Control: A Theory of Moral Responsibility*, Cambridge University Press, Cambridge. (Cited on p. 78.)
- 1998b *Responsibility and Control: A Theory of Moral Responsibility*, Cambridge University Press, Cambridge. (Cited on pp. 78, 82.)

Fischer, John Martin and Neal A. Tognazzini
- 2011 "The Physiognomy of Responsibility," *Philosophy and Phenomenological Research*, 82, 2, pp. 381–417. (Cited on p. 48.)

Fischette, Charles
- 2004 "Psychopathy and Responsibility," *Virginia Law Review*, 90, pp. 1449–1469. (Cited on p. 75.)

Fisher, Mark
- 1962a "A System of Deontic-Alethic Modal Logic," *Mind*, 71, pp. 231–236. (Cited on p. 165.)
- 1962b "Strong and Weak Negation of Imperatives," *Theoria*, 28, pp. 196–200. (Cited on p. 165.)

FitzPatrick, William J.
- 2008 "Moral Responsibility and Normative Ignorance: Answering a New Skeptical Challenge," *Ethics*, 118, 4, pp. 589–613. (Cited on p. 78.)

Fletcher, Joseph F.
- 1967 *Moral Responsibility*, Westminster Press, Philadelphia. (Cited on p. 78.)

Fonnesu, Luca
- 2013 "Geneaologie della responsabilità," in *Quando siamo responsabili? Neuroscienze, etica, diritto*, ed. by Mario De Caro, Andrea Lavazza, and Giovanni Sartori, Codice, Torino. (Cited on pp. vii, 25, 149.)

Frankfurt, Henry G.
- 1969 "Alternate Possibilities and Moral Responsibility," *The Journal of Philosophy*, 66, 23, pp. 829–839. (Cited on p. 127.)

Frede, Michael
- 1980 "The Original Notion of Cause," *Doubt and Dogmatism*, pp. 217–49. (Cited on p. 5.)
- 1987 *Essays in Ancient Philosophy*, University of Minnesota Press, Minneapolis. (Cited on p. 5.)

Freeman, Martin
- 2011 (ed. by)*Law and Neuroscience. Current Legal Issues*, 13, Oxford University Press, Oxford. (Cited on p. 84.)

Frege, Gottlob [Friedrich Ludwig Gottlob]
- 1918–9 "Der Gedanke: Eine logische Untersuchung," *Beiträge zur Philosophie des Deutschen Idealismus*, I, pp. 58–77. (Cited on pp. 164, 168.)

French, Peter A.
- 1984 "The Principle of Responsive Adjustment in Corporate Moral Responsibility: The Crash on Mount Erebus," *Journal of Business Ethics*, 3, 2, pp. 101–111. (Cited on p. 109.)

Frey, Gerhard
- 1957 "Idee einer Wissenschaftslogik: Grundzüge einer Logik imperativer Sätze," *Philosophia Naturalis*, 4, pp. 434–491. (Cited on p. 165.)

Frierson, Patrick
- 2008 "Empirical Psychology, Common Sense, and Kant's Empirical Markers for Moral Responsibility," *Studies in History and Philosophy of Science Part A*, 39, 4, pp. 473–482. (Cited on p. 80.)

Gardiner, P. L.
- 1955 "On Assenting to a Moral Principle," *Proceedings of the Aristotelian Society*, 55, pp. 23–44. (Cited on p. 164.)

Gardner, John
- 2003 "The Mark of Responsibility," *Oxford Journal of Legal Studies*, 23, 2, pp. 157–171. (Cited on p. 77.)
- 2005 "Wrongs and Faults," in *Appraising Strict Liability*, ed. by A. P. Simester, Oxford University Press, Oxford, pp. 51–80. (Cited on p. 92.)
- 2008 "Hart and Feinberg on Responsibility," in *The Legacy of H.L.A. Hart*, ed. by M. Kramer *et al.*, Oxford University Press, Oxford. (Cited on p. 61.)
- 2009 "Ethics and Law," in *The Routledge Companion to Ethics*, ed. by John Skorupski, Routledge, London. (Cited on p. 77.)
- 2012 *Law as a Leap of Faith*, Oxford University Press, Oxford. (Cited on p. 56.)

Garner, Richard T.
- 1971 "Some Doubts about Illocutionary Negation," *Analysis*, 31, pp. 106–112. (Cited on p. 171.)

Garrett, Jan Edward
- 1989 "Unredistributable Corporate Moral Responsibility," *Journal of Business Ethics*, 8, 7, pp. 535–545. (Cited on p. 109.)

Gauthier, David P.
- 1963 *Practical Reasoning: The Structure and Foundations of Prudential and Moral Arguments and Their Exemplification in Discourse*, Clarendon Press, Oxford. (Cited on pp. 164, 165.)

Gazzaniga, Mark S.
- 2008 "The Law and Neuroscience," *Neuron*, 60, 3, pp. 412–415. (Cited on p. 82.)

Geach, Peter Thomas
- 1958 "Imperative and Deontic Logic," *Analysis*, 18, pp. 49–56. (Cited on p. 164.)
- 1960 "Ascriptivism," *The Philosophical Review*, 69, 2, pp. 221–225. (Cited on pp. 144, 185.)
- 1965 "Assertion," *Philosophical Review*, 74, 4, pp. 449–465. (Cited on p. 166.)

Gensler, Harry J.
- 1990 *Symbolic Logic: Classical and Advanced Systems*, Prentice-Hall, Englewood Cliffs, NJ. (Cited on p. 165.)

Gentzen, Gerhard Karl Erich
- 1934/5 "Untersuchungen über das logische Schließen," *Mathematische Zeitschrift*, 39, pp. 176–210. (Cited on p. 172.)

Gernet, Louis
- 1917 *Recherches sur le développement de la pensée juridique et morale en Grèce*, Leroux, Paris. (Cited on p. 4.)

Gibbard, Allan
- 1990 *Wise Choices, Apt Feelings*, Harvard University Press, Cambridge (MA). (Cited on p. 166.)
- 2003 *Thinking How to Live*, Harvard University Press, Cambridge, MA. (Cited on p. 166.)

Gibbons, P. C.
- 1960 "Imperatives and Indicatives," *Australasian Journal of Philosophy*, 38, pp. 107–119. (Cited on p. 166.)

Gilbert, Margaret
- 2006 "Who's to Blame? Collective Moral Responsibility and its Implications for Group Members," *Midwest Studies in Philosophy*, 30, 1, pp. 94–114. (Cited on p. 108.)

Glannon, Walter
- 2008 "Moral Responsibility and the Psychopath," *Neuroethics*, 1, 3, pp. 158–166. (Cited on p. 80.)

Glover, Jonathan
- 1970 *Responsibility*, Routledge & Kegan Paul, London. (Cited on pp. 24, 64.)

Gommer, H.
- 2010 "From the 'Is' to the 'Ought': A Biological Theory of Law," *Archiv für Rechts- und Sozialphilosophie*, pp. 449–468. (Cited on p. 83.)

Gomolińska, Anna
- 1998 "On the Logic of Acceptance and Rejection," *Studia Logica*, 60, 2, pp. 233–251. (Cited on p. 168.)

González, Elsa
- 2002 "Defining a Post-Conventional Corporate Moral Responsibility," *Journal of Business Ethics*, 39, 1-2, pp. 101–108. (Cited on p. 109.)

Graham, Keith
- 2001 "The Moral Significance of Collective Entities," *Inquiry*, 44, 1, pp. 21–41. (Cited on p. 109.)

Graham, Keith
    2006 "Imposing and Embracing Collective Responsibility: Why the Moral Difference?" *Midwest Studies in Philosophy*, 30, 1, pp. 256–268. (Cited on p. 108.)

Graham, Peter A.
    forthcoming "A Sketch of a Theory of Moral Blameworthiness," *Philosophy and Phenomenological Research*. (Cited on p. 16.)

Grant, C. K.
    1968 "Imperatives and Meaning," in *The Human Agent*, St Martin's Press, New York, pp. 181–195. (Cited on p. 165.)

Green, Leslie
    2008 "Positivism and the Inseparability of Law and Morals," *New York University Law Review*, 83, pp. 1035–1058. (Cited on pp. 56, 77.)

Green, S.P.
    2005 "Six Senses of Strict Liability: A Plea for Formalism," in *Appraising Strict Liability*, ed. by A. P. Simester, Oxford University Press, Oxford, pp. 1–21. (Cited on p. 92.)

Greene, Joshua and Jonathan Cohen
    2004 "For the Law, Neuroscience Changes Nothing and Everything," *Philos Trans R Soc Lond B Biol Sci*, 359, 1451, pp. 1775–85. (Cited on pp. 42, 82.)

Greenspan, Patricia
    1987 "Unfreedom and Responsibility," in *Responsibility, Character, and the Emotions: New Essays in Moral Psychology*, ed. by Ferdinand Schoeman, Cambridge University Press, Cambridge. (Cited on p. 80.)
    2003 "Responsible Psychopaths," *Philosophical Psychology*, 16, 3, pp. 417–429. (Cited on p. 80.)

Grenander, M. E.
    1982 "The Fourfold Way: Determinism, Moral Responsibility, and Aristotelean Causation," *Theoretical Medicine and Bioethics*, 3, 3, pp. 375–396. (Cited on p. 80.)

Grue-Sørensen, Knud
    1939 "Imperativsätze und Logik. Begegnung einer Kritik," *Theoria*, 5, pp. 195–202. (Cited on pp. 164–166.)

Haji, Ishtiyaque and Stefaan E. Cuypers
    2004 "Moral Responsibility and the Problem of Manipulation Reconsidered," *International Journal of Philosophical Studies*, 12, 4, pp. 439–464. (Cited on p. 80.)

Hall, Everett W.

- 1947 "A Categorial Analysis of Value," *Philosophy of Science*, 14, pp. 333–344. (Cited on p. 165.)
- 1952 *What Is Value? An Essay in Philosophical Analysis*, Humanities Press, New York. (Cited on p. 165.)

Hamblin, Charles L.

- 1987 *Imperatives*, Oxford: Blackwell. (Cited on pp. 164, 165.)

Hansen, Jörg

- 2001 "Sets, Sentences, and Some Logics about Imperatives," *Fundamenta Informaticæ*, 48, pp. 205–226. (Cited on p. 165.)

Hare, Richard Mervyn

- 1952 *The Language of Morals*, Clarendon Press, Oxford. (Cited on pp. 164, 171.)
- 1972 "Practical Inferences," in *Practical Inferences*, University of California Press, Berkeley, CA, pp. 59–73. (Cited on p. 165.)
- 1989 "Some Sub-Atomic Particles of Logic," *Mind*, 98, pp. 23–37. (Cited on p. 171.)

Harrison, Jonathan

- 1991 "Deontic Logic and Imperative Logic," in *Logic and Ethics*, ed. by Peter Thomas Geach, Kluwer, Dordrecht, pp. 79–129. (Cited on p. 165.)

Hart, Herbert Lionel Adolphus

- 1948 "The Ascription of Responsibility and Rights," in *Proceedings of the Aristotelian Society*, 49, pp. 171–194. (Cited on pp. 20, 41, 83, 144, 145, 162, 185.)
- 1957 "Positivism and the Separation of Law and Morals," *Harvard Law Review*, 71, 593. (Cited on p. 77.)
- 1962 *Punishment and the Elimination of Responsibility*, University of London, Athlone Press, London. (Cited on pp. 44, 51.)
- 1964 *The Morality of the Criminal Law: Two Lectures*, Magnes Press, Hebrew University, Jerusalem. (Cited on pp. 50, 51.)
- 1982 *Essays on Bentham: Studies in Jurisprudence and Political Theory*, Clarendon Press, Oxford. (Cited on p. 121.)
- 2008 *Punishment and Responsibility*, in 2nd ed., Oxford University Press, Oxford. (Cited on pp. 3, 13, 16, 27, 42, 48–50, 52–54, 75, 76, 81, 84, 91, 92, 97, 99, 104, 144, 162.)
- 2012 *The Concept of Law, with a Postscript edited by Penelope A. Bulloch and Joseph Raz, and an Introduction and Notes by Leslie Green*, 3rd ed., Clarendon Press, Oxford. (Cited on pp. 77, 89, 147.)

Hart, Herbert Lionel Adolphus and Tony Honoré
- 1959 *Causation in the Law*, Clarendon Press, Oxford. (Cited on pp. 103, 117.)

Heller, Ágnes
- 1988 *General Ethics*, Basil Blackwell, Oxford/Boston. (Cited on p. 13.)

Henry, D. P.
- 1953 "St. Anselm on the Varieties of 'Doing'," *Theoria*, 19, pp. 178–183. (Cited on p. 170.)

Heyting, Arend
- 1930 *Die formalen Regeln der intuitionistischen Logik*, Sitzungsberichte der Preussischen Akademie der Wissenschaften, Physikalisch-mathematische Klasse, pp. 42–56. (Cited on p. 172.)

Hieronymi, Pamela
- 2008 "Responsibility for Believing," *Synthese*, 161, 3, pp. 357–373. (Cited on p. 16.)

Hindriks, Frank
- 2011 "Control, Intentional Action, and Moral Responsibility," *Philosophical Psychology*, 24, 6, pp. 787–801. (Cited on p. 80.)

Ho, Hsiu-Hwang
- 1969 *Some Semantical Problems in Deontic Logic and Imperative Logic*, PhD thesis, Michigan State University. (Cited on p. 166.)

Hoche, Hans-Ulrich
- 1995 "Do Illocutionary, or Neustic, Negations Exist?" *Erkenntnis*, 43, pp. 127–136. (Cited on p. 171.)

Hofstadter, Albert and John C. McKinsey
- 1939 "On the Logic of Imperatives," *Philosophy of Science*, 6, pp. 446–457. (Cited on pp. 164, 165.)

Hom, Christopher and Jeremy Schwartz
- 2013 "Unity and the Frege–Geach Problem," *Philosophical Studies*, 163, 1, pp. 15–24. (Cited on p. 166.)

Honoré, Tony
- 1999a *Responsibility and Fault*, Hart Publishing, Oxford. (Cited on p. 92.)
- 1999b "Responsibility and Luck — The Moral Basis of Strict Liability," in *Responsibility and Fault*, Hart Publishing, Oxford, chap. 2, pp. 14–40. (Cited on p. 98.)
- 2010 "Causation in the Law," in *The Stanford Encyclopedia of Philosophy*, ed. by Edward N. Zalta, Winter 2010. (Cited on pp. 104, 105.)

Horn, Laurence R.
- 1985 "Metalinguistic Negation and Pragmatic Ambiguity," *Language*, 61, 1, pp. 121–174. (Cited on p. 170.)
- 1989 *A Natural History of Negation*, University of Chicago Press, Chicago (Illinois). (Cited on pp. 167–170, 172, 174.)

Hume, David
- 1902 *An Enquiry Concerning Human Understanding (1748)*, Clarendon Press, Oxford. (Cited on pp. 24, 127.)
- 2011 *The Essential Philosophical Works*, Wordsworth, Ware (UK). (Cited on p. 24.)

Husak, D.N.
- 1995 "Varieties of Strict Liability," *Cananadian Journal of Law & Jurisprudence*, 8, pp. 189–225. (Cited on p. 92.)

Incurvati, Luca and Peter Smith
- 2010 "Rejection and Valuations," *Analysis*, 70, 1, pp. 3–10. (Cited on p. 168.)

Ingarden, Roman
- 1970 *Über die Verantwortung. Ihre ontischen Fundamente*, Reclam, Stuttgart. (Cited on pp. 21, 26.)
- 1987 *Książeczka o człowieku*, Wydawnictwo Literackie Kraków, Kraków. (Cited on p. 21.)

Irwin, Terence H.
- 1980 "Reason and Responsibility in Aristotle," in *Essays on Aristotle's Ethics*, University of California Press, Berkeley, pp. 117–155. (Cited on p. 5.)
- 2007–11 *The Development of Ethics*, Oxford University Press, Oxford. (Cited on p. 5.)

Isaacs, Tracy Lynn
- 2006 "Collective Moral Responsibility and Collective Intention," *Midwest Studies in Philosophy*, 30, 1, pp. 59–73. (Cited on p. 108.)
- 2011 *Moral Responsibility in Collective Contexts*, Oxford University Press, Oxford. (Cited on p. 108.)

Jackson, Bernard S.
- 1975 "Liability for Mere Intention in Jewish Law," in *Essays in Jewish and Comparative Legal History*, Brill, Leiden, pp. 202–340. (Cited on p. 16.)

Johanson, Arnold A.

    1988 "Imperative Logic as Based on a Galois Connection," *Theoria*, 54, pp. 1–24. (Cited on p. 165.)

    1996 "The Logic of Normative Systems," in *Deontic Logic, Agency and Normative Systems: ΔEON '96: Third international workshop on deontic logic in computer science, Sesimbra, Portugal*, ed. by M. A. Brown and J. Carmo, Springer, New York, pp. 123–133. (Cited on p. 165.)

    2000 *Principia Practica: The Logic of Practice*, Lanham, MD: University Press of America. (Cited on p. 165.)

Jørgensen, Jørgen

    1938a "Imperativer og Logik," *Theoria*, 4. (Cited on pp. 164–166, 195.)

    1938b "Imperatives and Logic," *Erkenntnis*, 7, pp. 288–296. (Cited on pp. 164–166.)

    1969 "Imperatives and Logic," *Danish Yearbook of Philosophy*, 6, pp. 9–17. (Cited on p. 164.)

Kalinowski, Jerzy *vel* Georges

    1953 "Teoria zdań normatywnych," *Studia logica*, 1, pp. 113–46. (Cited on p. 164.)

    1964 "Essai sur le caractère ontique du droit," *Revue de l'Université d'Ottawa*, 34, pp. 81–99. (Cited on p. 166.)

    1967 *Le problème de la vérité en morale et en droit*, Vitte, Lyon. (Cited on p. 166.)

Kane, Robert

    2011 *The Oxford Handbook Of Free Will*, Oxford University Press, Oxford. (Cited on p. 82.)

Kanger, Stig

    1971 "New Foundations for Ethical Theory," in *Deontic Logic: Introductory and Systematic Readings*, ed. by Risto Hilpinen, Reidel, Dordrecht, pp. 36–58. (Cited on p. 166.)

Kant, Immanuel

    1797 "Die Metaphysik der Sitten," in *Kants Werke [1907–1914]*, 6, de Gruyter, Berlin, pp. 203–492. (Cited on pp. 27, 28, 141.)

Karttunen, Lauri

    1976 "Discourse Referents," in *Syntax and Semantics Vol. 7*, ed. by James D McCawley, Academic Press, pp. 363–386. (Cited on p. 13.)

    1977 "Syntax and Semantics of Questions," *Linguistics and Philosophy*, 1, 1, pp. 3–44. (Cited on p. 13.)

Karttunen, Lauri and Stanley Peters
- 1979 "Conventional Implicature," in *Syntax and Semantics 11: Presupposition*, ed. by C.-K. Oh and D. Dinneen, Academic Press, New York, pp. 1–56. (Cited on p. 169.)

Kaufmann, Magdalena
- 2012 *Interpreting Imperatives*, Springer, Dordrecht. (Cited on pp. 164–166.)

Kelsen, Hans
- 1939 "The Emergence of the Causal Law," *Erkenntnis 8*, 8, pp. 69–130. (Cited on pp. 112, 114.)
- 1943 *Society and Nature: A Sociological Inquiry*, University of Chicago Press, Chicago, Illinois. (Cited on pp. 59, 112, 114.)
- 1949/2006 *General Theory of Law and State*, Transaction Publishers, New Brunswick/London. (Cited on p. 147.)
- 1960 *Reine Rechtslehre*, 2nd ed., Vienna: Franz Deuticke. (Cited on pp. 103, 112–116, 146–149, 166.)
- 1967 *Pure Theory of Law*, trans. by Max Knight, University of California Press, Berkeley. (Cited on pp. 112, 146–149.)
- 1973a "Causality and Accounting," in *Essays in Legal and Moral Philosophy*, ed. by Ota Weinberger, Reidel, Dordrecht, pp. 154–64. (Cited on pp. 112, 114.)
- 1973b "Derogation," in *Essays in Legal and Moral Philosophy*, D. Reidel, Dordrecht. (Cited on p. 151.)
- 1979 *Allgemeine Theorie der Normen*, Manz, Wien. (Cited on p. 166.)

Kershnar, Stephen
- 2004 "Moral Responsibility in a Maximally Great Being," *Philo*, 7, 1, pp. 97–113. (Cited on p. 78.)

King, Matt
- 2012 "Moral Responsibility and Merit," *Journal of Ethics and Social Philosophy*, 6, 2, pp. 1–17. (Cited on p. 78.)
- 2013 "Traction Without Tracing: A (Partial) Solution for Control-Based Accounts of Moral Responsibility," *European Journal of Philosophy*, 21, 1. (Cited on p. 78.)

King, Matt and Peter Carruthers
- 2012 "Moral Responsibility and Consciousness," *Journal of Moral Philosophy*, 9, 2, pp. 200–228. (Cited on p. 78.)

Kiparsky, Paul and Carol Kiparsky
- 1971 "Fact," in *Progress in Linguistics*, ed. by M. Bierwisch and K.E. Heidolph, Mouton, Den Haag, pp. 143–173. (Cited on p. 153.)

Klampfer, Friderik
    2004 "Moral Responsibility for Unprevented Harm," *Acta Analytica*, 19, 33, pp. 119–161. (Cited on p. 78.)

Knobe, Joshua and John Doris
    2010 "Responsibility," in *The Moral Psychology Handbook*, Oxford University Press, Oxford. (Cited on pp. 78, 80.)

Köbler, Gerhard
    1995 *Etymologisches Rechtswörterbuch*, Mohr, Tübingen. (Cited on p. 149.)

Koons, Robert
    2013 "Defeasible Reasoning," in *The Stanford Encyclopedia of Philosophy*, ed. by Edward N. Zalta, Spring 2013. (Cited on p. 145.)

Kripke, Saul Aaron
    1982 *Wittgenstein on Rules and Private Language: an Elementary Exposition*, Harvard University Press, Cambridge (MA). (Cited on p. 90.)
    2009 "Presupposition and Anaphora: Remarks on the Formulation of the Projection Problem," *Linguistic Inquiry*, 40, 3, pp. 367–386. (Cited on p. 13.)

Ladd, J.
    1992 "Bhopal: Moralische Verantwortung, normale Katastrophen und Bürgertugend," in *Wirtschaft und Ethik*, ed. by Hans Lenk and Matthias Maring, Reclam, Stuttgart, pp. 285–300. (Cited on p. 58.)

Lang, Wiesław
    1960 "Obowiązywanie normy prawnej w czasie w świetle logiki norm [*Diachronic validity of legal norm in the light of the logic of norms*]," *Zeszyty Naukowe Uniwersytetu Jagiellońskiego*, 31, 7, pp. 47–88. (Cited on p. 165.)
    1962 *Obowiązywanie prawa [Binding force of law]*, Warszawa: Państwowe Wydawnictwo Naukowe. (Cited on p. 165.)
    1985 "Responsibility and Guilt as Legal and Moral Concepts," *Archiv für Rechts- und Sozialphilosophie*, 24, pp. 262–268. (Cited on p. 78.)

Langford, C. H.
    1968 "The Notion of Analysis in Moore's Philosophy," in *The Philosophy of G. E. Moore*, 3rd ed., Open Court, La Salle, IL, pp. 321–342. (Cited on p. 166.)

Lec, Stanisław Jerzy
    2007 *Myśli nieuczesane wszystkie*, Noir sur blanc, Warszawa. (Cited on p. v.)

Lemmon, Edward J.
- 1965 "Deontic Logic and the Logic of Imperatives," *Logique et Analyse*, 8, pp. 39–71. (Cited on p. 165.)

Lenk, Hans and Matthias Maring
- 1993 "Verantwortung – normatives Interpretationskonstrukt und empirische Beschreibung," in *Ethische Norm und empirische Hypothese*, ed. by L. H. Eckensberger and U. Gähde, Frankfurt am Main, pp. 222–243. (Cited on pp. 15, 26, 58.)
- 2011 "Verantwortung," in *Historisches Wörterbuch der Philosophie*, ed. by Joachim Ritter, Karlfried Gründer, and Gottfried Gabriel, 11, Benno Schwabe, Basel, pp. 569–575. (Cited on p. 58.)

Leonard, Henry S.
- 1959 "Interrogatives, Imperatives, Truth, Falsity and Lies," *Philosophy of Science*, 26, pp. 172–186. (Cited on p. 166.)

Levy, Ken
- 2011 "Dangerous Psychopaths: Criminally Responsible But Not Morally Responsible, Subject to Criminal Punishment and to Preventive Detention," *San Diego Law Review, Vol. 48*, 48. (Cited on pp. 75, 79.)

Levy, Neil
- 2011 *Hard Luck: How Luck Undermines Free Will and Moral Responsibility*, Oxford University Press, Oxford. (Cited on p. 82.)

Levy, Neil and Michael McKenna
- 2009 "Recent Work on Free Will and Moral Responsibility," *Philosophy Compass*, 4, 1, pp. 96–133. (Cited on p. 77.)

Lewis, David Kellogg
- 1969 *Convention: A Philosophical Study*, Blackwell, Oxford. (Cited on p. 166.)
- 1983 "General Semantics," in *Philosophical Papers*, 1, Oxford University Press, New York, pp. 198–229. (Cited on p. 166.)
- 2000 "A Problem about Permission," in *Papers in Ethics and Social Philosophy*, Cambridge University Press, New York, pp. 20–33. (Cited on p. 166.)

Lewis, David Kellogg and Stephanie R. Lewis
- 1975 "Review of the book "Contemporary Philosophy in Scandinavia"," *Theoria*, 41, pp. 39–60. (Cited on p. 166.)

Libet, Benjamin
- 2004 *Mind Time: The Temporal Factor in Consciousness*, Harvard University Press, Cambridge (MA). (Cited on p. 82.)

Libet, Benjamin, Walter Sinnott-Armstrong, and Lynn Nadel
- 2011 *Conscious Will and Responsibility*, Oxford University Press, Oxford. (Cited on p. 82.)

Lippke, R.L.
- 2008 "No Easy Way Out: Dangerous Offenders and Preventive Detention," *Law and Philosophy*, 27, 4, pp. 383–414. (Cited on p. 75.)

Lorini, Giuseppe
- 2000 *Dimensioni giuridiche dell'istituzionale*, CEDAM, Padova. (Cited on p. 152.)
- 2001 *Il valore logico delle norme*, Adriatica Editrice, Bari. (Cited on pp. 164, 166.)
- 2013 "La verità come valore logico," in *The Value of Truth/The Truth of Value*, ed. by Stefano Colloca, LED, Milano, pp. 117–124. (Cited on p. 164.)

Luzzati, Claudio
- 1990 *La vaghezza delle norme. Un'analisi del linguaggio giuridico*, Giuffrè, Milan. (Cited on p. 132.)

Lynn, R. and T. Vanhanen
- 2002 *IQ and the Wealth of Nations*, Praeger Publishers. (Cited on p. 69.)

MacBride, Fraser
- 2013 "Truthmakers," in *The Stanford Encyclopedia of Philosophy*, ed. by Edward N. Zalta, Spring 2013. (Cited on p. 160.)

Macnamara, Coleen
- 2011 "Holding Others Responsible," *Philosophical Studies*, 152, 1, pp. 81–102. (Cited on p. 78.)

Magni, Sergio Filippo
- 2005 *Teorie della libertà*, Carocci, Roma. (Cited on pp. viii, 25, 28, 48, 62.)

Maibom, Heidi L.
- 2008 "The Mad, the Bad, and the Psychopath," *Neuroethics*, 1, 3. (Cited on p. 80.)

Mäkelä, Pekka
- 2007 "Collective Agents and Moral Responsibility," *Journal of Social Philosophy*, 38, 3, pp. 456–468. (Cited on p. 108.)

Malatesti, Luca and John McMillan
- 2010 *Responsibility and Psychopathy: Interfacing Law, Psychiatry, and Philosophy*, Oxford University Press, New York. (Cited on p. 80.)

Mally, Ernst
- 1926 *Grundgesetze des Sollens: Elemente der Logik des Willens*, Leuschner & Lubensky, Graz. (Cited on p. 164.)
- 1971 *Logische Schriften*, D. Reidel, Dordrecht. (Cited on p. 87.)

Martin, Mike W.
- 2010 "Personality Disorders and Moral Responsibility," *Philosophy, Psychiatry, and Psychology*, 17, 2, pp. 127–129. (Cited on p. 80.)

Marturano, Antonio
- 2012 *Il dilemma di Jørgensen*, Aracne Editrice, Roma. (Cited on p. 166.)

Mason, Elinor
- 2005 "Recent Work: Moral Responsibility," *Philosophical Books*, 46, 4, pp. 343–353. (Cited on p. 78.)

Mayerfeld, Jamie
- 1999 *Suffering and Moral Responsibility*, Oxford University Press, Oxford. (Cited on p. 80.)

Mazzoleni, Emil
- 2013 *Nomologica della impossibilità*, LL.MM. thesis, Università di Pavia. (Cited on p. 158.)

McGrath, Sarah
- 2005 "Causation by Omission: A Dilemma," *Philosophical Studies*, 123, 1-2, pp. 125–48. (Cited on p. 26.)

McKenna, Michael
- 2012 *Conversation & Responsibility*, Oxford University Press. (Cited on p. 91.)

McMillan, John and Grant R. Gillett
- 2005 "Moral Responsibility, Consciousness and Psychiatry," *Australian and New Zealand Journal of Psychiatry*, 39, 11, pp. 1018–1021. (Cited on p. 80.)

McNamara, Paul
- 2010 "Deontic Logic," in *The Stanford Encyclopedia of Philosophy*, ed. by Edward N. Zalta, Fall 2010. (Cited on p. 166.)

Meynen, Gerben
- 2010 "Free Will and Mental Disorder: Exploring the Relationship," *Theoretical Medicine and Bioethics*, 31, 6, pp. 429–443. (Cited on p. 80.)

Mill, John Stuart
- 1865 *An Examination of Sir William Hamilton's Philosophy and of the Principal Philosophical Questions Discussed in His Writings*, Longmans, London. (Cited on pp. 26, 28.)

Miller, Seumas
- 2001a "Collective Moral Responsibility for Omissions," *Business and Professional Ethics Journal*, 20, 1, pp. 5–24. (Cited on p. 108.)
- 2001b *Social Action: A Teleological Account*, Cambridge University Press, Cambridge. (Cited on p. 108.)
- 2006 "Collective Moral Responsibility: An Individualist Account," *Midwest Studies in Philosophy*, 30, 1, pp. 176–193. (Cited on p. 108.)

Miller, Seumas and Pekka Mäkelä
- 2005 "The Collectivist Approach to Collective Moral Responsibility," *Metaphilosophy*, 36, 5, pp. 634–651. (Cited on p. 108.)

Milo, Ronald D.
- 1976 "The Notion of a Practical Inference," *American Philosophical Quarterly*, 13, pp. 13–21. (Cited on p. 165.)

Moeschler, Jacques
- 2010 "Negation, Scope and the Descriptive/Metalinguistic Distinction," *Generative Grammar in Geneva*, 6, pp. 29–48. (Cited on p. 171.)

Mondolfo, Rodolfo
- 2012 *La comprensione del soggetto umano nell'antichità classica*, Bompiani, Milan. (Cited on p. 5.)

Moore, Geoff
- 1999 "Corporate Moral Agency: Review and Implications," *Journal of Business Ethics*, 21, 4, pp. 329–343. (Cited on p. 109.)

Moore, George Edward
- 1922 *Principia Ethica*, Cambridge University Press, Cambridge. (Cited on p. 33.)

Moore, Michael S.
- 1997 *Placing Blame: A General Theory of the Criminal Law*, Oxford University Press, Oxford. (Cited on pp. 75, 122.)
- 2009 *Causation and Responsibility*, Oxford University Press, Oxford. (Cited on pp. vii, 75, 103, 111, 122, 124, 132, 134.)

Moritz, Manfred
- 1941 "Gebot und Pflicht," *Eine Untersuchung zur imperativen Ethik. Theoria*, 7, pp. 219–257. (Cited on p. 165.)

Morse, Stephen J.

    1977 "Crazy Behavior, Morals, and Science: An Analysis of Mental Health Law," *S. Cal. L. Rev.*, 51, p. 527. (Cited on pp. 47, 69.)

    2008 "Psychopathy and Criminal Responsibility," *Neuroethics*, 1, 3. (Cited on p. 80.)

    2011a "Genetics and Criminal Responsibility," *Trends In Cognitive Sciences*, 15, 378. (Cited on p. 84.)

    2011b "Lost in Translation? An Essay on Law and Neuroscience," in *Law And Neuroscience, Current Legal Issues*, ed. by Martin Freeman, 13, Oxford University Press, Oxford. (Cited on p. 84.)

Moya, Carlos

    2005 *Moral Responsibility: The Ways of Scepticism*, Routledge, London. (Cited on p. 78.)

    2007 "Moral Responsibility Without Alternative Possibilities?" *Journal of Philosophy*, 104, 9, pp. 475–486. (Cited on p. 78.)

Mullane, Harvey

    1965 "Moral Responsibility for Dreams," *Dialogue*, 4, 02, pp. 224–229. (Cited on p. 16.)

Mulligan, Kevin, Peter Simons, and Barry Smith

    1984 "Truth-Makers," *Philosophy and Phenomenological Research*, 44, 3, pp. 287–321. (Cited on p. 160.)

Nadelhoffer, Thomas

    2004 "On Praise, Side Effects, and Folk Ascriptions of Intentionality," *Journal of Theoretical and Philosophical Psychology*, 24, 2, pp. 196–213. (Cited on p. 80.)

Nagel, Thomas

    1979 *Mortal Questions*, Cambridge University Press, Cambridge. (Cited on p. 98.)

    1986 *The View From Nowhere*, Oxford University Press, Oxford. (Cited on p. 163.)

Nahmias, Eddy A. *et al.*

    2005 "Surveying Freedom: Folk Intuitions About Free Will and Moral Responsibility," *Philosophical Psychology*, 18, 5, pp. 561–584. (Cited on pp. 80, 108.)

Nelkin, Dana K.

    2007 "Do We Have a Coherent Set of Intuitions About Moral Responsibility?" *Midwest Studies in Philosophy*, 31, 1, pp. 243–259. (Cited on p. 108.)

Nichols, Shaun and J. Knobe
- 2007 "Moral Responsibility and Determinism: The Cognitive Science of Folk Intuitions," *Noûs*, 41, 4, pp. 663–685. (Cited on p. 45.)

Nino, Carlos S.
- 1978 "Some Confusions around Kelsen's Concept of Validity," *Archiv für Rechts- und Sozialphilosophie*, 64, pp. 357–376. (Cited on p. 166.)

Nüssel, F.
- 2011 "Zurechnung," in *Historisches Wörterbuch der Philosophie*, ed. by Joachim Ritter, Karlfried Gründer, and Gottfried Gabriel, 12, Benno Schwabe, Basel, pp. 1446–1452. (Cited on p. 149.)

Oppenheim, Felix E. [Felix Errera]
- 1944 "Outline of a Logical Analysis of Law," *Philosophy of Science*, 11, pp. 142–160. (Cited on p. 165.)

Pace, Eric
- 1989 "Dr. Aleksander W. Rudzinski, 89, A Polish Diplomat Who Defected," Rudzinski's Obituary, http://www.nytimes.com/1989/04/08/obituaries/dr-aleksander-w-rudzinski-89-a-polish-diplomat-who-defected.html. (Cited on p. 193.)

Pardo, Michael S. and Dennis Patterson
- 2013 "Neuroscience, Normativity, and Retributivism," in *The Future of Punishment*, ed. by Thomas Nadelhoffer, Oxford University Press, Oxford. (Cited on p. 82.)

Parent, W. A.
- 1975 "The Nature of Moral Responsibility," *International Philosophical Quarterly*, 15, 1, pp. 111–114. (Cited on p. 78.)

Passerini Glazel, Lorenzo
- 2007 (ed. by)*Ricerche di Filosofia del diritto*, Giappichelli, Turin. (Cited on p. 18.)

Paul, Ellen Frankel, Fred Dycus Miller, and Jeffrey Paul
- 1999 *Responsibility*, Cambridge University Press, Cambridge. (Cited on p. 78.)

Paulson, Stanley L.
- 2004 "Zurechnung als apriorische Kategorie in der Rechtslehre Hans Kelsens," in *Zurechnung als Operationalisierung von Verantwortung*, ed. by Matthias Kaufmann and Joachim Renzikowski, Peter Lang, Frankfurt am Main, pp. 93–120. (Cited on p. 114.)

Peetz, Vera

 1979 "Illocutionary Negation," *Philosophia: Philosophical Quarterly of Israel*, 8, pp. 639–644. (Cited on p. 171.)

Perry, S.R.

 2001 "Honoré on Responsibility for Outcomes," in *Relating to Responsibility: Essays in Honour of Tony Honoré on his 80th Birthday*, ed. by Gardner John and Peter Cane, Hart Publishing, Oxford. (Cited on p. 92.)

Peters, Stanley

 1979 "A Truth-Conditional Formulation of Karttunen's Account of Presupposition," *Synthese*, 40, 2, pp. 301–316. (Cited on p. 13.)

Pink, Thomas

 2009 "Power and Moral Responsibility," *Philosophical Explorations*, 12, 2, pp. 127–149. (Cited on p. 78.)

Pitcher, George

 1960 "Hart on Action and Responsibility," *The Philosophical Review*, 69, 2, pp. 226–235. (Cited on pp. 144, 162.)

Pizarro, David A, Eric Uhlmann, and Paul Bloom

 2003 "Causal Deviance and the Attribution of Moral Responsibility," *Journal of Experimental Social Psychology*, 39, 6, pp. 653–660. (Cited on p. 80.)

Pokorny, Julius

 1994 *Indogermanisches etymologisches Wörterbuch*, Francke. (Cited on p. 168.)

Posner, Richard A

 1972 "A theory of negligence," *The Journal of Legal Studies*, 1, 1, pp. 29–96. (Cited on p. 121.)

 1973 "Strict Liability: a Comment," *The Journal of Legal Studies*, 2, 1, pp. 205–221. (Cited on p. 121.)

Prior, Arthur Norman

 1949 *Logic and the Basis of Ethics*, Clarendon Press, Oxford. (Cited on pp. 165, 166.)

 1968 "Imperatives and Truth," in *Akten des XIV. Internationalen Kongresses für Philosophie*, II, Herder, Wien, pp. 291–296. (Cited on p. 166.)

 1971 *Objects of Thought*, Clarendon Press, Oxford. (Cited on p. 165.)

Pufendorf, Samuel

1672/1934 *De jure naturae et gentium*, Clarendon Press-Humphrey Milford, Oxford-London. (Cited on p. 149.)

Ramírez, Miguel P.

2003 *Formal Pragmatic Model for Imperatives Interpretation*, Doctoral dissertation, University of Essex. (Cited on p. 165.)

Rand, Rose [Rozalia]

1939 "Logik der Forderungssätze," *Revue Internationale de la Théorie du Droit*, 1, pp. 308–322. (Cited on pp. 164, 165.)

1962 "The Logic of Demand-Sentences," *Synthese*, 14, pp. 237–254. (Cited on p. 164.)

Rawls, John

1955 "Two Concepts of Rules," *The Philosophical Review*, 64, 1, pp. 3–32. (Cited on p. 17.)

Raz, Joseph

2011 *From Normativity to Responsibility*, Oxford University Press, Oxford. (Cited on p. 76.)

Ricœur, Paul

1994 "Le concept de responsabilité: essai d'analyse sémantique," *Esprit*, 206, pp. 28–48. (Cited on pp. 25, 149.)

Ripley, David

2011 "Negation, Denial, and Rejection," *Philosophy Compass*, 6, 9, pp. 622–629. (Cited on p. 167.)

Risser, David T.

1985 *Corporate Collective Responsibility*, PhD thesis, Temple University. (Cited on p. 109.)

1996 "The Social Dimension of Moral Responsibility: Taking Organizations Seriously," *Journal of Social Philosophy*, 27, 1, pp. 189–207. (Cited on p. 78.)

2009 "Collective Moral Responsibility," in *Internet Encyclopedia of Philosophy*. (Cited on p. 108.)

Rodríguez-Pereyra, Gonzalo

2006 "Truthmakers," *Philosophy Compass*, 1, 2, pp. 186–200. (Cited on p. 160.)

Roskies, Adina L. and Shaun Nichols

2008 "Bringing Moral Responsibility Down to Earth," *Journal of Philosophy*, 105, 7, pp. 371–388. (Cited on p. 78.)

Ross, Alf [Alf Niels Christian]
- 1941 "Imperatives and Logic," *Theoria*, 7, pp. 53–71. (Cited on pp. 164–166.)
- 1957 "Tû-tû," *Harvard Law Review*, pp. 812–825. (Cited on p. 57.)
- 1959 *On Law and Justice*, University of California Press, Berkeley. (Cited on p. 86.)
- 1968 *Directives and Norms*, Humanities Press, New York. (Cited on pp. 41, 165, 166, 174.)
- 1975 *On Guilt, Responsibility, and Punishment* [Om skyld, ansvar og straf], University of California Press, Berkeley. (Cited on pp. 13, 57, 61, 83.)

Rosse, Stephen David
- 1973 *The Nature of Moral Responsibility*, Wayne State University Press, Detroit. (Cited on p. 78.)

Roversi, Corrado
- 2006 *La costitutizione della costitutività. Per una critica delle regole eidetico-costitutive.* PhD thesis, Università di Milano. (Cited on pp. 18, 87.)
- 2012 *Costituire. Uno studio di ontologia giuridica*, Giappichelli, Turin. (Cited on pp. 18, 57, 87.)

Rudziński, Aleksander Witold [*born* Witold Steinberg]
- 1947 *Z logiki norm*, Wydawnictwo Wydziału Prawa Uniwersytetu Jagiellońskiego, Kraków. (Cited on pp. 164, 165, 193.)

Russell, Bertrand
- 1905 "On Denoting," *Mind*, 14, 56, pp. 479–493. (Cited on p. 168.)

Russell, Paul
- 1995 *Freedom and Moral Sentiment: Hume's Way of Naturalizing Responsibility*, Oxford University Press. (Cited on p. 127.)
- 2002 "Responsibility and Control," *Canadian Journal of Philosophy*, 32, pp. 587–606. (Cited on p. 78.)
- 2008 "Hume on Free Will," in *The Stanford Encyclopedia of Philosophy*, ed. by Edward N. Zalta, Fall 2008. (Cited on p. 127.)

Ryle, Gilbert
- 1949 *The Concept of Mind*, University of Chicago Press, Chicago (Illinois). (Cited on p. 48.)

Saïd, Suzanne
- 1978 *La faute tragique*, F. Maspéro, Paris. (Cited on pp. 4, 5.)

Sankowski, Edward

    1990 "Two Forms of Moral Responsibility," *Philosophical Topics*, 18, 1, pp. 123–141. (Cited on p. 78.)

Santoni de Sio, Filippo

    2013 *Per colpa di chi*, Cortina, Milan. (Cited on p. 84.)

Sapolsky, R.M.

    2004 "The frontal cortex and the criminal justice system," *Philos Trans R Soc Lond B Biol Sci*, 359, 1451, pp. 1787–1796. (Cited on p. 42.)

Sartorio, Carolina

    2009 "Causation and Ethics," in Beebee *et al.* [2009]. (Cited on p. 133.)

    2012 "Two Wrongs Do Not Make A Right: Responsibility and Overdetermination," *Legal Theory*, 18, Special Issue 04, pp. 473–490. (Cited on pp. 127, 133.)

Scanlon, Thomas M.

    1998 *What We Owe to Each Other*, Harvard University Press, Cambridge (MA). (Cited on pp. 24, 33, 98, 163.)

    2014 *Being Realistic about Reasons*, Oxford University Press, Oxford. (Cited on pp. vii, 33, 166, 175.)

Scarpelli, Uberto

    1981 *Etica senza verità*, Il Mulino, Bologna. (Cited on p. 33.)

Schauber, Nancy

forthcoming "Complexities of Character: Hume on Love and Responsibility," *Hume Studies*. (Cited on p. 80.)

Schleim, Stephan, Matthias Tade Spranger, and Henrik Walter

    2009 *Von der Neuroethik zum Neurorecht?* Vandenhoeck & Ruprecht Verlag, Göttingen. (Cited on p. 83.)

Schleim, Stephan and Henrik Walter

    2007 "Cognitive Enhancement–Fakten und Mythen," *Nervenheilkunde*, 26, 1, p. 83. (Cited on p. 83.)

Schlick, Moritz

    1930 *Fragen der Ethik*, Julius Springer, Wien. (Cited on p. 65.)

Schmitt, Franciscus Saverius

    1936 *Ein neues unvollendetes Werk des hl. Anselm von Canterbury*, Aschendorff, Münster i W. (Cited on pp. 169, 191.)

Schoeman, Ferdinand
> 1987 *Responsibility, Character, and the Emotions: New Essays in Moral Psychology*, Cambridge University Press, Cambridge. (Cited on p. 80.)

Schroeder, Mark
> 2008a *Being For*, Oxford University Press, Oxford. (Cited on p. 166.)
> 2008b "How Expressivists Can and Should Solve Their Problem with Negation," *Noûs*, 42, 4, pp. 573–599. (Cited on p. 166.)
> 2008c "What Is the Frege-Geach Problem?" *Philosophy Compass*, 3, 4, pp. 703–720. (Cited on p. 166.)
> 2012 "Value Theory," in *The Stanford Encyclopedia of Philosophy*, ed. by Edward N. Zalta, Summer 2012. (Cited on p. 33.)

Schwyzer, Hubert
> 1969 "Rules and Practices," *The Philosophical Review*, 78, pp. 451–467. (Cited on p. 87.)
> 2012 "Regole del gioco e senso di gioco," in *Filosofie della norma*, ed. by Giuseppe Lorini and Lorenzo Passerini Glazel, Giappichelli, Torino, pp. 165–172. (Cited on p. 87.)

Searle, John Rogers
> 1964 "How to Derive "Ought" from "Is"," *The Philosophical Review*, 73, 1, pp. 43–58. (Cited on pp. 17, 18.)

Searle, John Rogers and Daniel Vanderveken
> 1985 *Foundations of Illocutionary Logic*, Cambridge University Press, New York. (Cited on p. 171.)

Sesonske, A.
> 1964 *Value and Obligation*, Oxford University Press, New York. (Cited on p. 33.)

Sheehy, Paul
> 2006 "Holding Them Responsible," *Midwest Studies in Philosophy*, 30, 1, pp. 74–93. (Cited on pp. 78, 108.)

Shen, F. et al.
> 2011 "Sorting Guilty Minds," *New York University Law Review*, 86, pp. 1306–1361. (Cited on p. 92.)

Shoemaker, David
> 2009 "Responsibility and Disability," *Metaphilosophy*, 40, 3-4, pp. 438–461. (Cited on pp. 80, 108.)
> 2011a "Attributability, Answerability, and Accountability: Toward a Wider Theory of Moral Responsibility," *Ethics*, 121, 3, pp. 602–632. (Cited on p. 80.)

Shoemaker, David
- 2011b "Psychopathy, Responsibility, and the Moral/Conventional Distinction," *Southern Journal of Philosophy*, 49, s1, pp. 99–124. (Cited on p. 80.)

Silver, David
- 2006 "Collective Responsibility, Corporate Responsibility and Moral Taint," *Midwest Studies in Philosophy*, 30, 1, pp. 269–278. (Cited on pp. 108, 109.)

Silvi, Marco Q.
- 2004a *Atto giuridico quale atto performativo*, PhD thesis, Università di Milano. (Cited on pp. 144, 162.)
- 2004b *Struttura giuridica del perdono*, Franco Angeli, Milan. (Cited on p. 151.)

Simester, A. P.
- 2005 (ed. by)*Appraising Strict Liability*, Oxford University Press, Oxford. (Cited on p. 56.)

Simons, K.W.
- 1997 "When Is Strict Criminal Liability Just?" *The Journal of Criminal Law and Criminology*, 87, 4, pp. 1075–1137. (Cited on p. 92.)

Singer, R.G.
- 1988 "The Resurgence of Mens Rea: III–The Rise and Fall of Strict Criminal Liability," *BCL Rev.*, 30, p. 337. (Cited on p. 92.)

Sinnott-Armstrong, Walter and Ken Levy
- 2011 "Insanity Defenses," in *Oxford Handbook of Philosophy and Criminal Law*, ed. by John Deigh and David Dolinko, Oxford University Press, Oxford, pp. 299–334. (Cited on p. 79.)

Skorupski, John
- 2010 *The Domain of Reasons*, Oxford University Press, Oxford. (Cited on pp. 33, 175, 183.)

Smiley, Marion
- 1992 *Moral Responsibility and the Boundaries of Community*, University of Chicago Press, Chicago (Illinois). (Cited on p. 78.)
- 2011 "Collective Responsibility," in *The Stanford Encyclopedia of Philosophy*, ed. by Edward N. Zalta, Fall 2011. (Cited on p. 108.)

Smiley, Timothy
- 1996 "Rejection," *Analysis*, 56, 1, pp. 1–9. (Cited on p. 168.)

Smith, Jeffery
forthcoming "A Political Account of Corporate Moral Responsibility," *Ethical Theory and Moral Practice*. (Cited on p. 109.)

Sneddon, Andrew
2005 "Moral Responsibility: The Difference of Strawson, and the Difference It Should Make," *Ethical Theory and Moral Practice*, 8, 3, pp. 239–264. (Cited on p. 80.)

Snell, Bruno
1946 *Die Entdeckung des Geistes*, Vandenhoeck & Ruprecht, Hamburg. (Cited on pp. 4, 5.)

Soares, C.
2003 "Corporate Versus Individual Moral Responsibility," *Journal of Business Ethics*, 46, 2, pp. 143–150. (Cited on pp. 108, 109.)

Sommers, Tamler
2009 "The Two Faces of Revenge: Moral Responsibility and the Culture of Honor," *Biology and Philosophy*, 24, 1, pp. 35–50. (Cited on p. 78.)
2012 *Relative Justice: Cultural Diversity, Free Will, and Moral Responsibility*, Princeton University Press, Princeton. (Cited on p. 80.)

Soon, C. S. *et al.*
2008 "Unconscious determinants of free decisions in the human brain," *Nature Neuroscience*, 11, pp. 543–545. (Cited on p. 82.)

Sorainen, Kalle [*born* Sandelin, Kaarle]
1939 "Der Modus und die Logik," *Theoria*, 5, pp. 202–204. (Cited on pp. 164, 166, 195.)

Sosa, Ernest
1964 *Directives: A Logico-Philosophical Inquiry*, PhD thesis, University of Pittsburgh. (Cited on p. 165.)
1966 "On Practical Inference and the Logic of Imperatives," *Theoria*, 32, pp. 211–223. (Cited on p. 165.)
1967 "The Semantics of Imperatives," *American Philosophical Quarterly*, 4, pp. 57–64. (Cited on p. 165.)
1970 "On Practical Inference," *Logique et Analyse*, 13, pp. 215–230. (Cited on pp. 165, 166.)

Speranza, J.L. and Laurence R. Horn
2010 "A Brief History of Negation," *Journal of Applied Logic*, 8, 3, pp. 277 –301, ISSN: 1570-8683, DOI: 10.1016/j.jal.2010.04.001, http://www.sciencedirect.com/science/article/pii/S1570868310000236. (Cited on p. 172.)

Stapleton, Jane
    2008 "Choosing What We Mean by 'Causation' in the Law," *Missouri Law Review*, 73, 2, pp. 433–480. (Cited on p. 122.)
    2009 "Causation in the Law," in Beebee *et al.* [2009]. (Cited on p. 122.)

Stockhammer, Morris
    1970 "Kausalität Und Zurechnung. Hans Kelsen Zum 90. Geburtstag," *Kant-Studien*, 61, 1-4. (Cited on p. 114.)

Strawson, Galen
    1994 "The Impossibility of Moral Responsibility," *Philosophical Studies*, 75, 1, pp. 5–24. (Cited on pp. 13, 26, 156.)
    2009 "The Impossibility of Ultimate Moral Responsibility," in *Free Will*, ed. by Derek Pareboom, Hackett, Indianapolis, p. 363. (Cited on pp. 13, 26, 156.)

Strawson, Peter Frederick
    1950 "Truth," *The Aristotelian Society: Supplementary Volume*, 24, pp. 129–156. (Cited on p. 165.)
  1968 (2008) *Freedom and Resentment and Other Essays*, Routledge, London. (Cited on pp. 17, 45.)

Swinburne, Richard
    1989 *Responsibility and Atonement*, Oxford University Press, Oxford, pp. 339–342. (Cited on p. 78.)

Sztykgold, Jerzy
    1936 "Negacja normy," trans. by Jerzy Wróblewski and Amedeo Giovanni Conte, *Przegląd filozoficzny*, 39, pp. 492–494. (Cited on pp. 165, 176, 197.)

Tamminga, Allard
    1994 "Logics of Rejection: Two Systems of Natural Deduction," *Logique et Analyse*, 146, pp. 169–208. (Cited on p. 168.)

Tesnière, Lucien
    1959 *Éléments de syntaxe structurale*, Klincksieck, Paris. (Cited on pp. 15, 58.)

Thomasius, Christian
  1718/1979 *Fundamenta iuris naturae et gentium (1705)*, 4th ed., Scientia, Aalen. (Cited on p. 149.)

Thomson, Judith Jarvis
    2003 "Causation: Omissions," *Philosophy and Phenomenological Research*, 66, 1, pp. 81–103. (Cited on p. 26.)

2007 "Normativity," in *Oxford Studies In Metaethics*, ed. by Russ Shafer-Landau, 2, Clarendon Press, pp. 240–265. (Cited on p. 33.)

2008 *Normativity*, Open Court, Chicago (Illinois). (Cited on pp. 33, 175.)

2010 "Normativity," *Analysis*, 70, 4, pp. 713–715. (Cited on p. 33.)

Tollefsen, Deborah Perron

2003 "Participant Reactive Attitudes and Collective Responsibility," *Philosophical Explorations*, 6, 3, pp. 218–234. (Cited on p. 108.)

Uckelman, Sara Lianna

2007 *Anselm's Logic of Agency*, Institute for Logic, Language and Computation (ILLC), University of Amsterdam, Amsterdam. (Cited on p. 170.)

2009 *Modalities in Medieval Logic*, Institute for Logic, Language and Computation, Amsterdam. (Cited on p. 170.)

Unwin, Nicholas

1999 "Quasi-Realism, Negation and the Frege-Geach Problem," *The Philosophical Quarterly*, 49, 196, pp. 337–352. (Cited on p. 166.)

2001 "Norms and Negation: A Problem for Gibbard's Logic," *The Philosophical Quarterly*, 51, 202, pp. 60–75. (Cited on p. 166.)

Vaan, Michiel de

2008 *Etymological Dictionary of Latin and Other Italic Languages*, Brill, Leiden. (Cited on p. 3.)

van den Beld, A.

2000 *Moral Responsibility and Ontology*, Kluwer. (Cited on p. 78.)

van Fraassen, Bas C.

1973 "Values and the Heart's Command," *The Journal of Philosophy*, 70, pp. 5–19. (Cited on pp. 33, 165.)

van Inwagen, Peter

1997 "Fischer on Moral Responsibility," *Philosophical Quarterly*, 47, 188, pp. 373–381. (Cited on p. 78.)

Vargas, Manuel

2010a "Are Psychopathic Serial Killers Evil? Are They Blameworthy for What They Do?" In *Serial Killers and Philosophy*, Blackwell, London. (Cited on p. 80.)

2010b "Responsibility in a World of Causes," *Philosophic Exchange*, 40, pp. 56–78. (Cited on p. 80.)

2013 *Building Better Beings: A Theory of Moral Responsibility*, Oxford University Press, Oxford. (Cited on pp. 23, 24, 27, 186.)

Vargas, Manuel

forthcoming "Situationism and Moral Responsibility: Free Will in Fragments," in *Decomposing the Will*, Oxford University Press, Oxford. (Cited on p. 80.)

Vasmer, Max

1958 *Russisches etymologisches Wörterbuch*, C. Winter, Heidelberg. (Cited on p. 168.)

Vegetti, Mario

2007a "Culpability, Responsibility, Cause: Philosophy, Historiography, and Medicine in the Fifth Century," in *Dialoghi con gli antichi*, ed. by Silvia Gastaldi *et al.*, Akademia Verlag, Sankt Augustin, pp. 93–109. (Cited on p. 5.)

2007b "L'io, l'anima, il soggetto," in *Dialoghi con gli antichi*, ed. by Silvia Gastaldi *et al.*, Akademia Verlag, Sankt Augustin, pp. 43–80. (Cited on pp. 4, 5.)

2010 "Io, persona e responsabilità. Tratti delle antropologie filosofiche antiche," in *Homo, caput, persona. La costruzione giuridica dell'identità nell'esperienza romana*, ed. by A. Corbino, M. Humbert, and G. Negri, Iuss Press, pp. 65–78. (Cited on pp. 4, 5.)

Velasquez, Manuel

2003 "Debunking Corporate Moral Responsibility," *Business Ethics Quarterly*, 13, 4, pp. 531–562. (Cited on pp. 108, 109.)

Vergilius, Publius Maro

Georgicon. (Cited on p. 103.)

Vernant, Jean-Pierre

1971 *Mythe et pensée chez les Grecs: études de psychologie historique*, F. Maspero, Paris. (Cited on pp. 4, 5.)

Vidal-Naquet, Pierre and Jean-Pierre Vernant

1972 *Mythe et tragédie en Grèce ancienne*, F. Maspéro, Paris. (Cited on pp. 4, 5.)

Vincent, Nicole

2008 "Responsibility, Dysfunction and Capacity," *Neuroethics*, 1, 3. (Cited on p. 80.)

2009 "On the Relevance of Neuroscience to Criminal Responsibility," *Criminal Law and Philosophy*, 4, 1, pp. 77–98. (Cited on pp. 81, 94.)

2013 (ed. by)*Neuroscience and Legal Responsibility*, Oxford University Press, Oxford. (Cited on p. 42.)

Vincent, Nicole, I. Van De Poel, and J. Van Den Hoven
  2011 *Moral Responsibility, Beyond Free Will and Determinism*, Springer Verlag, Berlin/Heidelberg. (Cited on pp. 13, 16, 48.)

Vranas, Peter B. M.
  2008 "New Foundations for Imperative Logic I: Logical Connectives, Consistency, and Quantifiers," *Noûs*, 42, 4, pp. 529–572. (Cited on pp. vii, 166.)
  2011 "New Foundations for Imperative Logic II: Pure Imperative Inference," *Mind*, 120, pp. 369–446. (Cited on p. 166.)
  2012 "New Foundations for Imperative Logic III: A General Definition of Argument Validity." (Cited on p. 166.)

Wallace, R. Jay
  1994 *Responsibility and the Moral Sentiments*, Harvard University Press, Cambridge (MA). (Cited on p. 26.)

Waller, Bruce N.
  2011 *Against Moral Responsibility*, MIT Press, Cambridge (MA). (Cited on pp. 13, 26, 82, 156.)

Wedeking, Gary A.
  1969 *A Critical Examination of Command Logic*, PhD thesis, Washington University, Saint Louis. (Cited on p. 165.)

Wedgwood, Ralph
  2007 *The Nature of Normativity*, Clarendon Press, Oxford. (Cited on p. 166.)

Weinberger, Ota
  1957 "Über die Negation von Sollsätzen," *Theoria*, 23, pp. 102–132. (Cited on p. 166.)
  1958 "Die Sollsatzproblematik in der modernen Logik," *Rozpravý Československé Akademie Věd*, 68, pp. 1–124. (Cited on pp. 165, 166.)

Weisberg, D.S. *et al.*
  2008 "The seductive allure of neuroscience explanations," *Journal of Cognitive Neuroscience*, 20, 3, pp. 470–477. (Cited on p. 83.)

Welch, John R.
  1992 "Responsabilidad Colectiva y Reduccionismo," *Pensamiento*, 48, pp. 49–68. (Cited on p. 109.)

Wigley, Simon
  2007 "Automaticity, Consciousness and Moral Responsibility," *Philosophical Psychology*, 20, 2, pp. 209–225. (Cited on p. 80.)

Wilder, Hugh T.
- 1980 "Practical Reason and the Logic of Imperatives," *Metaphilosophy*, 11, pp. 244–251. (Cited on p. 165.)

Williams, Bernard [Arthur Owen]
- 1963 "Imperative Inference," *Analysis*, pp. 30–42. (Cited on p. 165.)
- 1981 *Moral Luck: Philosophical Papers, 1973-1980*, Cambridge University Press, Cambridge. (Cited on p. 98.)
- 1993 *Shame and Necessity*, University of California Press, Berkeley. (Cited on p. 5.)

Williams, Garrath
- 2003 "Blame and Responsibility," *Ethical Theory and Moral Practice*, 6, 4, pp. 427–445. (Cited on pp. 78, 80.)
- 2004 "Praise and Blame," in *Internet Encyclopedia of Philosophy*. (Cited on p. 78.)
- 2006 "Responsibility," in *Internet Encyclopedia of Philosophy*. (Cited on p. 108.)
- 2008 "Responsibility as a Virtue," *Ethical Theory and Moral Practice*, 11, 4, pp. 455–470. (Cited on p. 78.)

Williamson, Timothy
- 1994 *Vagueness*, 81, 1, Routledge. (Cited on p. 132.)

Wilmot, Stephen
- 2001 "Corporate Moral Responsibility: What Can We Infer From Our Understanding of Organisations?" *Journal of Business Ethics*, 30, 2, pp. 161–169. (Cited on p. 109.)

Wilson, George and Samuel Shpall
- 2012 "Action," in *The Stanford Encyclopedia of Philosophy*, ed. by Edward N. Zalta, Summer 2012. (Cited on p. 185.)

Wittgenstein, Ludwig Josef Johann
- 1958 *The Blue and Brown Books*, Blackwell, Oxford. (Cited on p. 13.)
- 1970 *Zettel*, 2nd ed., Suhrkamp, Frankfurt am Main. (Cited on p. 87.)
- 2009 *Philosophical Investigations/Philosophische Untersuchungen*, ed. by Peter M. S. Hacker and Joachim Schulte, 4th ed., Wiley-Blackwell, Oxford. (Cited on pp. 90, 106, 111, 166.)

Wootton, Barbara
- 1963 *Crime and the Criminal Law: Reflections of a Magistrate and Social Scientist*, Stevens, London. (Cited on pp. 41, 43, 50, 51, 99.)

Wright, Georg Henrik von
- 1951 "Deontic Logic," *Mind*, 60, pp. 1–15. (Cited on p. 164.)

1968 "The Logic of Practical Discourse," in *Contemporary Philosophy: A Survey*, ed. by Raymond Klibansky, 1, La Nuova Italia, Firenze, pp. 141–167. (Cited on pp. 164, 165.)

1991 "Is There a Logic of Norms?" *Ratio Juris*, 4, pp. 265–283. (Cited on p. 166.)

1999 "Deontic Logic: A Personal View," *Ratio Juris*, 12, 1, pp. 26–38. (Cited on p. 166.)

Wright, Richard W.

2003 "The Grounds and Extent of Legal Responsibility," *San Diego Law Review*, 40, p. 1425. (Cited on p. 119.)

2008 "The Nightmare and the Noble Dream: Hart and Honoré on Causation and Responsibility," in *The Legacy of H. L. A. Hart: Legal, Political and Moral Philosophy*, ed. by M. Kramer *et al.*, Oxford University Press, Oxford. (Cited on p. 121.)

Yoshioka, Ghen-ichiro

1908 *A Semantic Study of the Verbs of Doing and Making in the Indo-European Languages*, Tokyo Tsukiji, Tokyo. (Cited on p. 16.)

Young, Robert

1974 "Moral Responsibility," *Journal of Value Inquiry*, 8, 1, pp. 57–68. (Cited on p. 78.)

Żełaniec, Wojciech

2008 "The Truth-Value of Norms," http://blog.centrodietica.it. (Cited on p. vii.)

Zellner, Harold M.

1971 *The Logic of Imperatives*, PhD thesis, The University of Miami. (Cited on p. 165.)

Zimmerman, Michael J.

1988 *An Essay on Moral Responsibility*, Rowman & Littlefield. (Cited on pp. 24, 78.)

Znamierowski, Czesław Gabriel Stanisław

1921 "O przedmiocie i fakcie społecznym," *Przegląd filozoficzny*, 24, pp. 1–33. (Cited on pp. 88, 150.)

1924 *Podstawowe pojęcia teorji prawa. Układ prawny i norma prawa*, Fiszer i Majewski, Poznań. (Cited on pp. 88, 150.)

1. Index of Subjects
2. Index of Names

INDEX OF SUBJECTS

A
aansprakelijk, 6
absolution
    legal, 158
    religious, 158
ábyrgð, 6
accomplice liability, 124
accomplice responsibility, 109
accountability, 6, 58
accusation, 3, 59, 153, 183
adkaznasć, 6
aitiologics, 4, 185
ansvar, 6, 9
ansvarlighed, 6, 59
answerability, 6
ascription, 141, 183
    vs. description, 159
    vs. prescription, 146
atbildība, 9
atsakomýbė, 9

B
behaviorism, 48
brute facts, 161

C
causation, 4, 59, 185
    and responsibility, 111, 134
cause, 4
    legal, 131
    proximate, 131
chaeg-im, 9
collective responsibility, 108
consequentialism, 28
constitutive rules, 18, 22, 91
context, 186

conventionalism, 26
conviction *vs.* sentence, 156
corporate responsibility, 109
counterfactual dependence, 127, 128
culpability, 67
cyfrifoldeb, 9

D
denial, 167
determinism, 49
disagreement, 78
duress, 20

E
eliminativism, 25
erantzukizun, 6
excuse, 55, 156, 183
expressivism, 166

F
felelősség, 6
forgiveness, 151
freagracht, 6
free will, 6, 20, 49
Frege-Geach problem, 166

G
group responsibility, 108
guilt, 47, 55, 57
    synonims and xenonyms, 55

H
Hamlyn Lectures, 43

I
imputability, 59, 67
institutional facts, 161

245

intention, 44
is-ought question, 83

J
Jørgensen's dilemma, 166
justification, 156, 183

K
Kausalität, 149

L
law as a game, 86
liability, 6
    criminal, 77
    strict, 85, 96

M
mala
    antiqua, 43
    in se, 43
    prohibita, 43
maximalism, 121
mens rea, 21, 41, 45, 54, 55, 73
    In Hart, 51
    in Lady Wootton, 50
mental illness, 47, 51
minimalism, 121
modularity, 186
moral luck, 24, 98

N
natural law, 60
negation, 167, 168, 183
    as denial, 168
    as rejection, 168
    illocutionary, 171
    internal *vs.* external, 168
    intuitionistic, 172
    law of double, 172
    logical, 168, 172
    metalinguistic, 170
    natural, 172
    neustic, 171
    normative, 173, 183
    prefixes of, 168
Neuroscience, 82, 83, 95

niesłuszność, 176
normativity, 14, 26
    axiological, 14, 30, 185
    nomophoric, 14, 30, 185
    of context, 183, 185
    predicates of, 164
    presupposition of, 178, 181

O
objectivism, 26
odgovornost, 6, 9
odpovědnost, 6
odpowiedzialność, 9
otgovornost, 6
otvetstvennost', 9

P
përgjegjësi, 6
pragmatics, 183, 186
    metapragmatics of
        responsibility, 161
psychopathy, 79
punishment
    censure as, 59
    justification, 56, 60

R
realism, 24
rejection, 167, 168
respondoiretat, 9
responsabilidad, 9
responsabilidade, 6, 9
responsabilità, 9
responsabilitat, 6
responsabilitate, 9
responsabilité, 6
responsibility
    accomplice, 109
    and causation, 111, 134
    as normative, 153, 183
    capacity, 73, 100
    collective, 108
    conceptions of, 23
    concepts of, 19
    conditions of, 21
    corporate, 109

criminal, 80
dimensions of, 28
elimination of, 47, 49
etymology of, 4
group, 108
in Afrikaans, 6
in Albanian, 6
in Arabic, 6
in A.Ross, 57, 61
in Basque, 6
in Belarusian, 6
in Bulgarian, 6
in Catalan, 6
in Chinese, 6
in Croatian, 6
in Czech, 6
in Danish, 6
in Dutch, 6
in English, 6
in Estonian, 6
in Finnish, 6
in French, 6
in Galician, 6
in German, 6
in Greek thought, 4
in Hebrew, 6
in Hindi, 6
in Hungarian, 6
in Icelandic, 6
in Irish, 6
in Italian, 9
in Japanese, 9
in Korean, 9
in Latvian, 9
in Lithuanian, 9
in Macedonian, 9
in Maltese, 9
in Modern Greek, 6
in Norwegian, 9
in Occitan, 9
in Persian, 9
in Polish, 9
in Portuguese, 9
in Romanian, 9
in Russian, 9
in Sardinian, 9
in Serbian, 9
in Slovak, 9
in Slovenian, 9
in Spanish, 9
in Swedish, 9
in Turkish, 9
in Ukrainian, 9
in Urdu, 9
in Welsh, 9
in Yiddish, 9
justification of, 27, 28
negation of, 153, 183
nomophoric, 17
non-nomophoric, 17
non-praxical, 16, 185
normative, 26
praxical, 16, 185
role-related, 18
shared, 108
vicarious, 109
xenonyms of, 5
retributionism, 27
Rule of Law, 54

S
sekinin, 9
shared responsibility, 108
sorumluluk, 9
spondeō, 3
strict liability, 44, 46, 50, 53, 56
słuszność, 176

T
theticity, 150, 161
toerekeningsvatbaar, 6

V
valency, 15
vastutus, 6
vastuu, 6
verantwoordelijkheid, 6
verantwoordelikheid, 6
Verantwortlichkeit, 6
Verantwortung, 6, 113
vicarious responsibility, 109

vidpovidal'nist', 9

voluntariness, 20, 45, 46, 82, 95, 96, 98, 120

Z
zérèn, 6
zodpovednost', 9
Zurechnung, 112, 113, 115, 149

INDEX OF NAMES

A

Adkins, William Arthur, 4, 203
Adler, Melvin J., 165, 203
Adshead, Gwen, 79, 203
Alchourrón, Carlos Eduardo, 166, 203
Alexander, Larry, 75, 82, 203
Anderson, Scott, 177, 203
Anselm of Canterbury, 169, 191, 203
Arendt, Johanna, 108, 204
Aristotle [Aristotélēs], 20, 204
Aspinwall, L. G., 83, 204
Atlas, Jay David, 13, 204
Austin, John Langshaw, 20, 84, 157, 179, 204
Azzoni, Giampaolo M., vii, 18, 19, 110, 204

B

Bacchini, Fabio, 213
Bacon, Francis, 103, 204
Balasubramanian, P., 13, 204
Bayertz, Kurt, 26, 204
Bazzoni, Mattia, 63, 144, 204
Beardsley, Elizabeth Lane, 165, 205
Beaver, David I., 13, 205
Beebee, Helen, vii, 103, 127, 205
Beekes, Robert S. P., 3, 4, 205
Benjamin, Martin, 108, 205
Bentham, Jeremy, 121, 205
Benveniste, Émile, 3, 205
Bergström, Lars, 165, 166, 205
Bernhauer, James, 204
Bhat, P. R., 164, 205
Bierwisch, M., 223

Björnsson, Gunnar, 2, 77, 177, 205, 206
Black, Max, 213
Blackburn, Simon, vii, 166, 206
Bloom, Paul, 80, 231
Bobbio, Norberto, 166, 206
Bobzien, Susanne, 108, 206
Bohnert, Herbert Gaylord, 165, 206
Bok, Hilary, 77, 206
Borchardt, Edward, 166, 206
Borges, Jorge Luis, 41, 141, 185, 206
Braham, Matthew, 77, 108, 206
Braude, Stephen E., 79, 206
Broad, Charlie Dunbar, 165, 206
Brouwer, Luitzen Egbertus Jan, 172, 207
Brown, M. A., 222
Brown, T. R., 83, 204
Brown, Vivienne, 77, 207
Brückner, Alexander, 168, 207
Bruckner, Donald W., 77, 207
Burns, J. M., 94, 207
Burrington, Dale E., 77, 207
Byrd, Jeremy, 77, 207

C

Callender, John S., 79, 207
Campbell, Joseph Keim, 77, 207
Cananzi, Daniele M., 210
Cane, Peter, 231
Caputo, Stefano, 213
Carcaterra, Gaetano, 18, 207
Cariani, Fabrizio, 213
Carmo, J., 222
Carruthers, Peter, 78, 223
Carston, Robyn, 13, 207

249

Caruso, Gregg, 78, 79, 108, 208
Cashmore, A.R., 42, 208
Castañeda, Héctor-Neri, 164, 165, 208
Chan, David K., 78, 208
Charlow, Nate, 166, 208
Ciocchetti, Christopher, 79, 208
Ciurria, Michelle, 78, 208
Clarke, Randolph, 78, 208
Coates, D. Justin, 78, 209
Cobb, John B. Jr, 78, 209
Cohen, Jonathan, 42, 82, 218
Cohen, L. Jonathan, 171, 209
Colloca, Stefano, vii, 91, 209, 226
Compton, E.S., 83, 209
Conte, Amedeo Giovanni, viii, 15–17, 30, 57, 87, 88, 91, 150–152, 154–156, 161, 166, 173, 209, 210
Copp, David, 78, 210
Corbino, A., 240
Corlett, J. Angelo, 108, 210
Cuypers, Stefaan E., 80, 218

D
Daniel-Rops, [Henri Petiot], 186, 210
Das, Ramon, 78, 210
De Brigard, Felipe, 78, 79, 210
De Caro, Mario, 215
de Haan, Jacob Israël, 5, 210
Deigh, John, 212, 236
Dell'Utri, Massimo, 213
Denaro, Pietro, 77, 78, 211
Devlin, Patrick, 43, 211
Devoto, Giacomo, 156, 211
Di Lucia, Paolo, vii, 5, 13, 16, 79, 150, 211
Dinneen, D., 223
Dodig-Crnkovic, Gordana, 78, 211
Dolinko, David, 212, 236
Doris, John, 78, 80, 224
Downie, R. S., 78, 211
Dubbink, Wim, 109, 211
Dubislav, Walter, 165, 211

Duff, Antony, 15, 58, 91, 92, 106, 211
Dummett, Michael A. E., 170, 212
Dworkin, Gerald, 75, 212

E
Eckensberger, L. H., 225
Edwards, Craig, 79, 212
Elliott, Carl, 79, 80, 212
Engliš, Karel, 176, 212
Epstein, R.A., 122, 212
Eshleman, Andrew, 77, 212
Espersen, Jon, 164–166, 212

F
Faraci, David, 80, 212
Faroldi, Federico L. G., vii, 107, 126, 164, 173, 195, 197, 212, 213
Feinberg, Joel, 24, 25, 49, 53, 75, 78, 83, 104, 108, 159, 162, 185, 213
Feis, Guglielmo, 79, 211
Ferrer Beltrán, Jordi, 145, 213
Ferzan, Kimberly K., 75, 203, 213
Fields, Lloyd, 80, 213
Fillmore, Charles J., 155, 156, 213
Fingarette, Herbert, 80, 213
Finlay, Stephen, 15, 30, 214
Finnis, John, 60, 214
Fischer, John Martin, 48, 77, 78, 82, 108, 214
Fischette, Charles, 75, 214
Fisher, Mark, 165, 214
FitzPatrick, William J., 78, 215
Fletcher, Joseph F., 78, 215
Fonnesu, Luca, vii, 25, 149, 215
Frankfurt, Henry G., 127, 215
Frede, Michael, 5, 215
Freeman, Martin, 84, 215, 229
Frege, Gottlob [Friedrich Ludwig Gottlob], 164, 168, 215
French, Peter A., 109, 215
Frey, Gerhard, 165, 215

Frey, R. G., 214
Frierson, Patrick, 80, 215

G
Gabriel, Gottfried, 225, 230
Gähde, U., 225
Gardiner, P. L., 164, 216
Gardner, John, 56, 61, 77, 92, 216
Garner, Richard T., 171, 216
Garrett, Jan Edward, 109, 216
Gastaldi, Silvia, 240
Gauthier, David P., 164, 165, 216
Gazzaniga, Mark S., 82, 216
Geach, Peter Thomas, 144, 164, 166, 185, 216, 219
Gensler, Harry J., 165, 216
Gentzen, Gerhard Karl Erich, 172, 217
Gernet, Louis, 4, 217
Geurts, Bart, 13, 205
Gibbard, Allan, 166, 217
Gibbons, P. C., 166, 217
Gilbert, Margaret, 108, 217
Gillett, Grant R., 80, 227
Glannon, Walter, 80, 217
Glover, Jonathan, 24, 64, 217
Gommer, H., 83, 217
Gomolińska, Anna, 168, 217
González, Elsa, 109, 217
Graham, Keith, 108, 109, 217, 218
Graham, Peter A., 16, 218
Grant, C. K., 165, 218
Green, Leslie, 56, 77, 218
Green, S.P., 92, 218
Greene, Joshua, 42, 82, 218
Greenspan, Patricia, 80, 218
Grenander, M. E., 80, 218
Grue-Sørensen, Knud, 164–166, 218
Gründer, Karlfried, 225, 230

H
Hacker, Peter M. S., 242
Haji, Ishtiyaque, 80, 218
Hall, Everett W., 165, 219
Hamblin, Charles L., 164, 165, 219
Hansen, Jörg, 165, 219
Hare, Richard Mervyn, 164, 165, 171, 219
Harrison, Jonathan, 165, 219
Hart, Herbert Lionel Adolphus, 3, 13, 16, 20, 27, 41, 42, 44, 48–54, 75–77, 81, 83, 84, 89, 91, 92, 99, 103, 104, 117, 121, 144, 145, 147, 162, 185, 219, 220
Heidolph, K.E., 223
Heller, Ágnes, 13, 220
Henry, D. P., 170, 220
Heyting, Arend, 172, 220
Hieronymi, Pamela, 16, 220
Hilpinen, Risto, 209, 222
Hindriks, Frank, 80, 220
Hitchcock, Christopher, 103, 205
Ho, Hsiu-Hwang, 166, 220
Hoche, Hans-Ulrich, 171, 220
Hofstadter, Albert, 164, 165, 220
Hom, Christopher, 166, 220
Honoré, Tony, 92, 103–105, 117, 220
Horn, Laurence R., 167–170, 172, 174, 221, 237
Humbert, M., 240
Hume, David, 24, 127, 221
Husak, D.N., 92, 221

I
Incurvati, Luca, 168, 221
Ingarden, Roman, 21, 26, 221
Invernizzi, Emanuele, 204
Irwin, Terence H., 5, 221
Isaacs, Tracy Lynn, 108, 221

J
Jackson, Bernard S., 16, 221
Johanson, Arnold A., 165, 222
John, Gardner, 231
Jørgensen, Jørgen, 164–166, 195, 222

K

Kalinowski, Jerzy *vel* Georges, 164, 166, 222
Kane, Robert, 82, 222
Kanger, Stig, 166, 222
Kant, Immanuel, 27, 28, 141, 222
Karttunen, Lauri, 13, 169, 222, 223
Kaufmann, Magdalena, 164–166, 223
Kaufmann, Matthias, 230
Kelsen, Hans, 59, 103, 112–116, 146–149, 151, 166, 223
Kershnar, Stephen, 78, 223
King, Matt, 78, 223
Kiparsky, Carol, 153, 223
Kiparsky, Paul, 153, 223
Klampfer, Friderik, 78, 224
Klibansky, Raymond, 243
Knobe, J., 45, 230
Knobe, Joshua, 78, 80, 224
Köbler, Gerhard, 149, 224
Koons, Robert, 145, 224
Kramer, M., 211, 216, 243
Kripke, Saul Aaron, 13, 90, 224

L

Ladd, J., 58, 224
Lang, Wiesław, 78, 165, 224
Langford, C. H., 166, 224
Lavazza, Andrea, 215
Lec, Stanisław Jerzy, v, 224
Lemmon, Edward J., 165, 225
Lenk, Hans, 15, 26, 58, 224, 225
Leonard, Henry S., 166, 225
Levy, Ken, 75, 79, 225, 236
Levy, Neil, 77, 225
Lewis, David Kellogg, 166, 225
Lewis, Stephanie R., 166, 225
Libet, Benjamin, 82, 203, 225, 226
Lippke, R.L., 75, 226
Lorini, Giuseppe, 152, 164, 166, 226, 235
Luzzati, Claudio, 132, 226
Lynn, R., 69, 226

M

MacBride, Fraser, 160, 226
Macnamara, Coleen, 78, 226
Magni, Sergio Filippo, viii, 25, 28, 48, 62, 226
Maibom, Heidi L., 80, 226
Mäkelä, Pekka, 108, 226, 228
Malatesti, Luca, 80, 226
Mally, Ernst, 87, 164, 227
Mandelbaum, Eric, 78, 79, 210
Marchei, Natascia, 211
Maring, Matthias, 15, 26, 58, 224, 225
Martin, Mike W., 80, 227
Martino, Antonio A., 166, 203
Marturano, Antonio, 166, 227
Mason, Elinor, 78, 227
Mayerfeld, Jamie, 80, 227
Mazzoleni, Emil, 158, 227
McCawley, James D, 222
McGrath, Sarah, 26, 227
McKenna, Michael, 77, 91, 225, 227
McKinsey, John C., 164, 165, 220
McMillan, John, 80, 226, 227
McNamara, Paul, 166, 227
Melchiorre, Virgilio, 210
Menzies, Peter, 103, 205
Meynen, Gerben, 80, 227
Milani, Daniela, 211
Mill, John Stuart, 26, 28, 228
Miller, Fred Dycus, 78, 230
Miller, Seumas, 108, 228
Milo, Ronald D., 165, 228
Moeschler, Jacques, 171, 228
Mondolfo, Rodolfo, 5, 228
Moore, Geoff, 109, 228
Moore, George Edward, 33, 228
Moore, Michael S., vii, 75, 103, 111, 122, 124, 132, 134, 228
Moritz, Manfred, 165, 228
Morris, C. W., 214
Morse, Stephen J., 47, 69, 75, 80, 84, 203, 229

Moya, Carlos, 78, 229
Mullane, Harvey, 16, 229
Mulligan, Kevin, 160, 229

N
Nadel, Lynn, 82, 203, 226
Nadelhoffer, Thomas, 80, 229, 230
Nagel, Thomas, 98, 163, 229
Nahmias, Eddy A., 80, 108, 229
Nakhnikian, G., 208
Negri, G., 240
Nelkin, Dana K., 108, 229
Nichols, Shaun, 45, 78, 230, 232
Nino, Carlos S., 166, 230
Nüssel, F., 149, 230

O
Oh, C.-K., 223
Oppenheim, Felix E. [Felix Errera], 165, 230

P
Pace, Eric, 193, 230
Pardo, Michael S., 82, 230
Pareboom, Derek, 238
Parent, W. A., 78, 230
Pasquali Cerioli, Jlia, 211
Passerini Glazel, Lorenzo, 18, 209, 210, 230, 235
Patterson, Dennis, 82, 230
Paul, Ellen Frankel, 78, 230
Paul, Jeffrey, 78, 230
Paulson, Stanley L., 114, 230
Peetz, Vera, 171, 231
Perry, S.R., 92, 231
Persson, Daniel, 78, 211
Persson, Karl, 2, 77, 177, 205, 206
Peters, Stanley, 13, 169, 223, 231
Pink, Thomas, 78, 231
Pitcher, George, 144, 162, 231
Pizarro, David A, 80, 231
Pokorny, Julius, 168, 231
Posner, Richard A, 121, 231
Prior, Arthur Norman, 165, 166, 231
Pufendorf, Samuel, 149, 232

R
Ramírez, Miguel P., 165, 232
Rand, Rose [Rozalia], 164, 165, 232
Ratti, Giovanni Battista, 145, 213
Ravizza, Mark, 77, 78, 82, 214
Rawls, John, 17, 232
Raz, Joseph, 76, 232
Renzikowski, Joachim, 230
Ricœur, Paul, 25, 149, 232
Righi, Roberto, 210
Ripley, David, 78, 79, 167, 210, 232
Risser, David T., 78, 108, 109, 232
Ritter, Joachim, 225, 230
Rodríguez-Pereyra, Gonzalo, 160, 232
Romenti, Stefania, 204
Roskies, Adina L., 78, 232
Ross, Alf [Alf Niels Christian], 13, 41, 57, 83, 86, 164–166, 174, 233
Rosse, Stephen David, 78, 233
Roversi, Corrado, 18, 57, 87, 233
Rudziński, Aleksander Witold [born Witold Steinberg], 164, 165, 193, 233
Russell, Bertrand, 168, 233
Russell, Paul, 78, 127, 233
Ryle, Gilbert, 48, 233

S
Saïd, Suzanne, 4, 5, 233
Sankowski, Edward, 78, 234
Santoni de Sio, Filippo, 84, 234
Sapolsky, R.M., 42, 234
Sartori, Giovanni, 215
Sartorio, Carolina, 127, 133, 234
Scanlon, Thomas M., vii, 24, 33, 98, 163, 166, 175, 234
Scarpelli, Uberto, 33, 234
Schauber, Nancy, 80, 234
Schleim, Stephan, 83, 234
Schlick, Moritz, 65, 234
Schmitt, Franciscus Saverius, 169, 191, 203, 234
Schoeman, Ferdinand, 80, 218, 235

Schroeder, Mark, 33, 166, 235
Schulte, Joachim, 242
Schwartz, Jeremy, 166, 220
Schwyzer, Hubert, 87, 235
Searle, John Rogers, 17, 18, 171, 235
Sesonske, A., 33, 235
Shafer-Landau, Russ, 239
Sheehy, Paul, 78, 108, 235
Shen, F., 92, 235
Shoemaker, David, 80, 108, 212, 235, 236
Shpall, Samuel, 185, 242
Silver, David, 108, 109, 236
Silvi, Marco Q., 144, 151, 162, 236
Simester, A. P., 56, 216, 218, 236
Simons, K.W., 92, 236
Simons, Peter, 160, 229
Singer, R.G., 92, 236
Sinnott-Armstrong, Walter, 79, 82, 203, 226, 236
Skorupski, John, 33, 175, 183, 216, 236
Smiley, Marion, 78, 108, 236
Smiley, Timothy, 168, 236
Smith, Barry, 160, 229
Smith, Jeffery, 109, 211, 237
Smith, Peter, 168, 221
Sneddon, Andrew, 80, 237
Snell, Bruno, 4, 5, 237
Soares, C., 108, 109, 237
Sommers, Tamler, 78, 80, 237
Soon, C. S., 237
Sorainen, Kalle [born Sandelin, Kaarle], 164, 166, 195, 237
Sosa, Ernest, 165, 166, 237
Speranza, J.L., 172, 237
Spranger, Matthias Tade, 83, 234
Stapleton, Jane, 122, 238
Stockhammer, Morris, 114, 238
Strawson, Galen, 13, 26, 156, 238
Strawson, Peter Frederick, 17, 45, 165, 238
Swenson, Philip, 78, 209
Swerdlow, R. H., 94, 207

Swinburne, Richard, 78, 238
Sztykgold, Jerzy, 165, 176, 197, 238

T
Tabery, J., 83, 204
Tamminga, Allard, 168, 238
Tesnière, Lucien, 15, 58, 238
Thomasius, Christian, 149, 238
Thomson, Judith Jarvis, 26, 33, 175, 238, 239
Tognazzini, Neal A., 48, 214
Tollefsen, Deborah Perron, 108, 239

U
Uckelman, Sara Lianna, 170, 239
Uhlmann, Eric, 80, 231
Unwin, Nicholas, 166, 239

V
Vaan, Michiel de, 3, 239
Van De Poel, I., 13, 16, 48, 241
van den Beld, A., 78, 239
Van Den Hoven, J., 13, 16, 48, 241
van Fraassen, Bas C., 33, 165, 239
van Hees, Martin, 77, 108, 206
van Inwagen, Peter, 78, 239
Vanderveken, Daniel, 171, 235
Vanhanen, T., 69, 226
Vargas, Manuel, 23, 24, 27, 80, 186, 239, 240
Vasmer, Max, 168, 240
Vegetti, Mario, 4, 5, 240
Velasquez, Manuel, 108, 109, 240
Vergilius, Publius Maro, 103, 240
Vernant, Jean-Pierre, 4, 5, 240
Vidal-Naquet, Pierre, 4, 5, 240
Vincent, Nicole, 13, 16, 42, 48, 80, 81, 94, 240, 241
Vranas, Peter B. M., vii, 166, 241

W
Wallace, R. Jay, 26, 241
Waller, Bruce N., 13, 26, 82, 156, 241
Walter, Henrik, 83, 234

Weber, Max, 69
Wedeking, Gary A., 165, 241
Wedgwood, Ralph, 166, 241
Weinberger, Ota, 165, 166, 223, 241
Weisberg, D.S., 83, 241
Welch, John R., 109, 241
Wigley, Simon, 80, 241
Wilder, Hugh T., 165, 242
Williams, Bernard [Arthur Owen], 5, 98, 165, 242
Williams, Garrath, 78, 80, 108, 242
Williamson, Timothy, 132, 242
Wilmot, Stephen, 109, 242
Wilson, George, 185, 242
Wittgenstein, Ludwig Josef Johann, 13, 87, 90, 106, 111, 166, 242
Wootton, Barbara, 41, 43, 50, 51, 99, 242

Wright, Georg Henrik von, 164–166, 209, 242, 243
Wright, Richard W., 119, 121, 243

Y
Yoshioka, Ghen-ichiro, 16, 243
Young, Robert, 78, 243

Z
Zalta, Edward N., 203, 205, 212, 220, 224, 226, 227, 233, 235, 236, 242
Żełaniec, Wojciech, vii, 243
Zellner, Harold M., 165, 243
Zimmerman, Michael J., 24, 78, 243
Znamierowski, Czesław Gabriel Stanisław, 88, 150, 243

COLOPHON

This document was typeset using `classicthesis` developed by André Miede.

Final Version as of June 3, 2014 at 6:53.

www.ingramcontent.com/pod-product-compliance
Lightning Source LLC
Chambersburg PA
CBHW051041160426
43193CB00010B/1025